Governing Through Pedagogy

This edited collection brings together researchers from education, human geography, sociology, social policy and political theory in order to consider the idea of the 'pedagogical state' as a means of understanding the strategies employed to re-educate citizens. The book aims to critically interrogate the cultural practices of governing citizens in contemporary liberal societies. Governing through pedagogy can be identified as an emerging tactic by which both state agencies and other non-state actors manage, administer, discipline, shape, care for and enable liberal citizens. Hence, discourses of 'active citizenship', 'participatory democracy', 'community empowerment', 'personalised responsibility', 'behaviour change' and 'community cohesion' are productively viewed through the conceptual lens of the pedagogical state. Chapters consider the spaces of schools, universities, the voluntary sector, civil society organisations, parenting initiatives, the media, government departments and state agencies as fruitful empirical sites through which pedagogy is worked and re-worked.

This book was originally published as a special issue of *Citizenship Studies*.

Jessica Pykett is a lecturer in Human Geography at the Institute of Geography and Earth Sciences, Aberystwyth University where she is researching the politics of governing through behaviour change, and the ascendance of libertarian paternalism in UK public policies.

Governing Through Pedagogy

Re-educating Citizens

Edited by
Jessica Pykett

Routledge
Taylor & Francis Group

LONDON AND NEW YORK

First published 2012
by Routledge
2 Park Square, Milton Park, Abingdon, Oxon, OX14 4RN

Simultaneously published in the USA and Canada
by Routledge
711 Third Avenue, New York, NY 10017

Routledge is an imprint of the Taylor & Francis Group, an informa business

British Library Cataloguing in Publication Data
A catalogue record for this book is available from the British Library

ISBN13: 978-0-415-69621-0

Typeset in Times New Roman
by Taylor & Francis Books

Publisher's Note
The publisher would like to make readers aware that the chapters in this book may be referred to as articles as they are identical to the articles published in the special issue. The publisher accepts responsibility for any inconsistencies that may have arisen in the course of preparing this volume for print.

Printed and bound in Great Britain by
TJI Digital, Padstow, Cornwall

Contents

CONTENTS

Notes on contributors

Michael Bailey teaches in the Sociology Department at the University of Essex. He is the editor of *Understanding Richard Hoggart: A Pedagogy of Hope* (2012), *The Assault on Universities: A Manifesto for Resistance* (2011), *Richard Hoggart: Culture and Critique* (2011), *Mediating Faiths: Religion and Socio-Cultural Change in the Twenty First Century* (2011) and *Narrating Media History* (2009). He has held visiting fellowships at Goldsmiths, the LSE and at the University of Cambridge.

John Clarke is Professor of Social Policy at the Open University, where he has worked for more than 30 years on the political and cultural struggles involved in remaking the relationships between welfare, states and nations. He has a particular interest in the ways in which managerialism and consumerism have been involved in reconstructing publics and public services. He is currently working with an international group on a project called *Disputing Citizenship*. His books include *Changing Welfare, Changing States* (2004); *Creating Citizen-Consumers* (with Janet Newman and others, 2007) and *Publics, Politics and Power: remaking the public in public services* (with Janet Newman, 2009).

Richard C. Fording is Professor of Political Science at the University of Alabama, Tuscaloosa. He has published numerous articles on welfare policy, race and politics, criminal justice policy, and state politics in such journals as the *American Political Science Review, American Sociological Review, American Journal of Political Science, American Journal of Sociology*, and the *Journal of Politics*, among others. He is the co-author (with Joe Soss and Sanford F. Schram) of *Disciplining the Poor: Neoliberal Paternalism and the Persistent Power of Race* (2011).

Richenda Gambles recently finished her PhD for which she studied at the Open University. She has previously worked as a Lecturer in the Department of Social Policy and Social Intervention, University of Oxford and now works at the Blavatnik School of Government, also at the University of Oxford. Her publications include *The Myth of Work-Life Balance* (with S. Lewis and R. Rapoport, 2006), and her contributions to edited collections include 'Going Public? Articulations of the personal and political on Mumsnet.com', in *Rethinking the Public* (eds. N. Mahony, J. Newman and C. Barnett, 2010) and 'Social Citizenship and the Question of Social Citizenship and the Question of Gender', in *Devolution and Social Citizenship* (ed. S. Greer, 2009).

Dan Hammett is a lecturer in the Department of Geography, University of Sheffield, and holds a research associate post at the Department of Geography, University of the Free State, South Africa. His research interests cover political and development geographies, with continuing projects addressing expressions of African state and nation-hood through political iconography, practices of resistance and political satire as challenges to excesses of African state power, and understanding the changing narratives and geographies of citizenship.

Linda Houser is an Assistant Professor at Widener University's Center for Social Work Education. Her research interests include state and federal workforce policies and supports, child care subsidies, and employment and care-giving in families of children with autism spectrum disorders.

Rhys Jones is Professor of Human Geography at Aberystwyth University. He is a cultural and historical geographer who works on the geographies of the state and its related group identities. His books include *People/States/Territories: The Political Geographies of British State Transformation* (2007) and *The Nature of the State: Excavating the Political Ecologies of the Modern State* (with Mark Whitehead and Martin Jones, 2007).

Maki Kimura is an Associate lecturer with the Open University and also teaches at University College London. Throughout her research career, she has engaged with the question of how differences and social exclusion based on class, gender, 'race' and ethnicity, nationality and sexuality are constructed in contemporary global society, and how subjectivity and agency emerges in this process. She is currently exploring the role of emotion and affect in the concepts and practices of citizenship and also examining the decision making process on nuclear security policy in different political systems.

Denise Meredyth is Deputy Pro Vice Chancellor Research and Professor in the College of Design and Social Context, RMIT (Royal Melbourne Institute of Technology). She was until recently the Deputy Director of the Institute for Social Research at Swinburne University; she is also a Chief Investigator in the ARC Centre of Excellence in Creative Industries and Innovation. She has a background in education history and policy, social policy, cultural policy and media and communications. Her books include *An Articulate Country*, with Kay Ferres (2001), and *Citizenship and Cultural Policy*, edited with Jeffrey Minson (2001).

Janet Newman is Emeritus Professor in the Faculty of Social Science at the Open University. Her research interests include new formations of governance, political and organisational change, and the remaking of publics and publicness. Publications include *Working the spaces of power feminism, activism and neo-liberalism* (2012); *Summoning the Active Citizen: responsibility, choice and participation* (with E. Tonkens, 2011); *Power, Participation and Political Renewal* (with M. Barnes and H. Sullivan, 2007); and *Modernising Governance: New Labour, Policy and Society* (2001).

Jessica Pykett is a lecturer in Human Geography at the Institute of Geography and Earth Sciences, Aberystwyth University where she is researching the politics of governing through behaviour change, and the ascendance of libertarian paternalism in UK public policies. Her research has been published in *Urban Studies, Critical Social Policy, Journal of Education Policy, Progress in Human Geography* and *Antipode*. She is currently writing (with Mark Whitehead and Rhys Jones) a book entitled *Changing Behaviour. On the Psychological Infrastructures of the State* (forthcoming, 2012).

Clarissa Rile Hayward, author of *De-Facing Power* (2000), is Associate Professor of Political Science at Washington University in St. Louis. This paper draws from her current book project, tentatively titled *Stories and Spaces: How Americans Make Race.*

Joe Soss is Cowles Professor for the Study of Public Service at the University of Minnesota, where he holds faculty positions in the Hubert H. Humphrey Institute of Public Affairs, the Department of Political Science, and the Department of Sociology. Along with Richard Fording and Sanford Schram, he is co-author of *Disciplining the Poor: Neoliberal Paternalism and the Persistent Power of Race* (2011).

Sanford F. Schram is Professor of social theory and social policy in the Graduate School of Social Work and Social Research at Bryn Mawr College. Some of his recent books include: *Disciplining the Poor: Neoliberal Paternalism and the Persistent Power of Race* (2011), co-authored with Joe Soss and Richard Fording; *Change Research: A Case Study on Collaborative Methods for Social Workers and Advocates* (2011), co-authored with Corey Shdaimah and Roland Stahl; and *Welfare Discipline: Discourse, Governance, and Globalization* (2006).

Lynn A. Staeheli is Professor of Human Geography at Durham University. Recent books include: *The People's Property. Power, Politics, and the Public* (with D. Mitchell, 2007); *Globalization and Its Outcomes* (with J. O'Loughlin and E. S. Greenberg, 2004); *Mapping Gender, Making Politics: Feminist Perspectives on Political Geography* (with E. Kofman and L. Peake, 2004). She has written several book chapters and journal articles, some of which include: 'Reconfiguring Citizenship in Transnational Perspective', in *The Other Cities* (ed. E. Kremer, 2005); 'Spaces of Public and Private: Locating Politics', in *Spaces of Democracy* (ed. C. Barnett and M. Low, 2004) and 'Citizenship and the problem of community', *Political Geography* (2008).

Introduction: the pedagogical state: education, citizenship, governing

Jessica Pykett

Institute of Geography and Earth Sciences, Aberystwyth University, Aberystwyth, UK

Introduction to special issue

Understanding state–citizen relations involves a multitude of spaces and actors, formal and informal political practices and the intricacies of subjectivity and citizen-formation. One emerging tactic by which both 'state' agencies and other non-state actors manage, administer, discipline, shape, care for and enable liberal citizens is that of governing through pedagogy. Schools, universities, the voluntary sector, civil society organisations, churches, commercial education and training providers, the media, government departments and state agencies offer fruitful empirical spaces through which the pedagogies of governing are worked and reworked. This special issue therefore brings together researchers from education, human geography, sociology, social policy and political theory in order to consider the idea of the 'pedagogical state' as a means of understanding the pedagogic strategies employed to govern citizens, both within and outside the formal education sphere.

The language of pedagogy can be useful in elaborating the sites of formal and informal education, the practices of teaching and learning and the subjectivities of teachers and learners in relation to governing tactics, with implications far beyond the immediate reach of formal education. Because pedagogy cannot be reduced to teaching, learning or education, it provokes us to consider not simply the disciplining and directive facets of education, but also the way pedagogy is used in order to develop competences and capabilities and to empower subjects in their future self-directed knowledge, experience and activities. Pedagogy also denotes a sense of the 'science' or 'arts of teaching', which prompts us to contemplate indirect and apparently contradictory modes of governing. Rather than presuming that pedagogical power will be characterised by domination and resistance, critically investigating interventions in the governability of liberal citizens can help us to reconsider the reflexive and sceptical ways in which citizens act, re-act and co-construct the cultural practices of governing. Such an approach can be useful in trying to avoid potentially simplistic critiques of bureaucracy, the 'nanny state', 'teacherly' or authoritarian state behaviours, the 'infantilisation' of adult citizens and the 'schooling' of society in so-called neoliberal times.

'The pedagogical state' as a concept, a theme and a research agenda requires developing and deconstructing from a variety of disciplinary perspectives, and contributors to this volume have engaged with and problematised the idea in equal measure. In the first article, Jessica Pykett introduces research which has explicitly developed the idea of the pedagogical state. Using the introduction of compulsory citizenship education in secondary schools in England as a case study, she explores what is at stake politically in competing narratives of pedagogy within the shifting realm of educational governance.

The next two papers offer further theoretical insights into our understandings of the politics of pedagogy. Contributors identify a number of pedagogical modes through which citizens govern and are governed. John Clarke highlights the way in which so-called ordinary people are enrolled into the architectures of governing, through policies of participation, inclusion, empowerment, emancipation, and through the 'coming of voice'. He shows how such policies in the realm of immigration and policing involve the evocation and constitution of 'ordinary people' and the performing (or failure to perform) of learnt identities of ordinariness, at the expense of political contestation. In an extension of her work on how power is exercised through pedagogy, Clarissa Rile Hayward discusses the way in which 'bad stories' are narrated through both personal and collective identity-work. She examines in particular how racialised identities in the US are translated into material and institutional forms through processes of social reproduction and a 'narrative pedagogy' employed by the state.

We then turn to some of the diverse spaces in which the concept of the pedagogical state offers explanatory purchase, beginning with the formal education system. In a study of citizenship education in South African Schools, Lynn A. Staeheli and Daniel Hammett explore how post-conflict states narrate and address particular histories (whilst omitting others) in constructing a sense of the nation and a felt history of 'cosmopolitan nationalism' through education. Again, the theme of 'narrative pedagogy' helps us to understand the relationship between education, citizenship discourses and governing practices. Michael Bailey takes us beyond formal schooling to consider the production of liberal worker subjectivities in early twentieth-century Britain, through an apparatus of educational organisations ranging from the Workers' Education Association, the University Extension Movement and the BBC. He demonstrates how this liberal form of governmentality relied on ensuring a regime of 'educated citizenship' and 'civil prudence'. Building on this relationship between media, education and politics, Richenda Gambles examines the making up of a particular pedagogic mode associated with the sensibilities of parenting, through the popular entertainment programme, *Supernanny*. She develops a nuanced account of 'a pedagogical state' to encompass the dispositions and moods associated with parental subjectivities as these are imagined through both government policy and popular culture.

The next three articles examine welfare and the discourse of 'empowerment' employed therein, in both UK and US contexts. Janet Newman introduces the idea of a 'pedagogy of public participation', highlighting its role in complicating the politics of 'progressive' agendas, the work of equalities and social justice activists, and the 'social investment state'. She identifies the behaviour-changing practices of 'informing, tutoring, developing and nudging', the subjects of this targeted pedagogy, and the political work accomplished by pedagogy as a kind of 'coercive voluntarism'. Rhys Jones reports on the way in which these very pedagogies play out within Citizens Advice Bureaux (CAB), 'in the shadow of the state'. He shows how the CAB's experience of both learning about the state through their advice work, and learning by the state through their social policy and campaigning work problematises easy distinctions between state/civil society; active/passive citizens and local/national polities. Finally, Sanford F. Schram, Joe Soss, Linda Houser and Richard C. Fording examine the (specifically anti-educational) pedagogical tactics of self-improvement, training and self-management, sanctions, compliance, punishment and forms of address in the realm of welfare policy in the US. The focus here on governing tactics reminds us of the significance of pedagogical modes of governing outside of formal educational institutions.

The final two papers further elaborate on the making up of pedagogical subjectivities in the context of higher education and in educational settings beyond the school. For Maki Kimura, contemporary narratives of key citizenship issues around multiculturalism, racism, religious extremism and global migration produced in academia are contrasted with existing policy and practice in UK Higher Education Institutions, and through consideration of the wider political, social and cultural imperatives of university-level education. Finally, Denise Meredyth explores 'Youthworx', a youth media/development project run by the Salvation Army in Australia. Her analysis of the ambiguous political rationalities of community and government agencies involved in the provision of youth services demands that we interrogate the professional and personal ethos, commitments and interests of specific actors in the making up of moral personalities and self-governing citizens, without reverting to critiques focussed on hidden norms and false freedoms.

The questions posed in this special issue help us to rethink the contemporary politics of governing in light of theoretical insights offered by the grammar of pedagogy. Governing through pedagogy plays out in a variety of empirical sites, employs a number of sometimes complementary and sometimes conflicting tactics, and narrates particular subject positions and social relations. Such governing also gives rise to unintended consequences. This special issue therefore aims to establish what kind of questions are worth asking within a research agenda focused on understanding governing through pedagogy. Two common missteps are perhaps worth guarding against in this venture. First, the ongoing question of the 'right' education for citizenship will necessarily remain unresolved. And second, the question of how governments 'get at' people through ever more dubious techniques and towards self-serving ends may serve only to obscure an important opportunity to ask where, when and what kinds of government interventions are legitimate and why.

Acknowledgements

This special issue is based on a symposium on 'The Pedagogical State' held at The Open University, Milton Keynes, 24–25 September 2008. In addition to the contributors here, I would like to thank all those who participated in the symposium and its organisation, including Melissa Butcher, Allan Cochrane, Roger Dale, Sarah Hall, José Hernandez, Engin Isin, Maki Kimura, Nick Mahony, Michele Marsh, Denise Meredyth, Gillian Rose, Don Rowe, Chris Wilson and Mike Saward. Clive Barnett and Doreen Massey also provided detailed comments and helpful critiques of my original paper. The symposium was funded by ESRC award PTA-026-27-1669, the Department of Geography and the Centre for Citizenship, Identities and Governance, for which I am very grateful.

Citizenship Education and narratives of pedagogy

Jessica Pykett

Institute of Geography and Earth Sciences, Aberystwyth University, Aberystwyth, UK

This paper argues that the concept of the 'pedagogical state' (Hunter 1994, Kaplan 2007) can be employed to better understand the cultural practices of governing through pedagogical means, and the evolving pedagogical relationship between state and citizen. The introduction of statutory Citizenship Education lessons in secondary schools in England in 2002 is used as a case study through which to develop the idea of the pedagogical state. It is argued that Citizenship Education makes manifest practices of citizen-formation, opens up a space in which teachers and pupils actively negotiate the tensions between freedom and government, and evokes a response which is often characterised by public scepticism. In this sense, it is inadequate to identify educational reforms and resultant citizen subjectivities as straightforwardly neoliberal without paying attention to the deeper and wider characteristics of pedagogical power.

It is often remarked that the UK's education sector is characterised by perpetual reform and restructuring, and that everyone is seen as an expert in educational matters. But scholars and commentators outside of the field of educational studies have remained rather quiet about drawing out the political, social, cultural and economic significance of contemporary educational practices. Where analysis of current educational reforms in the UK and elsewhere exists, such reforms are most often described as signifying a neoliberal political rationality in an increasingly economistic education sector. It is said that this rationality is aimed at 'responsibilizing' active, entrepreneurial and individualistic citizens whilst the state is 'rolling back' its own responsibilities towards the welfare of citizens. These accounts can neglect the distinctive nature of pedagogical power – both within and outside of the formal education sector – which is ambiguous in practice (its consequences are uncertain), which develops citizens' capacities to self-govern and which invites critique and public scepticism.

Citizenship Education provides an important case study through which to examine the changing facets of educational spaces, governance, practices and subjects. Secondary school pupils are taught 'key concepts' of 'democracy and justice', 'rights and responsibilities' and 'identities and diversity: living in the UK'. They learn a range of topics concerning rights, justice, law-making, government, democratic forms, freedom of speech, the media, voluntary sector, sustainable development, the economy, employers and employees, diversity, and the global community through 'key processes' of 'critical thinking and enquiry', 'advocacy and representation' and 'taking informed and responsible action'. Finally, they are offered 'curriculum opportunities' to debate, develop citizenship skills and participate in school and community decision-making, and individual and collective action (Qualifications and Curriculum Authority (QCA) 2007). The subject was introduced as part of New Labour's agenda for civil renewal (Blunkett 2003), the 'respect and responsibility' agenda, a response to perceived voter apathy, and as a rejoinder to alleged threats to 'British values' from an increasingly multicultural society. In this sense, it was presented by its main proponents, Sir Bernard Crick and David Blunkett, as a way to 'improve the health and future of British democracy' (QCA 1998, pp. 7–8) and to revitalise the public sphere, in a move which makes a presumption, as Newman and Mahony (2007, p. 53) have pointed out, that 'more democracy' is an unproblematic good.

The pedagogical state

What is school for? Some current educational reforms in the UK beg this question. The Government is busy extending its academies programme (DCSF 2008), which radically overhauls the way in which schools are funded and governed. This is aimed at regenerating inner city areas and 'raising aspirations in some of the most disadvantaged communities'. Available from: http://www.standards.dfes.gov.uk/academies/what_are_academies/whyacademies/?version=1 [Accessed 10 July 2008]. The expansion of state-maintained faith schools is being actively promoted (DCSF 2007a), indicating the expansion or return of schools into the spiritual realm. Schools have also been given new statutory duties to promote 'community cohesion' (DCSF 2007b), in response to unease concerning multi-culturalism, perceived security threats from British citizens and the revisiting of debates surrounding national identity. The education sector, like the health sector, is also carrying through the policy agenda of personalisation or 'personalised learning', which seeks to tailor education around the needs and aptitudes of diverse and individual learners. In this sense, schools are responsible for a major shift in the governance of the public services, and must face up to the apparent decline of the universal public ideal. In this context, the importance of schooling in society in general and the political significance of the introduction of Citizenship Education (QCA 1998) in particular should not be underestimated; this new national curriculum subject is concerned with the reformulation of state–citizen relations. Analysis of its content, implementation and pedagogy can inform our understandings of the political implications of educational reforms, contemporary practices of governing and formulations of citizenship.

These considerations have long been the concern of educational sociologists and critical educational theorists (Willis 1977, Ball 1987, McLaren 1989). They have argued that there is much to be gained from a sustained interrogation of the micro-politics of the school experience, curriculum, classroom practice, school architecture and routines, and the school in its social and spatial context. Recent accounts have focused on the neoliberalisation of education policy (Apple 2001, Fitzsimons 2002, Bonal 2003, Olssen 2004a, Davies and Bansel 2007) in the UK, US, Australia and New Zealand in particular. Mobilising Foucault's writings on governmentality, authors such as Olssen (2004a), Peters *et al.* (2000) and Davies and Bansel (2007, p. 254) aim to uncover the insidious way in which neoliberalism governs our actions, our conduct and our mentalities whilst promoting an illusion of freedom:

> We are interested in how the market works on students to shape them up as the consuming individuals it desires. How does the work of teachers transform students into less democratic, more neoliberal subjects who are at once more governable and yet believe themselves to be both autonomous and free? How do heightened competition, individualism and individual

responsibilization work along with the reduction in social responsibility to produce the entrepreneurial subjects best fitted for the neoliberal workplace? How does the calculated invisibility of neoliberalism work against our capacity to make a critique of it? These are some of the questions urgently in need of answers for those of us who work in the sphere of education.

A small but significant interest in the geographies of education has also recently developed (e.g. Butler and Hamnett 2007, Gulson and Symes 2007), alongside research into the geographies of children and young people (Valentine 2000, Weller 2003, 2007), which works towards gaining a better understanding of the role of space, place and scale in constituting school practices, politics and subjectivities. Such work (e.g. Weller 2007, p. 162) is often concerned with pointing out the apparent hypocrisies of schooling and education for citizenship where children are denied full citizenship rights and recognition:

> The rhetoric of citizenship education is concerned with developing responsible citizens in the future, whilst examples of teenagers' engagement within the informal school and in the wider community reveal alternative and often unrecognized acts of citizenship taking place in the here-and-now.

Further work in the geographies of education again highlights the neoliberal nature of educational reform regimes and the constitution of neoliberal subjectivities through schooling (Lewis 2003, Basu 2004). Mitchell (2006, p. 392), for instance, aims to show how EU educational philosophies, policies and experiences throughout the 1990s have shifted from democratic multiculturalism towards an individualised, responsibilized, flexibilized regime: 'in terms of the encouragement of individualized and self-regulating entrepreneurial behavior this shift dovetails well with the discourse and practices of neoliberal governmentality in general'. Mitchell (ibid., p. 390) identifies children and young people in particular as malleable and vulnerable to the pervasive forces of neoliberalism: 'students (that is, children) are particularly impressionable "subjects" whose formation in schools and families has historically been of great interest to hegemonic powers worldwide'. This shows how a conception of education as an invisible ideological force or 'power over' people who hold an illusion of freedom, informs much of the literature on schooling as a form of governmentality.

Without restating debates concerning the dominance of neoliberalism as an analytical category within the discipline of geography (see Peck and Tickell 2002, Larner 2003, Barnett 2005, Castree 2005), it is important to note that accounts of schooling and education policy reform are heavily reliant on the idea of neoliberalism – particularly presented through a Foucauldian frame – as an explanatory cause, context and/or consequence in terms of the governing of our conduct and mentalities through schooling. The distinctive nature of pedagogical power, the pedagogical relationship between state and citizen, and the particularities of schooling as a space, which both opens up critical debate and promotes the explicit governability of reflexive citizens, have all been somewhat neglected. In an interdisciplinary approach to the study of citizenship, I draw on anthropologists', cultural studies' and political theorists' analyses of schooling in order to further develop the concept of the pedagogical state as a means of discerning the pedagogic strategies employed by the state and 'non-state' agencies – both within and outside of the formal educational sphere – to govern citizens. I argue that an exploration of schooling should contribute more broadly to how we think about cultural practices of governing and the constitution of citizen subjectivities, and should throw into question some of the straightforward critiques of neoliberalism offered hitherto.

An emphasis on pedagogy and its enabling and inciting facets can illuminate some of the apparent paradoxes of governing. The pedagogical strategies employed both within and outside of the educational sphere are aimed *both* at the constraining practices of training, civilizing, governing, *and* at the enabling practices of developing skills, provoking knowledge and understanding and inculcating a sense of public doubt – through the nurturing of critical capabilities. The term 'pedagogy' is perhaps the current obsession of teacher-training courses and textbooks (Rogers 2002, Cowley 2003, Dixie 2003), interpreted as the need to understand tactics to control classroom behaviour and general principles to promote better learning. Others have noted that the 'science of teaching' has been notably absent from the English education system, which instead has favoured child development theories, intelligence testing and neuro-psychological approaches to teaching (Simon 1994). Whilst teaching is aimed at both controlling behaviour, and inviting critique, pedagogy is concerned with *thinking about* education and developing *understandings of* teaching. In this sense, pedagogy can be understood as a form of power which aims to unpack and rearticulate the best ways in which to develop competences, accrue knowledge and incite people to self-govern, rather than a simple case of teaching. Teaching on its own may indeed involve telling students 'how it is' and compelling students to act in particular ways through coercive means. However, we can learn something from the fact that the *paidagogos* of Greco-Roman education was not a controlling, state-sanctioned teacher, but a slave who watched over the children of the elite whilst they weren't at school (Atherton 1998, p. 230) – hardly a self-determining figure empowered to govern others through force or 'power over'.

The notion of the 'pedagogical state' tries to capture these enabling and inciting facets of pedagogy as a mode of *thinking about education*, and as a means by which state organisation, institutions, discourse, culture and affective modalities are being reformulated in the UK and elsewhere. Sociology (Turner 1993, Brenner 1999, Jessop 2001), political theory (Rhodes 1997, Stoker 2006), social policy (Clarke and Newman 1997, Clarke 2005, Newman 2005), political geography (Allen 2003, Painter 2005, Elden 2007) and citizenship studies (Isin 2004) have been fertile ground for important debates concerning the changing role of the state and citizen in an increasingly globalised world, the increasing role of non-state agencies in governing, and our evolving understandings of relations of power. However, missing from these accounts is direct analysis of the educational sector as a key site through which the state operates, through which citizen subjectivities are constituted and through which power is exercised. Exploring the pedagogical state is useful for examining the 'schooling' of citizen subjectivities, both within and outside of schools, and new forms of active citizenship which have consequences for the 'health' of democracy. It can also help us to investigate the extension of 'teacherly' or pedagogic practices into social life and the wider public sphere and to theorise the politics and geographies of pedagogical forms of power, pedagogical culture, 'psychagogy' or a 'totally pedagogised society'. The impact of current social, democratic, public service and educational reforms on the governing of citizens' conduct is important for understanding emerging forms of citizenship (active, neurotic, overactive, subversive, compliant, good) as well as the role and value of pedagogy and education in contemporary societies.

Research explicitly using the concept of the pedagogical state has thus far been rare and isolated – with little discernable cross-reference or common scholarship between key contributions. There are at least two conflicting notions of the pedagogical state. It could be argued that the first, provided by Kaplan (2007) and Bernstein (1996, cited in Bonal and Rambla 2003), overemphasises the efficacy of neoliberal forms of governing to determine citizens' subject positions and fails to address the question of how pedagogy both invites critique and develops citizens' capacities to act in the future. The second, named by Hunter

(1994) and alluded to by Hayward (2000), elaborates pedagogy as a distinctive modality of power which has consequences for the terms of critique on which critical scholars of education and schooling rely. The next section examines these two conceptions of the pedagogical state using the particular example of the introduction of Citizenship Education in secondary schools in England. I make specific reference to an extended period of multi-sited ethnographic research at a teacher-training course and schools in Bristol, South West England, undertaken between 2004 and 2006.

Citizenship Education and the pedagogical state

The introduction of Citizenship Education in secondary schools in England marked a new direction in educational governance. As has been noted, it was hailed by some as a form of even more pervasive social control; as part of an overarching ideological project of neoliberal globalisation. But what was really distinctive about Citizenship was that it made explicit the reflexive practices of citizen-formation – not that it constituted people as neoliberal subjects. Whilst it set out to define and delimit a notion of acceptable citizenly behaviour akin to the New Labour discourse of respect and responsibility, it also opened up a space within the secondary school for students and teachers to question this direct intervention in their governability and their constitution as citizens. The case of Citizenship Education therefore challenges dominant conceptions of education policy reform as decidedly neoliberal by posing the following three questions: do states succeed in 'pedagogizing our thinking' through the invisible forces of neoliberalism? Do states have governmental power over school students through the medium of teachers? Are school students transformed into neoliberal subjects through schooling? The responses to these questions have implications for how we might employ the concept of the pedagogical state to understand wider practices of governing outside of schools.

In an anthropological analysis of the 'pedagogical state' and the relationship between schooling, governance and subjectivity in modern Turkey, Kaplan (2007, p. 9) argues that 'schools are more than bureaucratic institutions serving the public. They are state projects both totalizing and individualizing', and that school systems have 'succeeded in "pedagogizing" our thinking of self, other, and world' (ibid., p. 227). He attributes a 'pedagogical culture' to modern states, and asserts that 'today, all countries are pedagogical states, or at least endeavour to be', and through which people's intimate selves are reconfigured to shape political and social identities. Whilst Kaplan is optimistic about the agency of children to carve out their own futures through this pedagogical sphere, his account tends towards a comprehensive notion of the state and elite control of individual private behaviours and the production of homogenised citizens, fostering 'allegiance to the national and obedience to state institutions and officials' (ibid., p. 219). He regards it only as *ironic* that the same curricula which ensure the inculcation of citizenship also conversely allow children to question power relations both within and beyond school (ibid., p. 220). His analysis of state power rests on the constraining and enabling remit of the educational sphere which, for him, holds a special significance in the case of schoolchildren (ibid., p. 225):

> Schoolchildren, and not their adult peers, are the ones most able to release themselves from the systematic discourses of modern governance, and thereby, accede to a state of maturity.

This account therefore shares much with common readings of the introduction of Citizenship Education and critique of the wider discourse of 'active citizenship' which is prevalent in contemporary governance practices. It portrays an overly romantic notion of childhood and a particularly pessimistic view of adult agency – and fails to recognise the distinctive nature of pedagogical power with which this paper is concerned. Current dismissals of Citizenship Education paint the subject as a failed and ineffectual programme of social control (deemed either a worthy or suspect cause). The concept of 'active citizenship' has become fundamental to debates concerning the purpose of education, curriculum reform, teaching and assessment methods. 'Key' and 'life' skills such as 'personal financial education,' 'confidence building' and 'parenting skills' are ever more important both in school curricula and adult education. Furthermore, the discourse of active citizenship, respect and responsibility becomes more wide-reaching as it affects an increasing variety of facets of social life. Commentators have therefore judged Citizenship Education to be: a more pervasive form of control employed by both state and non-state agencies (namely neoliberal interests); a means to cover up more divisive educational policies (Gillborn 2006); a mechanism for the 'schooling' of citizens who will demonstrate allegiance to the nation (Olssen 2004b, p. 276) and deference to the state (Mitchell 2003, p. 390). Indeed, education is often evoked as a 'technology of the self' by which the state seeks to ensure security and norms of civility and decency (Belsey 2005) through ever more invasive and underhand means.

Taken a step further, policy trends which promote active citizenship are commonly interpreted as indicating a 'nanny state' which seeks to increasingly interfere in the private lives of citizens, through such policies as 'parenting orders', Anti-Social Behaviour Orders, and the extension of schooling or 'teacherly' practices into traditionally non-educational spheres of social life. Society is regarded as increasingly 'schooled' and formerly autonomous adults 'infantilised' through intrusive and authoritarian social policies. Hence, the state ideology is seen to be promulgated through its meddling institutions and its bureaucratic machinery. As Michael Young (1996, p. vii). has commented, 'the government has become the schoolmaster or dominie of education', stating that state schooling in the UK has now become as controlling as he suggests other countries already are – 'an instrument for making children as uniform as possible – identikit citizens who would be easily governable'. Such interpretations are common in the popular press (O'Leary 1998, O'Hear 1999, Phillips 1999) as well as within critical research on education.

These criticisms converge with Bernstein's (1996, cited in Bonal and Rambla 2003, p. 169) account of the 'totally pedagogised society'. This idea outlines the importance of 'symbolic control', whereby pedagogues produce and maintain dominant discourses and forms of legitimation for state interests. The regulatory base serves as the foundation for a 'pedagogic modality' which transmits 'forms of consciousness, identity and desire' (ibid., p. 269). This strong pedagogic field is presented as recompense for the 'weak state of the global economy' (ibid., p. 175), and is exemplified by policies concerning lifelong learning, trainability and flexibility – through which formerly state responsibilities are personalised; that is, re-imagined as the personal responsibility of citizens themselves. Such conceptions of the pedagogical state beg the question of whether teachers and students 'captured' by a totally pedagogised society can have any agency, and hence whether education is a worthwhile pursuit at all.

Kaplan and Bernstein's renditions of the pedagogical state, shared by many analysts of Citizenship Education, critical and conservative alike, paint a picture in which schools serve to control the behaviour of citizens, to exercise state and elite power over people, and to produce particular kinds of constrained subjectivities. Hence, accounts of Citizenship Education focus on the controlling and constraining aspects of governing through pedagogical means, point out the hypocrisy or paradox of promoting 'governing through freedom' (Rose 1999, p. 62), and denounce the teaching of citizenship responsibilities to children who are – by virtue of being children – denied full citizenship rights. As Hunter and Meredyth (2001, p. 71) therefore point out, 'the discussion of liberal-democratic government oscillates helplessly between the insistence on free choice and anxiety about the role of government in forming the capacity for it'.

However, examples from Citizenship Education can be provided which testify to the contrary – that both teachers and students reject the idea of schooling as 'moral coercion' whilst recognising its role as a form of 'social governance' (Hunter and Meredyth 2001, p. 69). During my ethnographic research, for instance, year 10 pupils (aged 14–15), who participated in a 'UK Youth Parliament' training day as part of their school's Citizenship activities, spoke of how 'other' pupils in their classes disturbed their work and threatened their grades, if teachers could not control them. Similarly, a group of year 12 (aged 16–17) pupils, talking to me about their experiences of school, felt it was better to be in year 12 because all the 'louts' had left after their GCSEs. This may seem at first glance to signify that pupils comply with overly individualistic conceptions of education, with citizens being defined in terms of respect, good behaviour, self-regulation and educability. One of the risks of Citizenship Education is therefore the individualisation of blame, where individuals are blamed for social ills. However, these pupils remarked that it wasn't that 'other' pupils didn't 'fit' the education system, but that the system did not adequately cater for them. They sought social solutions to social problems and argued that a degree of teacher control was necessary to create the conditions in which they could all learn and develop. Furthermore, teachers often vigorously contested the notion that education should be about individual success, seeing their role as a chance to 'give pupils amazing experiences' that they wouldn't otherwise have. They didn't teach in order to fulfil government targets or agendas, and the curriculum didn't map out unproblematically onto the school. Such teachers saw themselves as social interventionists and viewed education as a means by which to reduce social inequalities, not to 'get ahead' of others. The idea that education should profit individuals through grades and competitive notions of success was greatly contested by these teachers, and Citizenship Education was seen as one means through which to counter dominant social trends towards individualism, commercialisation and selfishness, which they saw as prevalent amongst their pupils:

Jessica: What would you research if you were researching Citizenship Education?

Lauren: in relation to education[. . .]I'd actually focus on a balance between looking at those individuals that get strings and strings of GCSEs and A levels, and I'd say, um, what benefit is that to them? [. . .] so what, does that make you a better person? No, not really, so, what does make you a better person is having nice relationships with people and going and doing stuff for people, so I would actually look at those selfish people that kind of get, and this is really awful, this is really opinionated, but actually doing a study on those people that are like, really self-indulgent and do loads and loads of shit, and just get, loads of GCSEs and A levels, and make themselves ill doing it, because they just have to be perfect and have to be amazing, in comparison to those who perhaps spent a little bit of time giving something back and not just taking, taking, taking, so I'd so research on that.

(Lauren, Geography teacher, Crestway School,[1] interviewed 15 December 2004).

Neither teachers nor students are 'captured' by a 'totally pedagogised society', though they do – like everyone else – indeed exist in circumstances which attempt to shape their behaviours, values and actions. What is different about the education sector, and characterises pedagogical power in particular, is the way in which actions and behaviours are geared towards improving critical capacities, increasing knowledge, skills and capabilities, and inviting people to self-govern in a manifestly reflexive manner. So power in this sense is productive, and is not held by individuals but instead signifies the manifold ways in which all action is constrained by social relations. Through an ethnography of schooling, political theorist, Clarissa Rile Hayward (2000, p. 46) finds fault with conceptions of power held by critical pedagogy scholars, in that they presume power to have a 'face'. They view pedagogy as the 'content and design of both the formal and hidden curriculum, through which particular forms of knowledge and student subjectivity are produced and legitimized'. Such authors, she argues, therefore attribute both too much and too little power to teachers and students, suggesting that 'teachers who have power need only be exhorted to recognize its effects and to use it to challenge, rather than reproduce and legitimize social hierarchies' (ibid., p. 49) at the same time as describing a 'totally pedagogised society' in which teachers can only be complicit. This account of the transformative potential of 'hegemonic intellectuals' obscures the way in which power 'without a face' operates relationally and is conditioned by particular social environments, in which free subjects act.

We cannot say that state power – reflecting neoliberal interests or otherwise – is held over school students through the governmental technology of Citizenship Education. This is because the curriculum itself was developed by an alliance of often conflicting interests, involving non-state, peripheral state and state agencies and actors. In practice, the subject is shaped by state-trained teachers who have been taught by non-state actors (university-based teacher training lecturers), and in schools, Citizenship Education is 'delivered' by a range of actors varying from non-governmental organisations, teachers, voluntary associations and educational consultants, using a variety of texts, materials and resources produced by private publishing companies, NGOs, educational cooperatives, pressure groups and so on. As Painter (2006, p. 756) points out, the state is no longer coterminous with public value and state institutions, and its effects are always open, uncertain and fallible (ibid., p. 761). It is therefore difficult to claim that a policy such as Citizenship Education portrays a unified state agenda. Teachers and their own teacher-trainers play a hugely important mediatory role, and cannot be considered as either totally autonomous or merely automatons. The following teacher-trainer demonstrated commonly held views about the social role of teachers in defining the purpose of Citizenship Education itself:

> well our students write a mission statement for citizenship education in their first week of the [Citizenship] course, because although you've got our official definition, you also need to have your own definition that you feel comfortable with, and I mean, my definition is, education about political issues and skills, students are to become involved in their community, in local, national and international politics

(Jill Rutter, London Metropolitan University, interviewed 12 February 2004).

Defining citizenship in their own terms is equally important for student-teachers. During his Citizenship PGCE course, one such student-teacher presented to his colleagues on what he thought Citizenship Education should be about, outlining that he would be teaching his school-placement class about globalisation, fair trade, multinational companies, Structural Adjustment Programmes (SAPs), George Bush's relationship with the Saudi regime, Michael Moore, and the role of 'adbusters' (a direct action advertisement saboteur group) in bringing such politics to the attention of the wider public. Whilst it would be easy to dismiss Citizenship Education as a means for ensuring state control over the behaviour of citizens, here it was being used as a vehicle through which teachers could raise awareness of what they perceived to be pressing political issues, global injustices and inequalities.

If we are to account for this apparent subversion of Citizenship Education, a more complex explication of the pedagogical state is therefore required, and it is to this second notion of the pedagogical state that I now turn. Ian Hunter describes the emergence of mass-schooling in eighteenth Century Europe as part of an intentionally contradictory 'pastoral bureaucracy' which was essential to the survival of a peaceful state. Like Kaplan and Bernstein, he considers the rationale for pedagogy as serving the interests of the state. But rather than presuming these interests to be those of an elite, and contrary to the interests of citizens, he regards pedagogy as integral to the very definition of state interests and the constitution of the social. Central to his argument is that schooling was by design a disciplinary technology aimed at the separation of the person from the citizen. On the one hand, the administrative state aimed to pacify the population (in response to the ravages of civil war and religious factions), and provided the discipline and training necessary for people to act capably as citizens. On the other hand, Christian pastoral techniques were employed to shape the comportment of the self-reflective person (Hunter 1994, p. 61). These apparently contradictory rationales were held together by non-principled institutional arrangements (ibid., p. 90). *Constituting people as governable citizens* was indeed what made the functioning of government possible, to improve the security of the state and thereby the well-being of its citizens (p. 39); instigating a thoroughly public value in education. Hence, we can analyse pedagogical power by confirming its enabling and inciting functions, reflecting Foucault's assertion that power is exercised through discursive means – i.e. through our ability to articulate how we are made governable. It is no irony, therefore, that in his unpacking of the dominant history of sexuality as one of repression, Foucault (1981, p. 8, my emphasis) points out that we live in a society which:

> has been *loudly castigating* itself for its hypocrisy for more than a century, which *speaks verbosely* of its own silence, takes great pains to *relate in detail* the things it does not say, *denounces* the powers it exercises, and *promises* to liberate itself from the very laws that have made it function

So whilst critics have condemned Citizenship Education as a means of governing citizens more effectively, of promoting social and moral conformity, it could also be argued that such accounts overestimate the power of the state to govern citizens through schooling, and underestimate the way in which teachers and pupils both articulate and respond to what can be regarded as a direct and explicit intervention in their governability. Indeed, it can be asserted that Citizenship Education itself makes manifest practices of citizen-formation, opens up a space in which teachers and pupils actively negotiate the tensions between freedom and government, and evokes a response which is often characterised with public scepticism, if not cynicism. Hence, Citizenship Education cannot simply be understood as a means through which the state exercises more effective and coercive powers by educating people to repress themselves.

Textbooks commonly used in the teaching of Citizenship Education testify to some of the ambiguity of the moral and behavioural agenda within the subject. Whilst such books are preoccupied with the values and competences and behaviours of young people, notions of the active citizen are relatively open – it is for the readers themselves to do the active and reflexive work through which they become citizens. The ideal citizen posited by such texts is one who critically reflects on the education s/he receives. Indeed, teachers are urged to go one step further, and to always reflect and critique the resources, curricula and common-sense understandings of Citizenship Education they receive from various sources. One 'viewpoint' article in the ACT (Association for Citizenship Teaching) Journal, *Teaching Citizenship* ('Tom' 2006, p. 26), is a clear example of the 'public doubt' demonstrated by one pupil, and is worth quoting at some length:

> I am a year 11 pupil who has been taught Citizenship for the past five years, but for me the concept remains unengaging [...] we are presented with concepts such as 'democracy' and

asked to debate them. However, the emphasis is not on *whether* democracy is good but *why* it is good – the important question has been decided before we even discuss it. In this way, ideas are implicitly labelled 'good' or 'bad' – democracy and charity are 'good' while dictatorship is 'bad'. In effect, rather than learning how to discriminate between ideologies, we are being *given* an ideology [...] Such complexity reveals problems with the fixed concepts of Citizenship: is 'participation' (considered one of Citizenship's 'good' words) then the action of a good citizen, or is 'resistance'? To whom is one's loyalty due? [...] Often, the effect is to make children cynical: either subscribing to these ideas without really understanding them, or carelessly disregarding them.

This pupil is clearly sceptical of Citizenship Education, and believes he is being 'brainwashed' by the ideology of the taught curriculum, and unfounded, opinionated relativism in class discussions, or indeed unsubstantiated 'faith' in binary concepts such as 'good' and 'bad'. He is offering insight into the reflexive complexity of teaching and learning democracy, and asking questions about ethics, politics and justice that he feels Citizenship as a subject closes down. The existence of such an article (in a publication supported indirectly by the government, through the ACT) demonstrates that teachers and pupils are not being coaxed into 'swallowing' the citizenship curriculum, implementing it unquestioningly and act out its recommendations by force or coercion. However, it is this student's education itself which has provided the very forum in which he is able to loudly castigate the government and denounce its intervention in the curriculum. Seen by some as mere paradox, this invitation to public scepticism, I argue, is at the heart of the education of citizens, which is concerned with developing the reflexive capacities of people to govern themselves in order to achieve social peace (Hunter 1994, Hunter and Meredyth 2001, p. 86). Even key citizenship resources for teachers sanctioned by a Government department, such as the recent handbook, *Making Sense of Citizenship* (Huddleston and Kerr 2006, p. 14), exemplify an enabling and inciting form of power. Citizenship Education is not 'optional' so is part of a direct government intervention in the curriculum, but it is 'about helping young people to think for themselves' – this is a distinctly pedagogical form of power which is concerned with developing particular active and reflexive competences to enable people to govern themselves. Furthermore, what is posited as the 'ideal citizen' in many citizenship textbooks is not some individualistic, self-responsible, entrepreneurial (neoliberal) consumer, but a highly sophisticated, reflexive, always questioning, critical, socially aware, *socially* responsible, politicised citizen (e.g. Culshaw *et al.* 2002, p. 5, emphasis added):

> Citizenship is about *learning to live together* as a community, both within your own country and beyond. Citizenship Education gives people the knowledge they need to play a full part in society. Understanding *how society works* will help you to *live better* within it, and *give you the power* to make things better for other people too.

Citizenship Education, as both Hunter (1994) and Hayward (2000) suggest, is therefore concerned with what makes government possible. It is aimed at improving the health of democracy by equipping citizens with the skills, knowledge and disposition to become active participants in their own government. In the reflexive practices of Citizenship Education, teachers and pupils *learn about* citizenship as well as *learning to be* citizens. By contrast, the approach of both Bernstein (1996) and Kaplan (2007) fails to deal adequately with the question of subjectivity, and posits education as an apparatus of ideological state control – rather than as something integral to personhood which has proliferative potential. Theorising the education of citizen subjectivities should rely neither on an unfounded faith in human good, nor a privileged 'view from above' which claims to uncover the real sources of dominating power, but should acknowledge that citizen autonomy necessitates compromise, hypocritical actions and contradictions, and sceptical orientations. Pedagogical power does not therefore produce freedom nor rely on an illusion of freedom, as critics of neoliberalism suggest. Pedagogy is concerned with how best to improve people's capacity to act in the future as a means by which to ensure the welfare of people living together in societies. In this sense, it has very little to do with freedom, and everything to do with social welfare.

The pedagogical state beyond schools

The way in which we employ the idea of the 'pedagogical state' as a means of understanding the pedagogic strategies employed by the state and non-state agencies to govern citizens within the formal educational sphere has implications for how we theorise state power, state–citizen relations and the cultural practices of governing in the wider social sphere. Whilst critical educational theorists have made influential contributions to the interpretation of so-called 'public pedagogy' (Giroux 2004, p. 74, McLaren 2008, p. 476), they have thus far relied on an approach which seeks only to uncover the neoliberal agenda lying behind 'the educational force of culture [which] negates the basic conditions of critical agency' (Giroux 2004, p. 74). Investigating pedagogical sites such as sports and entertainment media, cable television networks, churches and channels of elite and popular culture such as advertising (ibid., p. 75), they find only dominating power which serves to placate ignorant publics and perpetuate social injustices. Their account therefore presumes that lessons from schooling as an ideological apparatus can be applied to the wider social sphere without modification. In contrast, the account offered here interprets Citizenship Education as a site in which 'the state' invites public scepticism, promotes the future capabilities of citizens to reflexively self-govern and aims to assure social order and the welfare of citizens. This analysis provokes us to rethink critical interpretations of 'active citizenship' policies and the pedagogical practices of governing found in the UK at this time.

Pedagogical strategies commonplace in schools can be found in local authority relationships with parents, in criminal justice, and in welfare policies. The Every Child Matters green paper, for instance, (HMSO 2003, p. 29, emphasis added) promoted extended schools, which should act as:

> the hub for services for children, families and other members of the community. Extended schools offer the community and their pupils a range of services (such as childcare, adult learning, health and community facilities) that *go beyond their core educational function.*

In addition, this green paper (2003, p. 41) proposed a set of measures aimed at providing advice for all parents, support targeted at certain parents, such as 'parent education programmes . . . where parents are trained in behavioural techniques'. The Children's Plan (DCSF 2007c, p. 6) outlines a 'partnership with parents' as a key theme in children's services. It proposes to compel local authorities to provide 'Parent Support Advisers' and aims to ensure a new involved relationship between parents and schools (ibid., p. 8). The plan outlines a place for 'Family Intervention Projects' and a new telephone advice services, 'Parent Know-How'. It also describes the idea of using 'Acceptable Behaviour Contracts as a measure to prevent young people engaging in antisocial behaviour and to ensure young people receive support to improve their behaviour at the same time as an Antisocial Behaviour Order' (ibid., p. 13). Further afield, in welfare policies, benefit claimants are obliged to demonstrate a range of behaviours before they are considered eligible for a bare minimum of state assistance. More generally, 'paternalist' governing practices and participatory governance strategies in the spheres of health, community regeneration, environmental responsibility, the provision of community legal advisory services such as the Citizens Advice Bureaux and personal finance education, both in the UK and the US (e.g. Thaler and Sunstein 2008), are growing in political prominence. Such policies are themselves based on a pedagogical relationship between state and citizen, and our understandings of their significance would benefit from an interdisciplinary interrogation of school-based practices, educational policy reform and the educational sector.

Conclusions

Education is a significant sphere through which to understand contemporary governance and the cultural and governmental practices of the state and non-state agencies. It is argued that pedagogy is a way of thinking about teaching and a set of considerations about the appropriate way to teach people to govern themselves and others. It is not a form of monolithic, coercive power, but holds within it the conditions for its own challenge. Pedagogical power is not repressive but enables us to articulate the conditions in which we are made governable, and Citizenship Education is perhaps the most stark example of a policy technology replete with hypocrisy, contradiction, and the incitement to a sceptical, reflexive response. Schoolchildren do not therefore occupy a privileged position of having not *yet* been colonised by the 'totally pedagogised society', as has been suggested by critical scholars. Both Kaplan's and Bernstein's conceptualisations of the pedagogical state provide somewhat deterministic and totalising accounts of the strategies pursued by states to govern spaces, subjects and practices through pedagogical means. This results in a narrative, shared by proponents of critical pedagogy, that renders individuals responsible for their own 'emancipation' from various hidden curricula exercised through the ideological state apparatus of both schooling itself, and school-like practices employed outside of the formal educational sphere.

The second approach followed by both Hayward and Hunter is distinctive in its analysis of pedagogical power and freedom. They thus help to make visible *the social conditions of freedom which comprise the cultural and governmental environment* in which pedagogical subjects are produced – that is, the making and shaping of a people who are governable but not unproblematically governed. This also helps us to consider how there is 'no spatial beyond of the state, and there are no subjects outside power' (Li 2005, p. 385). In her critique of Scott's work on development and global welfare: *Seeing Like a State* (Li 2005, p. 383), Li is concerned with the way in which state and 'non-state' agencies position people as subjects, serve a number of contingent and competing interests, and constantly reassemble their configurations in order to govern, not according to some 'master plan' (ibid., p. 386), but through 'local tactics of education, persuasion, inducement, management, incitement, motivation, encouragement' (Li 2005, p. 386). Rather than identifying a master plan or closing down (or reserve for enlightened 'transformative intellectuals', or not-yet-captured schoolchildren) the possibility of critique, the analysis of power and subjectivity outlined here through the case of Citizenship Education generates novel questions about how the pedagogical state reframes the state and citizen, what forms of address state and non-state agencies use to call forth citizen-subjects, and in what spheres and to what ends particular people are invoked as pedagogical subjects.

Such an explanation understands education, after Hunter, as a purposefully *unprincipled* domain which serves to separate the principled private actions and subjectivities of persons from public impartial ones. It views the governability of citizens as actually quite a good thing, and therefore leads us out of the moralised realm of dead-end questioning as to whether education is being privatised, neoliberalised, or employed as a form of social control. This is both too obvious and too deterministic a conclusion, and it ignores the distinctive nature of pedagogical power. Instead, we should ask questions about how people are made governable through Citizenship Education, and about the relationship between citizenship, education and governance beyond the classroom.

We could interrogate the increasingly moralised discourse of 'participation through personalisation' (Leadbeater 2004), through which educational failures become the personal responsibility of pupils and their families as they are disentangled from their socio-spatial contexts. We could ask how new educational actors negotiate the everyday ethical dilemmas involved in educational policy-making, decision-making, management and governance. City academies, trust schools, faith schools, the charitable status of private education, home-schooling, parental involvement policies and the emergence of non-state educational actors (opinion-formers, think-tanks, quangos, educational NGOs, non-governmental public bodies, advisory groups, young people's representatives, educational consultants) all provide fruitful sites, practices and subjects for the analysis of new forms of educational governance. These sites illuminate emerging forms of pedagogical power – not all of them necessarily desirable, but none reducible to the hegemonic forces of neoliberalism alone.

We may therefore draw lessons from the pedagogical strategies employed by the state and 'non-state' actors to govern citizens *outside* of the formal educational sphere. Pedagogy can be understood as both shaping behaviour and inviting critique, and thus as an enabling and productive mode of power. Pedagogical power is employed by 'state', 'non-state' and peripheral state actors, recognising a blurring of the boundaries between state and citizen as entities (Painter 2006), and problematising analyses which seek to name a unified state agenda. Schools constitute people as governable citizens in the context of social constraints on freedom. These constraints comprise the cultural and governmental environment in which pedagogical subjects are discursively framed, invoked and yet exhibit proliferative potential. Interrogation of such social constraints would be fruitful avenues for critical research. The case of Citizenship Education in UK schools shows how the practices of citizen-formation are made explicit through schooling – shaping 'schooled' behaviours whilst at the same time inviting a response of public scepticism. Research on the discourse of active citizenship, state–citizen relations and the changing practices of governing could benefit from the implications of this pedagogical form of power both within and beyond the school gates. An interrogation of the characteristics of pedagogy can help us to divest ourselves of the tendency to claim privileged insights into how *other* people are fooled by the invisible ideologies of governmental power.

Note

1. All names are pseudonyms.

References

Allen, J., 2003. *Lost geographies of power*. Oxford: Blackwell Publishing.

Apple, M.W., 2001. Comparing neo-liberal projects and inequality in education. *Comparative education*, 37 (4), 409–423.

Atherton, C., 1998. Children, animals, slaves and grammar. *In*: Y. Lee Too and N. Livingstone, eds. *Pedagogy and power. Rhetorics of classical learning*. Cambridge: Cambridge University Press, 214–244.

Ball, S.J., 1987. *The micro-politics of the school: towards a theory of school organization*. London: Methuen.

Barnett, C., 2005. The consolations of 'neoliberalism'. *Geoforum*, 36 (1), 7–12.

Basu, R., 2004. The rationalisation of neoliberalism in Ontario's public education system, 1995–2000. *Geoforum*, 35, 621–634.

Belsey, T., 2005. Foucault, truth-telling, and technologies of the self in schools. *Journal of educational enquiry*, 6 (1), 76–89.

Bernstein, B., 1996. *Pedagogy, symbolic control and identity. Theory, research, critique.* London: Taylor & Francis.

Blunkett, D., 2003. *Civil renewal: a new agenda. The CSV Edith Kahn memorial lecture, 11th June 2003.* London: Home Office Communication Directorate.

Bonal, X., 2003. The neoliberal educational agenda and the legitimation crisis: old and new state strategies. *British journal of sociology of education*, 24 (2), 159–175.

Bonal, X. and Rambla, X., 2003. Captured by the totally pedagogised society: teachers and teaching in the knowledge economy. *Globalisation, societies, education*, 1 (2), 169–184.

Brenner, N., 1999. Beyond state-centrism? Space, territoriality and geographical scale in globalization studies. *Theory and society*, 28 (2), 39–78.

Butler, T. and Hamnett, C., eds, 2007. The geography of education. *Urban studies*, 44 (7), 1161–1174.

Castree, N., 2005. The epistemology of particulars: human geography, case studies and 'context'. *Geoforum*, 36 (5), 541–544.

Clarke, J., 2005. New labour's citizens: activated, empowered, responsibilized, abandoned? *Critical social policy*, 25 (4), 447–463.

Clarke, J. and Newman, J., 1997. *The managerial state. Power, politics and ideology in the remaking of social welfare.* London: Sage.

Cowley, S., 2003. *How to survive your first year in teaching.* London: Continuum.

Culshaw, C., Wales, J., Clarke, P. and Reaich, N., 2002. *Citizenship today.* London: HarperCollins.

Davies, B. and Bansel, P., 2007. Neoliberalism and education. *International journal of qualitative studies in education*, 20 (3), 247–259.

DCSF, 2007a. *Faith in the system*, Department for Children, Schools and Families (DCSF) Publications, Nottingham. Available from: www.dcsf.gov.uk/publications/faithinthesystem/ [Accessed 3 March 2008].

DCSF, 2007b. *Guidance on the duty to promote community cohesion.* Nottingham: DCSF Publications. Available from: http://publications.teachernet.gov.uk/ [Accessed 3 March 2008].

DCSF, 2007c. *The children's plan. Building brighter futures.* Norwich: TSO.

DCSF, 2008. Academy programme to be further accelerated with lower set up costs as part of a new 'national challenge' programme DCSF Press Notice, 29 February 2008. Available from: www.dfes.gov.uk/pns/DisplayPN.cgi?pn_id=2008_0036 [Accessed 3 March 2008].

Dixie, G., 2003. *Managing your classroom (classmates).* London: Continuum.

Elden, S., 2007. Rethinking governmentality. *Political geography*, 26 (1), 29–33.

Fitzsimons, P., 2002. Neoliberalism and education: the autonomous chooser. Available from: http://radicalpedagogy.icaap.org/content/issue4_2/04_fitzsimons.html [Accessed 12 September 2003].

Gillborn, D., 2006. Citizenship education as placebo. 'Standards', institutional racism and education policy. *Education, citizenship and social justice*, 1 (1), 83–104.

Giroux, H.A., 2004. Cultural studies and the politics of public pedagogy: making the political more pedagogical. *Parallax*, 10 (2), 73–89.

Gulson, K.N. and Symes, C., eds, 2007. *Spatial theories of education. Policy and geography matters.* London: Routledge.

Hayward, C.R., 2000. *De-facing power.* Cambridge: Cambridge University Press.

HMSO (Treasury), 2003. *Every child matters.* Norwich: TSO.

Huddleston, T. and Kerr, D., eds, 2006. *Making sense of citizenship. A continuing professional development handbook.* London: Hodder Education.

Hunter, I., 1994. *Rethinking the school. Subjectivity, bureaucracy, criticism.* St. Leonards, Australia: Allen and Unwin.

Hunter, I. and Meredyth, D., 2001. Popular sovereignty and civic education. *In*: D. Meredyth and J. Minson, eds. *Citizenship and cultural policy.* London: Sage.

Isin, E.F., 2004. The neurotic citizen. *Citizenship studies*, 8 (3), 217–235.

Jessop, B., 2001. Bringing the state back in (yet again): reviews, revisions, rejections, and redirections. *International review of sociology*, 11 (2), 149–173.

Kaplan, S., 2007. *The pedagogical state. Education and the politics of national culture in post-1980 Turkey.* Stanford: Stanford University Press.

Larner, W., 2003. Neoliberalism? *Environment and planning D: society and space*, 21 (5), 509–512.

Leadbeater, C., 2004. *Participation through personalisation.* London: Demos. Available from: http://www.demos.co.uk [Accessed 6 September 2007].

Lewis, N., 2003. Embedding the reforms in New Zealand schooling: after neoliberalism? *GeoJournal*, 59, 149–160.

Li, T.M., 2005. Beyond 'the state' and failed schemes. *American anthropologist*, 107 (3), 383–394.

McLaren, P., 1989. *Life in schools: an introduction to critical pedagogy in the foundations of education*. London: Longman.

McLaren, P., 2008. This fist called my heart: public pedagogy in the belly of the beast. *Antipode*, 40 (3), 472–481.

Mitchell, K., 2003. Educating the national citizen in neoliberal times: from the multicultural self to the strategic cosmopolitan. *Transactions of the institute of British geographers*, 28 (4), 387–403.

Mitchell, K., 2006. Neoliberal governmentality in the European Union: education, training and technologies of citizenship. *Environment and planning D: society and space*, 24 (3), 389–407.

Newman, J., ed., 2005. *Remaking governance. Peoples, politics and the public sphere*. Bristol: Policy Press.

Newman, J. and Mahony, N., 2007. Democracy and the public realm: towards a progressive agenda? *Soundings*, 36 (summer), 52–62.

O'Hear, A., 1999. Enter the new robot citizens. Labour's plans for classes in citizenship pose an insidious threat to all of us. *Daily Mail (London)*, 14 May.

O'Leary, J., 1998. Indoctrination fear over lessons on citizenship. *The Times*, 23 March.

Olssen, M., 2004a. Neoliberalism, globalisation, democracy: challenges for education. *Globalisation, societies, and education*, 2 (2), 231–275.

Olssen, M., 2004b. From the Crick Report to the Parekh Report: multiculturalism, cultural difference, and democracy – the re-visioning of Citizenship Education. *British journal of sociology of education*, 25 (2), 179–192.

Painter, J., 2005. State: society. *In*: P. Cloke and R.J. Johnston, eds. *Spaces of geographical thought: deconstructing binaries*. London: Sage, 42–60.

Painter, J., 2006. Prosaic geographies of stateness. *Political geography*, 25 (7), 752–774.

Peck, J. and Tickell, A., 2002. Neoliberalizing space. *Antipode*, 34 (3), 380–405.

Peters, M., Marshall, J. and Fitzsimons, P., 2000. Managerialism and education policy in a global context: Foucault, neoliberalism and the doctrine of self-management. *In*: N.C. Burbules and C.A. Torres, eds. *Globalization and education. Critical perspectives*. London: Routledge, 109–132.

Phillips, M., 1999. The indoctrination of citizen Smith Jr. *Sunday Times (London)*, 7 March.

Qualifications and Curriculum Authority (QCA), 1998. *Education for citizenship and the teaching of democracy in schools. Final report of the advisory group on citizenship* ('The Crick Report'). London: QCA.

QCA, 2007. *Citizenship. Programme of study: key stage 4*. Available from http://www.qca.org.uk/qca_12208.aspx [Accessed 3 December 2007].

Rhodes, R.A.W., 1997. *Understanding governance: policy networks, governance, reflexivity and accountability*. Buckingham: Open University Press.

Rogers, B., 2002. *Classroom behaviour: a practical guide to effective teaching, behaviour management and colleague support*. London: Paul Chapman Publications.

Rose, N., 1999. *Powers of freedom. Reframing political thought*. Cambridge: Cambridge University Press.

Simon, B., 1994. Why no pedagogy in England? *In*: B. Moon and S. Meyes, eds. *Teaching and learning in the secondary school*. London: Routledge, 10–22.

Stoker, G., 2006. *Why politics matters. Making democracy work*. Basingstoke: Palgrave Macmillan.

Thaler, R.H. and Sunstein, C.R., 2008. *Nudge. Improving decisions about health, wealth and happiness*. London: Yale University Press.

'Tom', 2006. Cynical citizens. *Teaching citizenship*, 14 (Spring), 26.

Turner, B.S., ed., 1993. *Citizenship and social theory*. London: Sage.

Valentine, G., 2000. Exploring children and young people's narratives of identity. *Geoforum*, 31, 257–267.

Weller, S., 2003. Teach us something useful: contested spaces of teenagers' citizenship. *Space and polity*, 7 (2), 153–172.

Weller, S., 2007. *Teenagers' citizenship. Experiences and education*. Abingdon: Routledge.

Willis, P., 1977. *Learning to labour: how working class kids get working class jobs*. Farnborough: Saxon House.

Young, M., 1996. Foreword. Go for diversity! *In*: F. Carnie, M. Large and M. Tasker, eds. *Freeing education. Steps towards real choice and diversity in schools*. Stroud: Hawthorn Press, vii–viii.

Enrolling ordinary people: governmental strategies and the avoidance of politics?

John Clarke

Department of Social Policy, Faculty of Social Sciences, The Open University, Walton Hall, Milton Keynes, UK

Recent strategies for 'governing the social' have placed a premium on recruiting ordinary people to their processes. This commitment to the value of ordinary people links UK initiatives in public services and citizenship to innovations in development strategies in the global south. This paper asks what it is that makes ordinary people such a desired object of governmental strategies and suggests that it is their assumed a-political character and their capacity to bring values, knowledge and other resources that are beyond the state. This article suggests that keeping politics out of governing may be a governmental ambition, but ordinary people cannot be relied on to perform in such ways.

What is it about ordinary people that makes them the focus of innovative strategies of governing the social? From political participation schemes to the burgeoning world of micro-credit models of development, from empowering communities to creating 'choice and voice', new processes of governance place 'ordinary people' at the centre. So, who are these ordinary people? What makes them such valued subjects? What are the governmental and political dynamics of their enrolment? These questions link a number of different places, politics, policies and practices in which ordinary people are the focus of governmental excitement.

In this paper, I explore the widespread enthusiasm for enrolling ordinary people into new strategies for governing the social, leading to an examination of what value such people are seen to add to the processes of governing. In the third section, I consider the problematic relationship between politics and governing through recent UK policy initiatives. This leads to a consideration of the role of ordinary people's voices in the construction of policy texts (in what I term vernacular ventriloquism). This paper concludes with a discussion of the problematic relationships between pedagogies, politics and power in governing the social.

New modes of governing the social

In the 1980s and 1990s, what might be called market-centric models dominated the national and international reform agendas in relation to welfare systems, public service provision and development programmes. Such changes have attracted various descriptions: neo-liberalism, the Washington consensus, market fundamentalism and the new public management. These changes shared some organising assumptions: that the market was an efficient and innovative means of coordinating human activity; that individuals were active, and rational, choice makers; that incentives energised 'entrepreneurial' action and that public institutions, government programmes and state systems were, at best, cumbersome, slow and unresponsive (at worst, they were colonised and monopolised by producer power).

Such developments produced arguments that both the political and the social domains of societies had been eviscerated, reduced or subordinated to the logics and mechanisms (and interests) of the economic (Clarke 2007). However, this focus on the subordination of politics and the social has rather distracted attention from other processes of processes of governmental reform and innovation. These range from the massive extension of state powers and capacities around national and international 'security', sometimes identified as the punitive turn or the culture of control (e.g. Garland 2001, Crawford 2006, Cochrane and Talbot 2009) to the proliferation of strategies for enrolling 'ordinary people' into governing the social on which I focus here.

When such innovations are discussed, they are frequently reduced to the corrupt fruit of neo-liberalism as it enlarges its scope or reach. While not wanting to suggest that such innovations are innocent, or even form progressive alternatives to the marketising or economising projects of the last three decades, something is lost if they are treated as merely the continued extension of the neo-liberal project. In particular, such reductive views miss out *other* politics. In particular, they are over-focused on the dominant elements of politics and policy and thus neglect what Williams (1977) calls the residual and emergent elements of a conjuncture. Williams argued that 'real', rather than 'epochal', historical analysis had to address the coexistence of multiple tendencies and the relations between them. For me, this points to the importance of other politics and to treating innovation as the response to the failures of earlier strategies – especially those of marketisation or economisation in terms of both their contradictory consequences and their failure to command adequate popular political support or attachment. A disorganised or disorderly field of the 'social' generates antagonisms, tensions and forms of disaffection that present problems of governmental authority, the mobilisation of political consent and (party) political calculation (Clarke 2004).

It is in this landscape that the enrolment of 'ordinary people' acquires its significance. Ordinary people – in their many governmentalised incarnations – provide a new locus for governing the social. They seem to represent an alternative to 'old style' government, to the anonymity and contractualism of markets, and to the problematic world of 'politics'. Ordinary people both bring and create value in the process of governing the social. In a recent book (Newman and Clarke 2009), we have argued that 'ordinary people' have been addressed as the embodiment of three particular formations: communities, civil society and voluntary/non-governmental organisations:

> [C]ommunity is a concept that bridges spatial and political-cultural processes of reassembling the nation; it also encompasses a variety of material and symbolic resources on which political and governmental projects attempt to draw in recomposing the public. Civil society condenses multiple political projects and brings into view different conceptions of what it might mean to act publicly beyond the state. The 'third sector' includes a plurality of organisational types and forms, from the community group to the large voluntary sector organisation, charity or non governmental agency, all seen as repositories of social, moral or cultural resources. Each has become valued as a site where people can govern, provision and manage themselves beyond the structures of state systems. As a result we will be paying rather more attention to how these sites are identified, valorized and recruited in the process of governing than to their

diverse political and historical roots. Each is an *object of desire*, representing important moral, social or civic virtues that are assumed to be valuable or productive. Each is deeply implicated in strategies for state reform: viewed as alternatives to state services, as ways of mediating state projects, and as ways of drawing on resources beyond the state. They are all are assumed to contain subjects – ordinary people – who can be summoned as partners or participants in new assemblages of power. (Newman and Clarke 2009, p. 46)

This is not to claim that these three sites exhaust the ways in which ordinary people are sought out, solicited and enrolled into contemporary strategies for governing the social. On the contrary, the range of such strategies is extensive: we could trace this valorisation of ordinary people as governance actors in such diverse sites as tenant empowerment in the governance of social housing (McKee and Cooper 2007, McDermont *et al.* 2009); exercises in public participation and citizen deliberation (Barnes *et al.* 2007, Mahony 2008); or administrative bodies that create lay voices to set alongside expert or professional views (Davies *et al.* 2007). We might also include processes of installing choice and/or voice in the management of public services – education, health care and social care, for example (Clarke *et al.* 2007). While these have tended to focus on the creation of a consumer-like choice through markets or market-mimicking devices, they also involve the elevation of 'lay' knowledge (at least that of being an 'expert of one's own condition') and the displacement of bureau-professional welfare articulations of knowledge and power.

We can also trace this valorisation of ordinary people in the shifting approaches to economic and social development in societies outside the Euro-North American developmental norm, particularly in policies intended to enhance or empower 'civil society'. Innovations designed to enrol 'ordinary people' sometimes speak in the language of discovering and realising the social and cultural capital of the poor (especially but not only in the micro-credit boom that followed the success of the Grameen Bank). Here, people are re-imagined as 'enterprising selves', able to insert themselves into the circuits of value of a global economy by means of turning themselves, their knowledges, their cultural habits into forms of capital (Elyachar 2005). Excluded and marginalised 'ordinary people' thus become both the object and the means of modernisation. In the process, the problems of earlier political, institutional or state-centred models of development are acknowledged – so that 'failure' is seen as an effect of sclerotic states or forms of political corruption that distorted development possibilities.

In a similar way, US aid flows to the countries of the former Soviet Union after its break-up sought channels of circulation that avoided the state – and the political actors associated with it (Wedel 2001). As a result, 'civil society' actors and organisations were clearly identified as the preferred conduits and connections. Wedel's study points to the contradictory effects of this mapping of the societies in question. She argues that the emerging organisations of Eastern European civil society included the formation of elite cliques and clubs whose 'can do' qualities appealed to funding agencies. Their connections to Western funders in turn enlarged their standing and capacity to act:

The initiatives of the big men were often more informed by politics than the donors expected. Western funding reinforced the ability of certain influential groups to shape all aspects of economy, politics and society, undeterred by the rule of law. What did this portend for the efforts of Western donors, whose stated goal was to encourage the development of a civil society? Because many funds went to groups that were exclusive, informal, de facto political clubs, they helped to reinforce the clubs rather than widen political participation or to 'build democratic institutions'. Some funds empowered entrenched political and economic cliques and power brokers, in some cases undercutting legitimate state institutions and governance. (Wedel 2001, p. 108)

Both of these examples point to a critical relationship between 'politics' and the recruitment of 'ordinary people' (whether as micro-entrepreneurs or civil society actors). Ordinary people are seen as a counterbalance to the dangers and 'dirtiness' of politics – they are not contaminated with the corruption, collusion and cynicism of existing politics. This conception of politics as something to be avoided is visible elsewhere, not least in the nations emerging from the former Yugoslavia. There, the common conception of politics as dirty or corrupt was intensified by its articulation with ethno-nationalism, war and 'ethnic cleansing' strategies. Writing about the conditions of, and constraints on, women's activism, Helms argues that:

> Ordinary Bosnians generally view politics with a large dose of scepticism, especially when they see political parties as working against their own interests. Politicians are derided as corrupt schemers, only out for personal gain and engaged in dark deals and morally compromising activities.... Since the dissolution of socialist Yugoslavia, politics have also been reviled for producing the politicized ethnic hatred which fuelled and preceded the war and which continues, in the eyes of many Bosnians, to underlie obstacles to the (re)establishment of peace and prosperity...

> Despite such negative associations, however, when the question arises as to whether women should or can be effective politicians, it becomes clear that politics is nevertheless regarded as a source of prestige and power, and one meant primarily for men.... (Helms 2006, p. 4)

In this setting, the demarcation of politics as a male preserve is constituted through a complex articulation of gendering and sexualising representations. Helms argues that women are expected to prioritise home and children (albeit while having access to waged work), but 'politics is nevertheless seen as too demanding and "dirty" for women'. She goes on:

> For women, this dirtiness implies not only dishonesty but sexual immorality. Monika, a nineteen year old political activist and candidate for the Zenica municipal assembly, told me that her boyfriend was now resigned to her involvement in politics but that, 'at the beginning he would make [critical] comments, he thought it wasn't right. You know, they say politics is a whore and a woman in politics is therefore a whore'. In this very common formulation, politics is feminized, but as a disreputable, immoral female – the whore. 'She' corrupts good men, compelling them to engage in immoral acts. Politicians are similarly cast as prostitutes who sell themselves and their moral principles for personal gain. The masculinity of male politicians, however, is not damaged through their participating in politics. Indeed, they engage in some of the most quintessentially masculine arenas: the public and the political. Even metaphorically, men's masculinity (virility) is enhanced rather than diminished though their association with a 'whore', through the sexualised double standard... Thus, politics as a whore does not feminize or emasculate male politicians so much as point to the corruption and immorality of their profession. Women, however, are doubly excluded from this realm, both because they are not male and because, as females, association with such immorality calls their own moral reputations into question. (Helms 2006, p. 5)

Women must negotiate this heavily structured conception of the gendering of politics if they wish to be publicly active. For many, Helms argues, the NGO form provides a way of negotiating this exclusionary definition of politics. NGOs are 'humanitarian', not 'political', organisations and thus serve as a site where women may reasonably pursue social objectives without being seen to 'meddle' in politics. In practice, such distinctions were less securely founded, but it is precisely the rise of the NGO form (especially in the fields of transnational governance) that both permitted some forms of activism, and acted as a constraint on the struggle for 'politics'. The gendering of politics, however, produced possibilities of representing women as more closely identified with the social, moral and humanitarian dimensions of social life and need (by comparison with the more abstracted or distant world of politics). Women, too, were seen as more likely to promote common interest and build alliances (including across ethnic boundaries) than male politicians (see also Helms 2003).

Women, then, sometimes hold a contingently privileged position when the 'ordinariness' of ordinary people becomes an issue. This has also been true in terms of economic and social development models in the South and for models of Social Investment as a post-welfarist orientation in the North. For example, Esping-Andersen (2002) has argued that a 'New Welfare State' needs to be organised around 'child-centred investment' and a new 'gender contract' in which public child care enables full-time waged work for women (producing a virtuous circle of work, taxation and investment). At the same time, women are characteristically the targets of programmes of volunteering and community activation – since they are both embedded in the everyday local and are likely to act on its networks of relationships (Newman 2010).

What marks these enrolments of ordinary people to governmentalised locations is not their reduction to an economised subjectivity, but how they blur conventional distinctions between realms and roles. No doubt, in some of these strategies, 'ordinary people' are being addressed as, or induced to be, economic actors (producers, consumers, entrepreneurs and so on). They are also, in some cases, invited to become the 'self-governing' subjects of neo-liberal rationality (Rose 1999, see also Maasen and Sutter 2007). But they are also invited to become co-producers of welfare, care, community and the 'social fabric'. They are solicited as co-governors of the social, standing for and representing other ordinary people ... as members of the public, service users, residents, citizens or bearers of the 'lay perspective'.

Without erasing the differences of enrolment and empowerment that certainly exist in different policies and governance assemblages, I want to consider the intricate relationship between ordinary people, politics and governance as a set of motifs that animates many of these innovations. In particular, this set of motifs constructs the value of ordinariness for contemporary governmental strategies. In this valorisation of ordinariness, we can see the effects of many of the anti-statist and 'bottom-up' movements of earlier decades that challenged the domination of the powerful and powerful institutions in the name of the oppressed, excluded and dominated. There are three connecting threads visible here:

1. the top-down/bottom-up distinction, which sometimes is translated into varieties of anti-elitism, including the anti-elitism of what Frank (2001) calls 'market populism';
2. the question of power and its strained relationship to the discourse of empowerment (Cruikshank 1999, Sharma 2008) and
3. the framing device of 'voice' as both a marker of participation and a strategic demand for inclusion on behalf of the excluded.[1]

Governing through ordinary people

These innovations often have a neo-liberal or market-centric character – consumerist models of choice, micro-credit approaches to development or even independent budgets in social care might all be read in these terms. Certainly, these are strategies that seek to imagine people as economic agents, acting as entrepreneurs of the self and engaging themselves in market or market-like transactions and relationships. But there is something more about this valorisation of ordinary people across the range of strategies that demands analytic attention: the problematic relationship between governing and politics. In particular, I want to point to a genealogical puzzle about these strategies: their ethos of enrolling and empowering ordinary people has roots in a variety of anti-statist popular movements. From the disabled people's movement's demands for independent living (and their critique of professional power) to challenges to 'top-down' models of economic development or feminist struggles with patriarchal (state, market and professional) systems of health care – a whole range of struggles and demands have insisted on the importance of 'bottom-up' approaches that are grounded in the needs, demands and perspectives of 'ordinary people'.

The UK government itself signalled concerns about declining political participation and the need for 'democratic' and 'constitutional renewal' in a Green Paper on *The Governance of Britain* (Ministry of Justice 2007), while a recent White Paper on *Communities in Control* evoked the history of struggles from below as part of its narrative of transferring 'real power' to 'real people' (see also Newman 2010):

> British history is punctuated by debates about the nature of democracy and the struggles for political power to be extended to greater numbers of the population – from the Putney Debates during the English Civil War which paved the way for our civil liberties, to the Chartists' campaign in the nineteenth century to extend the vote to working people and from the demands of the Suffragettes for votes for women, to the campaigns in the 1960s and 1970s for more involvement by industrial workers, students, council house tenants and users of social services. More recently the mass campaign mobilising people in the call to 'Make Poverty History' reminds us that the way our democracy works has always been subject to *pressure from below*. (Department of Communities and Local Government 2008, p. 14, para. 1.6; my emphasis)

Let me stress that this is a genealogical puzzle, not a claim that such struggles have provided the motifs or discourses for neo-liberal politics and governmental strategies. The puzzle concerns how different orientations, discourses and political projects might become part of governmental 'assemblages' in the present (Newman and Clarke 2009). In one sense, political projects and governmental strategies are rarely coherent entities with only one singular character or voice. They are, rather, better thought of in terms of articulations – both in the social constituencies they attempt to identify, address and mobilise (or demobilise); and in the 'voices' that they use in the process of addressing those constituencies. Studies of neo-liberalism have tended to concentrate on the dominant elements of the project (and discourse) or on its alliances with one or two other political tendencies (neo-conservatism, social democracy, perhaps), but have rarely explored the diversity of encounters that are at stake in trying to govern the social in neo-liberal times and terms (Clarke 2004). It is hardly surprising that earlier 'social' movements should provide some of the resources for addressing the failures of neo-liberal rule, for revitalising and rethinking it, and even for imagining 'after neo-liberalism' (Larner and Craig 2005).

As I suggested above, perhaps the most significant attribute of ordinary people that makes them an object of governmental desire is their relationship to politics. In an era of (generally) growing disaffection from, or disenchantment with, institutionalised forms, organisation and practices of politics, the conduct of politics has seemed increasingly problematic. In particular, there are concerns about 'political classes' who appear excessively detached from the populations that they (claim to) represent; about the rise of corruption, collusion and the distortions wrought by power, wealth and celebrity; and about the significance of forms of 'regressive' populist politics based around racism, xenophobia and nationalism that debase liberal pubic culture and its norms of political conduct (see, for example, Stoker 2006). In the context of these concerns about 'actually existing politics', ordinary people are valorised *because they are not political*. They are seen as occupying positions that are above or below politics: below, because they are seen to be concerned with more 'everyday' issues; above, because they are not engaged in the venal, corrupt or collusive pursuit of power and self-interest in the manner of politicians.

'Anti-elitism' has been a distinctive theme of New Labour's approach to public service reform – whether challenging patterns of recruitment to 'elite' universities or insisting that ordinary people should have the chance to exercise choice in their lives. This anti-elitist populism connects a variety of innovations in public service reform, the institutions of governing and the activation of citizens and communities. Ordinary people deserve to exercise choice and voice. They should be encouraged and enabled to take part in processes of decision making – albeit localised to particular places or particular services. They deserve to be included in the 'governance of Britain' rather than being excluded by concentration of power and influence. In a speech in 2005, David Miliband MP articulated New Labour's commitment to engaging ordinary people – the public – in the continuing reform of public services. He argued that:

There are three main reasons why the public is coming centre stage:

– We live in an increasingly diverse country, where not only are needs and aspirations different, but people are more confident that they have a right to an opinion about how they are treated.

– The 'active welfare state' is based on rights and responsibilities for the individual as well as the state. More and more of what Government wants to achieve requires the engagement of the citizen. Think of public health, or safe neighbourhoods, or raising pupil performance: all depend on public services, but all depend too on the way citizens help themselves.

– Third and most important, there is increasing evidence that services which have gone from improvement to transformation have done so through concerted engagement with service users. Public services can only help people take up opportunity and feel more secure if they give confidence as well as care, empowerment as well as standards. (Miliband 2005, p. 3)

Here, we see the British version of the active or activated citizen: as a co-producer of outcomes, as an assertive claims maker and as an empowered partner in public service processes. The state *needs* ordinary people in this sense. However, as with so many other facets of citizenship, this activated engagement is conditional. The needs and desires of these active and energetic citizens should not point in the direction other than those already envisaged by government (or their agents). The 2008 White Paper on welfare reform exemplified the tortured relationship between governmental direction and the harnessing of the desires and energies of citizens around the issue of conditionality and enforcement:

To make the most of the opportunities available, we need to support everyone to achieve their own aspirations of a return to work, and match this with increased obligations on the individual to take up this help. This means recognising that everyone is different and tailoring support to their own personal needs, but also that nothing can be achieved without individual effort. (Department of Work and Pensions 2008, p. 21)

Ordinary people are not only constituted as these active users of public services, they are solicited into governance roles in local deliberations and in the governance of services or areas of 'public concern' (such as health care, housing and policing: Martin 2007, Clarke 2009, McDermont *et al.* 2009). Here, ordinary people are recruited precisely because they are not the established authorities or recognised experts. Rather, they bring other perspectives or other voices to deliberations about policy, planning and service delivery (in education through parent governors; and housing, in the form of tenant representatives on governing bodies). In health care, there have been a variety of schemes at local and national level designed to expand the involvement of 'lay' representatives. Graham Martin has explored some of these developments in relation to the Campaign for

Public and Patient Involvement in Health (CPPIH). Indeed, he suggests that the summoning of members of the public and patients to participation puts in play a multiplicity of desired qualities – in which specific expertise is solicited alongside the expertise of experience; and where a person's representativeness can be a product of either ordinariness or difference.[2]

> Perhaps the strange mix of representativeness, diversity, ordinariness, knowledge and expertise to which these materials appeal to is best summed up in a passage repeated in several CPPIH leaflets:
>
> > Forum members will be champions for health and make the views of patients and the public heard.
> >
> > That's why we need people like you – people who know their communities and will give their time to make a real difference.
> >
> > *Can you help to bring better health to your community?*
>
> What is required, above all, is this mystical quality of knowing one's 'community' – which is something, apparently, which people like you possess! You are ordinary enough, motivated enough and knowledgeable enough to take on the duties of a PPI Forum member – but of course you could be anyone who has picked up (and, perhaps crucially, read) a leaflet while attending a local health service. The materials appeal to 'local people', 'ordinary people', 'people who know their communities', seeking to link personal concern with individual health to a common communitarian consciousness that demands collective responsibility and collective action.
>
> 'Ordinariness' and commonality with the 'wider community' have a special place in these appeals: not only do they provide particular insights unavailable through other mechanisms, but they also enhance the ability of Forum members to perform their role of accessing the local population to uncover its views and needs in ways that public-health research, apparently, cannot. (Martin 2007, pp. 46–47)

Ordinary people are thus summoned to engage in multiple – and multi-directional – pedagogic relationships. Although providing the authentic voice of everyday experience, they may need tutoring in the process of coming to voice. For example, the Green Paper on the Governance of Britain claims that 'Citizenship education ensures young people become informed citizens and develops their skills of participation and *responsible action*' (Ministry of Justice 2007, p. 55; my emphasis). In more service-specific settings, ordinary people may need to acquire the knowledge and skills that make them active or expert (learning the medical knowledge appropriate to being an expert patient, for example). In governance arrangements, they may have to be trained in the knowledge and skills that enable them to be 'effective' participants. McDermont *et al.* (2009) point to how 'experience' is not enough for tenant representatives in housing governance. Rather, they have to learn the legal, financial and managerial expertise that is valued in the good governance of such organisations.

But these tend to be top-down conceptions of pedagogy – in which ordinary people are invited to learn. But Martin's study points to a different dynamic in which ordinary people are involved in a sort of *inverse pedagogic practice* – in which their role is to teach the state (and its agencies) what it cannot know by itself, or at least has trouble discovering through other means. The ordinary people recruited to participatory and deliberative processes thus enable everyday knowledge to become visible/audible to the state – with the promise that this access to new knowledge will allow the state and its agents to better respond to the needs and concerns of ordinary people. This is something beyond the constitution of the active and responsible citizen as the subject/object of government (Rose 1999). Here, we see the solicitation of ordinary people as the medium or agent of government, populating the emerging apparatuses of governing the social.

Vernacular ventriloquism: governing through the voice of ordinary people

There is a further dynamic in the relationship between governing, politics and policy visible in some recent UK policy documents which present a distinctively New Labour mode of textual/governmental work: the summoning of ordinary people as active agents in the process of constructing governmental problems and solutions.[3] Nowhere has this been more visible than in the contentious questions of Britishness and citizenship. The Green Paper on The Governance of Britain identified the questions of identity, Britishness and British values as a critical area for engagement between government and the people:

> Above all, this process will be a dialogue with the people of Britain and between the people of Britain. This will require time, careful coordination and planning to ensure the nation feels genuinely engaged in the debate on Britain's values. The end point will be a British statement of values that reflects the voices of citizens across the country. The debate will also provide valuable insights into national views on citizenship and Britishness, which may be published after a period of dialogue and feedback (Ministry of Justice 2007, p. 59)[4]

This 'dialogue' may appear to be nothing more than an exercise in governmental 'listening', but the process of developing a White Paper on citizenship (Home Office 2008) involved commissioning research on public attitudes and holding focus groups to solicit the view of ordinary people (here inscribed as the public):

> To understand in detail the values that the public feels should be at the heart of our immigration system, we held nine public listening sessions around Britain, talking to hundreds of people about the kind of changes they wanted to see.

> The public is very clear that it wants to see a much simpler, more straight-forward set of rules governing the way newcomers become citizens, with a much clearer set of rights and responsibilities. (Home Office 2008, p. 14)

The document uses these voices of ordinary people to construct a set of concerns and policy solutions. This is a rather different device to the conventional mode of governmental address in which governments speak for and to the public. In this respect, it also differs from more conventional forms of political populism. Here, the public itself (appears to) establish the policy agenda:

> It is a common observation that British people hold only a loose sense of what shared values are – until people faced with something that looks like a direct challenge to norms like 'tolerance' and 'freedom of speech'.

> But people give a sense of what's important to them when asked what they would miss if they emigrated. The NHS was commonly cited, as were our values of tolerance, fairness and freedom of speech, a healthy disrespect for authority yet a keen sense of order ...

> *It's hard to pin down [what a good citizen is]. You don't want migrants to lose their identity. But you do get big culture clashes. People need to accept and fit in at some level and fundamentally show respect for the country.*

Newcastle participant

> *Multiculturalism is a two-way street – they must accept us and change too.*

Aberdeen participant

> There was a general acceptance that people from different backgrounds could have different cultural traditions and practices and that these differences should be respected. But people

were concerned that cultural differences could obstruct integration and that 'integrating' was not just about understanding British laws but also learning about everyday behaviour . . .

In sum, the prevalent point of view was a genuine desire to be welcoming, tempered by a belief that the welcome should not be unconditional. The views we received were unambiguous on three points in particular: it is important to *speak the common language, make an economic contribution* to the country and *obey the law*. (Home Office 2008, pp. 14–15; emphasis in original)

It is striking that so many of the quoted participants share the words and frame of reference that New Labour has sought to establish around the contentious issues of citizenship and Britishness. There are no visible outbursts of racism or mean-spirited nationalism visible in this text. The terms of engagement are those of a liberal and tolerant society bent on establishing a 'post-multiculturalist' approach to immigration and citizenship (see also Pitcher 2009). Finally, the requirements of economic contribution, law-abidingness and a common language are themselves well-established elements at the core of New Labour conceptions of the active citizen.

Nevertheless, there is something distinctive about this mode of formulating policy discourse. It grounds policy in the 'common sense' of the public (rather than in the hands of politicians or experts). It summons ordinary people as experts of Britishness. By calling this 'vernacular ventriloquism', I do not mean to detract from its innovative character. Even if it is a cynically calculated piece of governmental discursive practice, it is significant that this shift to the vernacular has been thought either necessary or advantageous. The enrolment of ordinary people into the process of setting policy changes their place and changes the relationships between knowledge, power and policy. However, as with older forms of political and media populism, there are significant questions about the relationship between democratic and demotic voice. Although many contemporary social and political trends are signified as 'democratic' (from the internet to reality TV voting), it seems that these might be better understood as the *demoticisation* of contemporary popular and political culture in which the 'voice of the people' acts as a particular sort of device. That is to say, there are many sites in which the voice(s) of the people might be heard, but these have tenuous and tortuous relationships to politics and power. The proliferation of demotic voicings – ventriloquised by government, solicited in countless surveys, engaged by governance processes, expressed through web sites – poses, but does not resolve, some serious questions about who constitutes the people and how they are to be represented.

Conclusion: paradoxical pedagogies and problematic politics

Finally, I want to reflect on the problems associated with this governmentalisation of ordinary people – in particular, their links to pedagogies and politics. This governmental strategy is a process of de-politicisation through addressing and engaging ordinary people as those who are above and below politics. De-politicisation, as Wendy Brown argues, is a process that:

involves construing inequality, subordination, marginalization and social conflict, which all require political analysis and political solutions, as personal and individual, on the one hand, or as natural, religious or cultural on the other . . . Although depoliticization sometimes personalizes, sometimes culturalizes, and sometimes naturalizes conflict, these tactical variations are tethered to a common mechanics, which is what makes it possible to speak of depoliticization as a coherent phenomenon. Depoliticization involves removing a political phenomenon from comprehension of its *historical* emergence and from a recognition of the *powers* that produce and contour it, No matter its particular form and mechanics, depoliticization always eschews power and history in the representation of its subject. (Brown 2006, p. 15; emphasis in original)

Recruiting ordinary people for their a-political 'common sense' appears as a device for de-politicisation, or for 'taking the politics out of things'. Ordinary people are represented as grounded in everyday life, rather than being driven by the abstractions of political ideologies or the single-minded pursuit of narrow political interests. Here, we see one version of the problem of politics in which the critical insistence that 'everything is political' runs up against the cynical realist view of politics as dirty. Thus, 'taking politics out of things' can be read as a process of depoliticisation or as the avoidance of corrupting practices and people, and the restoration of human and humane values (as embodied in ordinary people). But there is a risk of narrowing our understanding of politics if we reduce it to this juxtaposition. In particular, I would suggest that the discussion of ordinary people here has thrown up three other aspects of politics that are worth attention.

First, I argued earlier that the enrolment of ordinary people drew on a wide range of political discourses and movements that could not be reduced to a singular political, governmental or state strategy. Such political richness – requiring us to consider the residual and emergent tendencies as well as the dominant elements of a cultural formation – is significant for thinking about how governmental strategies are assembled and how they attempt to address, engage and mobilise their desired subjects. Popular movements have celebrated, defended and championed 'ordinary people' in powerful ways (as have forms of populist discourses). There is, as Sharma (2008) has argued, no singular and coherent strategy of empowerment – rather empowerment is a mobile and varying assemblage, drawing together elements of very different conceptions of people, power and politics and articulating them with objectives, strategies, practices and techniques. These include a variety of pedagogic relationships and practices in which ordinary people are invited to learn how to perform their ordinariness, represent other ordinary people and help to govern the social.

Second, pedagogies are themselves sets of techniques and technologies that are both 'depoliticising' (in the Wendy Brown sense) and political. That is, they take relationships and issues and abstract them from the conditions of power and politics in which they are produced, while involving a complex of political dynamics. The deployment of pedagogic techniques and technologies in the work of governing combines what we might call governmental and political calculation: governmental logics are not necessarily the same as (party) political desires and objectives. But pedagogies also put into play dynamics of power and politics in the relationships and practices they imagine and institutionalise. These are embodied in the roles allocated (educator/educated); the modes of interaction and the developmental view of the relationship (as well as the specific 'learning outcomes' being sought). I have tried to show how the enrolment of ordinary people might have quite different pedagogies in use.

Thirdly and finally, it turns out that ordinary people are not wholly reliable – or predictable – governmental agents. Sometimes, they are even difficult to find. For example, Elyachar (2002, pp. 505–506) reports a desperate search for 'ordinary women' to show to funders and sponsors of micro-credit enterprise schemes in Cairo. Ordinary people have to be discovered and enrolled into the practices and relationships of governmental strategies. They also have to know how to *perform* as ordinary people. Indeed, one might argue that one of the pedagogical dimensions of this process of enrolling ordinary people involves teaching them 'how to behave' – as ordinary people, as representatives, as voices. They need induction into the expectations of their performance:

the rules of the game, the acceptable voicings, the places that they should come to occupy in a field of positions and relationships (and their hidden but emergent architectures of power). Sometimes, such attempts to 'conduct conduct' fail: ordinary people step out of their place and perform 'inappropriately'. Sharma (2008, pp. 99–107) study of an empowerment NGO in India relates a performance to be staged for national and international observers by the NGO and the women with whom it worked. Despite warnings that the event needed a 'perfect presentation' of the programme (Sharma 2008, p. 101) and to 'avoid mentioning development problems or needs in front of the visitors' (Sharma 2008, p. 105), the women's performance ended with them presenting written demands for new village facilities to the governmental Chief Development Officer (Sharma 2008, p. 107).

Ordinary people may seek to *repoliticise* issues, events and relationships – restoring the dimensions to view that made them problematic in the first place. This is a significant issue for studies of governmental strategies: we should not assume that they succeed or that they deliver the subjects whom they seek to summon. Politics – in its many forms – is rarely containable. Politics (and not necessarily progressive politics) always threatens the would-be orderly world of de-politicised government.

Acknowledgements

I am grateful to Jessica Pykett, both for organising the original event and for thinking that this particular puzzle was worth pursuing. It draws on the work of, and conversations with, a number of friends and colleagues, notably Julia Elyachar, Elissa Helms, Janet Newman, Anu Sharma, Paul Stubbs and Janine Wedel. I hope I have not bent their ideas too far. I am also grateful to the reviewers for *Citizenship Studies* for their suggestions about how to clarify and improve the analysis being presented.

Notes

1. The concept of voice thus links US political theory and social movement politics, e.g. Hirschman (1970), Gilligan (1982), Fine (1992), Verba *et al.* (1996) and Fishkin (1997). The concept – at least in the plural form – is also significant for critical approaches to social action derived from Mikhail Bakhtin: see for example, Wertsch (1991) and Holland and Lave (2001).
2. Representativeness is itself the subject of highly contested claims making in particular settings. Since it can be used to both claim and deny 'voice'. Individuals or organisations may claim to be voice of 'ordinary people' or, more contentiously, the 'excluded'. Public organisations may recognise or refuse such claims, not least on the grounds of 'unrepresentativeness'. See Barnes *et al.* (2007) and, more generally, Saward (2009), on non-elected claims to representation.
3. This is an unsubstantiated observation, given that I have not undertaken either historical or comparative analysis of policy documents to establish its validity. Nevertheless, I am struck by the use of ordinary people particularly in documents around citizenship and Britishness. A more systematic investigation of the styles and modes of address of policy documents in the UK would also have to attend to the recent extensive use of visual representations of 'ordinary people' in them, not least for their expression of 'diversity' as a visible characterization of the social.
4. Note that in 63 uses of the word 'people' in the text, only three qualifiers are used: *British* people, *local* people and *young* people (who emerge as a particular object of concern because of potential distance from the political process, institutions and culture).

References

Barnes, M., Newman, J. and Sullivan, H., 2007. *Power, participation and political renewal: case studies in public participation*. Bristol: Policy Press.
Brown, W., 2006. *Regulating aversion: tolerance in the age of identity*. Princeton, NJ: Princeton University Press.
Clarke, J., 2004. *Changing welfare, changing states: new directions in social policy*. London: Sage.
Clarke, J., 2007. Subordinating the social? Problems of post-welfarist capitalism. *Cultural studies*, 21 (6), 974–987.

Clarke, J., 2009. 'The people's police? Citizens, consumers and communities'. *In*: R. Simmons, M. Powell and I. Greener, eds. *The consumer in public services*. Bristol: The Policy Press.

Clarke, J., Newman, J., Smith, N., Vidler, E. and Westmarland, L., 2007. *Creating citizen-consumers: changing publics and changing public services*. London: Sage.

Cochrane, A. and Talbot, D., eds, 2009. *Security: welfare, crime and society*. Maidenhead: The Open University Press in association with the Open University.

Crawford, A., 2006. Networked governance and the post-regulatory state? Steering, rowing and anchoring the provision of policing and security. *Theoretical criminology*, 10 (4), 449–479.

Cruikshank, B., 1999. *The will to empower*. Ithaca, NY: Cornell University Press.

Davies, C., Wetherell, M. and Barnett, E., 2007. *Citizens at the centre: deliberative participation in health care decisions*. Bristol: Policy Press.

Department of Communities and Local Government, 2008. *Communities in control: real people, real power*. London: The Stationery Office (CM 7428).

Department of Work and Pensions, 2008. *Raising expectations and increasing support: reforming welfare for the future*. London: The Stationery Office (CM 7506).

Elyachar, J., 2002. Empowerment money: The World Bank, non-governmental organizations, and the value of culture in Egypt. *Public culture*, 14 (3), 493–513.

Elyachar, J., 2005. *Markets of dispossession: NGOs, economic development, and the state in Cairo*. Durham, NC: Duke University Press.

Esping-Andersen, G., 2002. *Why we need a new welfare state*. Oxford: Oxford University Press.

Fine, M., ed., 1992. *Disruptive voices: the possibilities of feminist research*. Ann Arbor, MI: University of Michigan Press.

Fishkin, M., 1997. *The voice of the people*. New Haven, CO: Yale University Press.

Frank, T., 2001. *One market under god: extreme capitalism, market populism and the end of economic democracy*. New York: Anchor Books.

Garland, D., 2001. *The culture of control: crime and social order in contemporary society*. Chicago, IL: University of Chicago Press.

Gilligan, C., 1982. *In a different voice: psychological theory and women's development*. Cambridge, MA: Harvard University Press.

Helms, E., 2003. Women as agents of ethnic reconciliation? Women's NGOs and international intervention in postwar Bosnia-Herzogovina. *Women's studies international forum*, 26 (1), 15–33.

Helms, E., 2006. 'Politics is a whore': women, morality and victimhood in post-war Bosnia-Herzogovina. *In*: X. Bougarel, E. Helms and G. Duijzings, eds. *The New Bosnian mosaic: identities, memories and moral claims in a post-war society*. Aldershot: Ashgate.

Hirschman, A., 1970. *Exit, voice and loyalty*. Cambridge, MA: Harvard University Press.

Holland, D. and Lave, J., 2001. History in person: an introduction. *In*: D. Holland and J. Lave, eds. *History in person: enduring struggles, contentious practices, intimate identities*. Santa Fe, School of American Research; Oxford: James Currey Ltd.

Home Office, 2008. *The path to citizenship: next steps in reforming the immigration system*. London: Home Office Border and Immigration Agency.

Larner, W. and Craig, D., 2005. After neoliberalism? Community activism and local partnerships in Aotearoa New Zealand. *Antipode*, 37 (3), 402–424.

Maasen, S. and Sutter, B., eds, 2007. *On willing selves: neoliberal politics vis-à-vis the neuroscientific challenge*. Basingstoke: Palgrave Macmillan.

Mahony, N., 2008. *Spectacular political experiments*. Thesis (PhD). Milton Keynes: The Open University.

Martin, G., 2007. 'Ordinary people only': knowledge, representativeness and the publics of public participation in healthcare. *Sociology of health and illness*, 30 (1), 35–54.

McDermont, M., Cowan, D. and Prendergast, J., 2009. Structuring governance: a case study of the new organisational provision of public service delivery. *Critical social policy*, 29 (4), 677–702.

McKee, K. and Cooper, V., 2007. The paradox of tenant empowerment: regulatory and liberatory possibilities. *Housing, theory and society*, 25 (2), 132–146.

Miliband, D., 2005. Putting the public back into public services. Speech to the Guardian Public Services Summit by The Minister of State, Cabinet Office, 2 February.

Ministry of Justice, 2007. *The Governance of Britain*. London: The Stationery Office.

Newman, J. and Clarke, J., 2009. *Publics, politics and power: remaking the public in public services*. London: Sage.

Newman, J., 2010. Towards a pedagogical state? Summoning the 'empowered' citizen. *Citizenship studies*, 14 (6), 711–723.

Pitcher, B., 2009. *The politics of multiculturalism: race and racism in contemporary Britain*. Basingstoke: Palgrave Macmillan.

Rose, N., 1999. *Powers of freedom: reframing political thought*. Cambridge: Cambridge University Press.

Saward, M., 2009. Authorisation and authenticity: representation and the unelected. *The journal of political philosophy*, 17 (1), 1–22.

Sharma, A., 2008. *Logics of empowerment: development, gender and governace in neoliberal India*. Minneapolis, MA: University of Minnesota Press.

Stoker, G., 2006. *Why politics matters: making democracy work*. Basingstoke: Palgrave Macmillan.

Verba, S., Schlozman, K. and Brady, H., 1996. *Voice and equality: civic voluntarism in American politics*. Cambridge, MA: Harvard University Press.

Wedel, J., 2001. *Collision and collusion: the strange case of western aid to Eastern Europe*. New York: Palgrave Macmillan.

Wertsch, J.V., 1991. *Voices of the mind: a sociocultural approach to mediated action*. Cambridge, MA: Harvard University Press.

Williams, R., 1977. *Marxism and literature*. Oxford: Oxford University Press.

Bad stories: narrative, identity, and the state's materialist pedagogy[1]

Clarissa Rile Hayward

Department of Political Science, Washington University in Saint Louis, St Louis, MO 63130, USA

How do state actors teach citizen-subjects collective identities? In this article, the author argues that one important way they do so is by teaching subjects to weave into their personal stories of 'who I am' shared or public narratives of 'who we are'. But, although story-telling is an important part of how states *produce* identities, it is not the only way they help *reproduce* them. States help reproduce identity narratives by institutionalizing them: by building them into laws and norms and policies. States help reproduce identity narratives by objectifying them, as well: by building them into material forms. Illustrating with the example of racial identities in the twentieth century United States, the author argues that when states institutionalize and objectify identity-narratives, they lend them a resilience they would not otherwise enjoy.

In the present essay, I ask how states shape the identities of citizen-subjects. Throughout, I use the term 'pedagogy' in the very broadest sense. My starting point is the premise that the educative work states do is never fully contained in institutions of formal schooling, never isolated from larger social and political processes. I understand pedagogy, what is more, to be a two-way process. The work states do in educating citizens is less a matter of compelling them to behave in certain ways, than inducing them to *govern themselves*: teaching them, not simply to act in this way rather than that, but also to value, to desire, to perceive in this way rather than that, by enlisting them as agents in the ongoing process of their subjectification.

To the question *how* states shape identities, I offer a two-part answer. In the first section, I draw on theories of narrative identity to make the case that one important way states influence subject formation is by teaching people to weave into the stories they tell about who they are as unique individuals – into their narratives of personal identity – shared narratives of collective identity. Identification, I argue, is inherently *selective, exegetical, productive*, and *competitive*. Together, these four characteristics account for the centrality of narrative to processes of identification, and also for the unavoidably political quality of identity narratives.

If the first section highlights the insights work on narrative identity offers into the pedagogical state, the second underscores the limits of that approach. Here, my claim is that, although story-telling is an important part of how actors – including state actors – *produce* identities, it is not the only, and it is not the most significant way they *reproduce* them. Social and political actors, including state actors, help reproduce identities, not just by telling and retelling the stories from which they have been constructed, but also by *institutionalizing* and *objectifying* those stories. Illustrating with the example of racial identities in the twentieth century United States, I argue that states build identity-narratives into laws and other institutions. They build them into material forms, as well, for example, racialized urban and suburban spatial forms. They thus enable their practical reproduction, lending them resilience in the face of challenge and critique.

Identity and stories

How do states shape identities? To tackle this question, I want to start with the observation – now all but commonplace in social and political theory – that people construct both their personal identities, and also their civic and other collective identities, and that they do so in specifically *narrative* form.[2] Seyla Benhabib, to cite one prominent example, writes, 'We are born into webs of interlocution or webs of narrative – from the familial and gender narratives to the linguistic one to the macronarrative of one's collective identity. We become who we are by learning to become a conversation partner in these narratives' (Benhabib 1999, p. 344).[3]

Story-telling, the claim is, is how people construct their identities: their understandings of who they are as unique individuals, and also as members of particular groups or collectivities. It is how people make sense of the social world, and of their place in that world. But why do actors create identities *as stories*? And how do states intervene in identity formation? In this first section, I draw on theories of narrative identity to sketch what I want to suggest are four key characteristics of identification, which shed light on the process of narrative identity construction and on the pedagogical role states play in that process.

Identification is selective

First, identification is selective. Imagine a set comprised of all the things that happened to you since you woke up this morning: all the actions you took; all the decisions you made; all the relationships in which you participated; all the traits, impulses, and dispositions you exhibited. Now, estimate how many days you have lived, up to and including today. Even if, on average, only a single memorable thing happened to you each day of your life, for you to recount any one of these as you construct your understanding of (to recall Benhabib's language) 'who [you] are' would be to highlight an infinitesimally small fraction, or subset, of what happened.

But this is precisely what you do each time you offer an account of your lived experience. As you construct your understanding of the life you have lived up to this moment, as you construct your understanding of your identity (of 'who you are'), you do not catalog everything that happens to you: everything you do and observe and feel, moment to moment. You do not keep a running tally of 'what happens at time t and what happens at time $t + 1 \ldots$ what happens at time $t + n$' and refer to that log as an objective record. You do not process your experience that way. Nor do you remember it that way. Instead, in the moment, you attend to some of what happens, but not all, making running judgments about significance and meaning. When the moment has passed, and you reflect back upon what it is that you recall, you make additional judgments. You construct events from your recollections. You relate those events to one another through plots, which, typically, you elaborate only after the fact. You thus *narrativize* your lived experience, constructing a (selective) personal identity story.[4]

Collective identification is selective, no less so than is personal identification: selective not only of actions, experiences, and dispositions, but of *persons* as well. Thus, shared understandings of 'who we are' – as an American people, for example, or as

African-Americans, or women, or Catholics – constitute some, but not other, past actors and past actions as definitive of 'our' history. They identify some, but not other, contemporary people, practices, and values as component parts of 'who we are'. Just as personal identity-narratives are the mode through which individuals construct their self-understandings, collective identity-narratives are the mode through which these shared understandings are made.

Consider the following (notorious) example: in the early decades of the twentieth century, leading up to the passage of the Immigration Act of 1924, elected officials in the United States; eugenicists, including those who served as advisors to the state; and other political actors told stories of American identity that centered on a putative Anglo-Saxon racial heritage. 'Who we Americans are', (this story went) was *not* the 'blacks' or the 'Asians' who were physically present in the American territory. It was not the practices in which those persons engaged, the ways they dressed and spoke, their experiences and traditions. Nor were would-be immigrants from Southern or Eastern European countries part of the American 'we'. Instead, Americans were, to quote, Dr Harry Laughlin, expert advisor to the congressional House Committee on Immigration, 'a race of white people'.[5]

Of course, not all collective identities are racist identities. All are selective, however, and necessarily so, since to identify particular persons as *X*s (and particular actions and attributes as *X*-like) is always to cull from a larger set of possibilities, a smaller subset. It is through narrative that social and political actors perform this work of identitarian selection.

Identification is exegetical

Identification is selective, then. It is exegetical as well. As the political theorist Alasdair MacIntyre has argued, the actions and interactions that serve as the material from which identities are constructed, must, if they are to be meaningful, be interpreted (MacIntyre 2007, Chap. 15). Suppose, for example, you have spent countless hours pounding with your fingers on the keys of your computer, while staring intently at the marks that appear on its screen. To include the *action* you thus performed as a component part of your account of 'who you are', you would need to do more than simply recount this behavior. You would need to say something about *why* you behaved in the way you behaved: what it was you thought you were doing, what your beliefs were (and are) about this behavior, what your purposes were, what you intended to accomplish. What is more, because your beliefs and intentions are not free standing – because they are related to other beliefs and intentions you hold, and because they are shaped by beliefs you share with others, and by practices and institutions in which you participate with others – you could not stop there.

'I was pounding the keys of the keyboard', you might say, 'because I was writing about narrative and identity'. You might add: 'I was writing part of a book I was working on, and which I intended to publish. I intended to do so in part because I wanted to communicate with an audience of readers, whom I imagined as I wrote; in part because publishing books is what people do when they engage in the practice of academic political philosophy; in part because the university that employs me encourages and rewards book publishing' – etc. To paraphrase MacIntyre, one cannot interpret actions without reference to beliefs and intentions, and to what he calls the 'settings' that lend beliefs and intentions subjective and intersubjective intelligibility. Narrative is among the discursive forms that best enable such interpretation (MacIntyre 2007, p. 206).

Collective identification is no less exegetical than is personal identification. Every narrative of 'who we are' is but one (contestable) interpretation of the meaning of the data from which it is comprised. Consider again the racialized story of American national identity, cited above. That narrative did not simply *select* persons and actions and attributes, it also *interpreted* them. If the raw data from which the story was made included phenotypical variation, for example – variation in skin tone, variation in the color and the texture of people's hair – if it included variation in observed behaviors – for instance, differences in how well different persons maintained their places of residence – a crucial part of the twentieth century American racial narrative was its interpretation of those data.

In the early decades of the century, phenotypical variation was widely understood to be a manifestation of biological type, which itself was thought an important *cause* of variation in traits and behaviors (Banton 1998). Specifically, people categorized 'black' were widely understood to be a distinct racial group from 'whites', and their (biologically rooted) race a cause of undesirable traits and dispositions.[6] Among the latter was an incapacity for responsible home ownership, and hence a tendency to adversely affect, by the mere fact of their residence in a place, the value of property there.[7]

This understanding, needless to say, was an *interpretation* – and a highly contestable interpretation, at that. A more plausible interpretation of the same data might have been that, due to widespread housing discrimination, Southern migrants to Northern cities were unable to purchase new and/or well-maintained homes. They were confined to overcrowded and physically deteriorated rental housing units, which – because they were discriminated against in hiring and lending – they very often could not afford to repair.

But it was the former, not the latter, interpretation that achieved dominance in the early twentieth century United States. It was the racist narrative that was circulated in the discourse of business elites: among real estate agents, in particular, and real estate lenders and appraisers (Helper 1969). It was the racist narrative that circulated in popular discourse, as well, for example, in local newspapers and in magazines such as *Good Housekeeping* (Abrams 1955). Moreover, it was the racist narrative that circulated among American state actors: among elected officials, members of the nascent profession of city planners, and eventually officers of key New Deal housing agencies, such as the Home Owners Loan Corporation and the Federal Housing Administration (FHA) (Jackson 1985).

Identification is productive

The role of actors such as these – American state actors who told and who retold twentieth century racial narratives – highlights the third trait of identification that I want to underscore: its productivity. Processes of identity construction are productive in the very most basic sense of that word. When people tell stories of 'who I am' and 'who we are', they do not simply retrieve data from the past and report it, building an historical record of what happened. Instead, by naming or 'our heroes' and 'our achievements' – or, in the case of personal identity stories, 'my intentions' and 'my purposes' – they *shape* present and future perception, evaluation, and action. If part of how I understand 'who I am', for instance, is 'I am a person who writes books', or if part of how we define 'who we are' is, 'we are white Americans', then we will think, feel, and value – and we will act – differently than we otherwise would.[8]

The early twentieth century racialized narrative of American national identity was a narrative state actors taught citizen-subjects. They taught it through formal educative processes, for instance though public schooling in civics. They taught it through the informal education of public political speech as well. State actors taught citizens stories of race and investment risk, what it is more, for instance through the underwriting standards put in place by the FHA, which defined as unacceptably high risk – indeed, as uninsurable – mortgages for homes occupied by black persons, and for white-occupied homes located in neighborhoods where black people lived.[9]

The political import of these stories was enormous. Stories of Americans as 'a race of white people' legitimized the exclusion from citizenship of whole categories of persons whom they named unassimilable.[10] At the same time, stories of race and investment risk effectively excluded American blacks from the market in real estate – a crucial avenue for wealth accumulation for whites in the postwar years – while producing a dramatic shift in America's racial geography. As is well known, black ghettos did not exist in almost any American city at the close of the nineteenth century. At that time, black city dwellers lived in wards that were, on average, only 27% black (Cutler *et al.* 1999). Just a half century later, a full 55 US cities included neighborhoods that, according to the most commonly used indices of racial segregation, qualified as ghettos (ibid).[11] By then, black American city dwellers lived in neighborhoods that were, on average, 43% black (ibid).

Identification is competitive

How is it that a collective identity story can produce such politically significant outcomes? How is that, simply by telling a story, a political actor can influence who is included in, and who is excluded from, a political society, or even the patterns of residence and land use within that society? I want to answer this question, first, by exploring a response suggested by theories of narrative and identity. In the second section, I want to problematize and complicate that response.

Political theoretical work on identity and narrative suggests that political actors, including state actors, will shape subject formation through collective identity stories if and when individuals incorporate those stories into the personal identity stories they tell. If individual citizens in the early twentieth century United States were to weave into the narratives they told about their own lives state-promulgated narratives of nation and of race, for instance, if individual home buyers and home sellers were to weave into their stories state-promulgated narratives of race and investment risk, then those collective identity stories would shape the judgments and choices those individuals made. If, in short, some substantial number of individuals were to tell themselves, 'I am a white American', then racial stories would shape their perception, their judgment, and their action. It is just such a process Anthony Appiah has in mind when he writes that 'becoming who we are' involves citing in our personal identity narratives shared or public narratives of collective identity: 'Identification often has a strong narrative dimension. By way of my identity I fit my life story . . . into larger stories – for example, of a people, a religious tradition, or a race' (Appiah 2002, p. 243).

It is important to underscore, however, that to the extent that the state's pedagogy takes this particular form – to the extent that it works *as a narrative* and *through* the narratives individuals tell – states are constrained to teach identity stories that citizens will incorporate into their life-stories. States are thus constrained to teach narratives that conform with relatively widely held empirical beliefs about the world as it is, or at least stories that do not clearly conflict with such beliefs. States are constrained to teach narratives that conform with relatively widely held normative beliefs about the world as it should be, or at least do not clearly conflict with such beliefs.

Imagine that in the 1920s, the Congressional House Committee on Immigration had tried to circulate a very different story of American identity than the one that it circulated. Imagine it had proffered a story radically at odds with the putatively scientific claims of the eugenists of that day – perhaps a constitutional patriotic story, which incorporated an explicitly constructivist view of 'race'. Or suppose that in, the 1930s, the FHA had worked to circulate a very different racial narrative than the one that it circulated: a story that flew in the face of the claims of early twentieth century land economists, perhaps one asserting that there was *no* relation between investment risk and race. If these narratives had struck most individuals as incorrect, or if they had struck them as morally illegitimate, then one would expect those individuals *not* to incorporate those stories into their narratives of personal identity. One would expect them, instead, to reach for some alternative collective identity story as they constructed their narratives of personal identity.

This thought experiment illustrates the fourth and final characteristic of identification I want to highlight. Identification is a *competitive* process. There is never simply one story on offer – *the* story of 'who we Americans are' (or we African-Americans, or we women, or we Catholics). Instead the processes by which collective identity narratives are produced and reproduced take the form of political *contests*. Different actors, with different beliefs, desires, and interests, are differently served by competing versions of 'the' story of almost every group: nation, race, caste, class, and community. These multiple narratives very often contrast with one another on important dimensions. In many cases, they directly contradict one another. They typically serve the interests of, and/or or reflect the beliefs or the values of, some, but not other, agents.[12]

Indeed, it is this competitive quality that accounts for the relation of mutual constitution between, on the one hand, collective, and on the other hand, personal identity-stories. Just as the latter can attain intelligibility only if they incorporate the former, so the former can take root, they can survive, only if they are incorporated into the latter. To the extent that identities are produced and reproduced *as narratives*, collective identities must work *through* stories of personal identity. Collective identity stories can succeed, theories of narrative identity suggest, only if some substantial number of individuals build them into their stories of personal identity.

Bad stories

One might, therefore, expect only those collective identities to succeed that take the form of *good stories*. By 'good' stories I mean stories that accord with, or at least do not conflict with, widely held empirical beliefs and widely endorsed moral and/or ethical principles.[13] One might expect only those collective identities to succeed that take the form of stories that are 'good' in this very minimal sense, because one might think people would find collective identity stories that were *not* good stories to be jarring. One might expect, as individuals told their personal identity stories, that they would not incorporate such 'bad' collective stories into them. Hence, MacIntyre's claim that not only scientists and philosophers, but also 'ordinary agents' – people like you, or me, or mid-twentieth century American home buyers – find themselves thrown into what he calls 'epistemological crises' when faced with the fact that part or all of the narratives they have been telling themselves about the world, and about their lived experience, cannot comprehend some datum or data (MacIntyre 1997).

MacIntyre conceives the trigger of such crises in terms of a new experience: one which challenges some extant (and the implication is: some extant *good*) narrative. Suppose, for instance, an early twentieth century American who identified as 'white' were to move to a racially integrated neighborhood and to observe that the people there with phenotypical characteristics associated with 'blackness' in fact kept their yards neatly manicured and their homes in excellent repair. By MacIntyre's account, at that point that individual should experience 'radical interpretive doubt' (MacIntyre 1997, p. 455). She should wonder how it is that the racial identity story she had incorporated into her personal life-story could have been so predictively inaccurate on this point. She would then face the task, MacIntyre's claim is, of rewriting the story she tells herself (and others) about her identity: reinterpreting all the relevant experiences that she previously had interpreted, but now in a way that accounts for both her black neighbors' proclivity to maintain their property in excellent condition *and* her previous beliefs that, due to their 'racial heritage and tendencies', they would not.

The (unstated) premise is that 'ordinary agents', much like good scientists, have a relatively low tolerance for dissonance between, on the one hand, the stories they tell about the world and their experience in it, and on the other, their considered ontological and evaluative beliefs. In practice, however, people often are *not* thrown into epistemological crises when new data contradict old identity stories. People often do not revise even those identities – such as, at the turn of the twenty-first century, racial identities – that seem in desperate need of revision. They often do not create new identities, using more credible and more legitimate narratives, even when they are faced with evidence that directly contravenes the stories from which their identities were made.

Why not?

Change and stasis

The year 1940 marked the start of a decade one might have expected to be a turning point in dominant understandings of race in America, and in American racial practices.[14] It was in the 1940s that the collective identity story of race as biological difference – the story that had rationalized, by providing an allegedly scientific basis for, the differential treatment of persons based on race – was decisively undermined at the level of scientific discourse. By the end of that decade, scientists in the United States and in Europe had arrived at consensus on what has since been dubbed the 'evolutionary synthesis': an explanation of purportedly categorical, and permanent, racial differences in terms of gradual genetic shifts engendered by evolution within reproductively isolated populations (Banton 1998, Chap. 4). Phenotypical variation among individuals, which to that point had been widely assumed a mark of distinct racial types, was now recognized to be continuous, rather than categorical. There is no biologically rooted difference, scientists came to agree, which separates humans into discrete 'races', and which produces specifically racial traits, qualities, and dispositions.[15]

At roughly that same time, the normative stories that had legitimized racial hierarchies through mid-century came under siege. The association of racism with Naziism made American racial beliefs and practices appear to those who self-identified as opponents of Hitler, not just empirically misguided, but also morally repugnant. In 1944, the widely circulated Fourth Report of the Commission to Study the Organization of the Peace (CSOP) underscored that 'The cancerous Negro situation in our country gives fodder to enemy propaganda and makes our ideals stick like dry bread in the throat'. 'Through revulsion against Nazi doctrines', the report continued, 'we may ... hope to speed up the process of bringing our own practices ... more in conformity with our professed ideals'.[16] Gunnar Myrdal, writing that same year, took a similar stance. Predicting that 'The War [would be] crucial for the future of the Negro', Myrdal averred, 'There is bound to be a redefinition of the Negro's status in America as a result of this War'(Myrdal 1944, p. 997).

The latter change (the change in the normative discourse surrounding race in America) made *racist* narratives (such as the narrative that legitimized the ghettoization of blacks), to recall the language introduced above, 'bad stories'. The former (the change in empirical beliefs about racial identity and difference) did the same for the larger set of early twentieth century *racial* narratives. Theories of narrative identity would lead us to expect, in the wake of these changes, dramatic shifts in how Americans identify racially. They would lead us to expect dramatic shifts in American racial practices as well, as one individual after the other experienced 'radical interpretive doubt' and rewrote her personal identity story.

But at mid-century, Americans did not do away with racial – or for that matter, with racist – identity thinking. They did not reconstruct their identities, using exclusively good (that is to say, credible and legitimate) stories. To be sure, one can imagine such a reconstruction. Lionel McPherson and Tommie Shelby (2004), for instance, make the case that an African-American identity based on feelings of racial solidarity, and on a sense of shared political interests and collective political will, is not only morally legitimate, but also compatible with an (empirically credible) understanding of race as socially significant, but not biologically grounded. Such an understanding of is not, however, the understanding most Americans employ. Most Americans, well after the middle years of the twentieth century, continue to comprehend 'race', not only in social and political terms, but also as a marker of shared biological heritage. Indeed, even people who are fully aware of the speciousness of claims about race as biological type often adopt this commonsensical understanding. 'Her mother is black, but she looks white', I might remark to you in conversation, even though I would studiously avoid in my scholarly work any suggestion that 'black' and 'white' racial identities are categorically discrete biological inheritances, made plain through phenotypical variation.

Indeed, were I to make such a remark, it would likely strike you as anything but extraordinary. People very often reach for, people very often use, as they interpret and negotiate the social world, collective identities that, when spelled out in storied form, are not good stories. People often use such identities even when they know on some level – even when, if prompted, they would readily acknowledge – that the stories undergirding them are not credible and not legitimate. People often use identities that are supported by bad stories, not only to characterize the beliefs of others, but also as component parts of the stories they tell about their own lives, about their own identities.

Identities and institutions

Social actors often use identities made from 'bad stories' because, although (as theories of narrative identity underscore) people typically *produce* identities as narratives, they very often do not *reproduce* them in narrative form. To be sure, I sometimes learn and relearn my collective identities by learning the story of who 'we Americans' are (or we African-Americans, or we women, or Catholics). But I also learn my identities *practically*. I learn them through everyday action in institutional contexts that have been shaped by narratives of collective identity, and through everyday contact with material forms that embody those narratives.

To illustrate, I want to consider, first, the *institutionalization*, and then the *objectification*, of early twentieth century racial stories. Recall the claim (from section one, above) that collective identity construction is a competitive process. As actors create and circulate identity stories, they compete with other actors, who offer other stories of who 'we' are (as a race, a nation, and a people). When a given narrative emerges successful from such competition – when, for instance, in the early decades of the last century, the new story of race and investment risk was incorporated into the personal life-stories of a critical mass of individuals who self-identified as 'white' – social and political actors do not simply continue to tell and retell that narrative. Thus actors, including American state actors, did not simply circulate (in civics classrooms and in texts and in public political speeches) the early twentieth century American racial narrative. They also institutionalized that narrative. They built it into laws and other institutions, that is to say. Social and political actors, including state actors, build successful stories into institutions, which define norms and standards, and which distribute rewards and sanctions accordingly.

A case in point is the racial zoning laws that were passed in many American cities in the second decade of the twentieth century.[17] These is one instance of an institution – in this case a legal ordinance – which codified, and which backed with the force of legal sanction, a story about the incompatibility of 'the black and white races'. A second example is racially restrictive covenants: deed restrictions from roughly that same era, which, although privately enacted, were publicly enforced.[18] Racial covenants, like racial zoning laws, codified the collective identity story that emerged as dominant in the early twentieth century United States, enforcing it with rewards (state protection of property rights for those who conformed to deed restrictions) and sanctions (legal punishment for covenant violators).

A third example is state policies, such as FHA policies, which also institutionalized racial identity narratives. As noted above, the FHA actively circulated stories of race and investment risk in its publications, including its *Underwriting Manual*. But the agency did much more than that. By building those stories into its underwriting guidelines and allowing them to strongly shape its investment policies, the agency ensured that federal loan guarantees were distributed as those stories prescribed: to whites disproportionately, that is to say, and in particular to whites who purchased houses in racially exclusive enclaves.[19]

Imagine a prospective home buyer in the early postwar years who rejects early twentieth century racial narratives. Imagine a home buyer who refuses to incorporate those stories into her own story of who she is as a unique individual. Let us stipulate that this home buyer is socially ascribed 'white' racial identity, but imagine that (because she is aware of recent shifts in the scientific discourse on race) she finds the stories the FHA cites and circulates not to be credible. Imagine, furthermore, that (because she is persuaded by the normative critique of racist practices that emerged from the war with Nazi Germany) she finds the stories the FHA cites and circulates not to be legitimate.

Even if this home buyer does not incorporate the FHA-endorsed narrative of race and investment risk into her personal life-story, because the agency has institutionalized that narrative, it will nonetheless shape her field of possible action. If she wants to qualify for a federally backed mortgage for a house (or, for that matter, if she wants to be certain she can secure a mortgage on the private market), even if she *wholly rejects* the racial narrative, she must act *as if* she accepts it. She must purchase her house in a racially exclusive enclave, that is to say. If she does not – if she buys in a black ghetto, or if she buys in a racially integrated neighborhood – she will face nontrivial sanctions.

I do not mean to imply, by proposing this thought experiment, that all Americans revised their identity stories in the middle of the last century. No doubt, the postwar United States was characterized by a wide range of racial beliefs and attitudes. Some Americans, no doubt, did change the stories they told in response to shifts in dominant racial narratives, while others no doubt clung to now-discredited racial stories. But even if every single American had revised her identitarian story-telling, I want to underscore, absent corresponding changes to the institutions old stories had shaped, American racial practices would not have radically changed. *The institutionalization of identity stories lends them resilience in the face of challenge and critique.*

Identities and spaces

Their *objectification* lends them added resilience. By 'objectification' (a term I borrow from Pierre Bourdieu), I mean their translation into object form, or into material form. Bourdieu

(1977, Chap. 2) introduces this notion in his famous study of the Kabyle built environment, in which he argues that the division between the Kabyle house and the public world, along with the divisions of space interior to the house itself, objectify identity categories and the social meanings actors attach to those categories. Objectification in the Kabyle case consists in actors designating 'male' spaces – spaces of politics, production, and exchange – and 'female' spaces – spaces of domestic work, sex, and reproduction. When people engage in practical activities in such spaces, Bourdieu's claim is – when those identified as 'men' sow and reap in the field, when those identified as 'women' cook and care for the sick and the dying in the house – they learn and they re-learn, implicitly, the identities objectified in those forms.

Central to Bourdieu's argument is his claim that such learning is, at least in part, corporeal.[20] It happens, not only through explicitly thematized identity narratives, in other words, but also through material forms, which work directly on the muscles, the nerves, the tendons that make up a human body. Think of how you learned (and how, if you tried, you might now recall) strongly gendered narratives from your childhood, such as the tale of *The Princess on the Pea*. Then try, if you can, to remember how you learned (and think how, daily, as if by instinct, you are recalled) to perform your gender well – as you walk, as you talk, as you exhibit (or as you refrain from exhibiting) sensitivity to discomfort. The latter differs from the former qualitatively in that it is an instance of, not consciously and explicitly citing a narrative, so much as mastering *practically* a social competence. If, like Kabyle men and women, you perform well your gender identity, you do so, not only and not necessarily because you endorse the narratives from which that identity was constructed, but also, and significantly, because you have acquired what Bourdieu calls 'a feel for the game' (Bourdieu 1990, p. 11).[21]

In the twentieth century United States, social and political actors, including democratic state actors, not only institutionalized racial identities in laws and in policies. They also inscribed those identities in urban and suburban spatial forms, such as the black ghettos and the white enclaves that were the product of racial zoning ordinances, racial covenants, and racist housing policies. Racial identity stories changed dramatically in the middle years of the century. Even institutions changed as, for instance, the US Supreme Court ruled racial zoning laws unconstitutional, and racially restrictive covenants unenforceable (*Buchanan v. Warley* 1917, *Shelley v.* Kraemer 1948). Yet, state actors helped maintain racialized spaces with new institutions: with zoning laws which, even though not explicitly racially targeted, had predictably racially segregating effects, and with policies, such as Urban Renewal/Redevelopment, which, in Arnold Hirsch's words, 'played a key role in fostering, sustaining, and, not infrequently, intensifying the separation of the races even in the absence of Jim Crow legislation' (Hirsch 1998, viii). State actors helped maintain racialized spaces, as well, through omissions of action: for instance, by failing effectively to enforce the fair housing legislation passed in the late 1960s.[22]

Recall that, in 1890, only one of those American cities with a thousand or more black residents included a neighborhood that, according to commonly used indices of racial segregation, were 'black ghettos'. In 1990, 98 of those same cities did: a full 96% of the original set (Cutler *et al.* 1999). In those cities as a whole, the average black resident lived in a census tract that was 61% black (ibid).

At the start of the twenty-first century, it remains colloquial to speak of the 'black' and the 'white' parts of town. Those individuals who identify – and who *are identified* – as 'black' or as 'white' need not explicitly cite in their life-narratives collective stories of racial identity, in order to know, and to *feel*, when they are 'out of place'. Through the actions and the failures to act that contribute to the maintenance of racialized space, the American state teaches its citizens 'a feel for the (racial) game'. As citizen-subjects act and interact in racialized urban and suburban spaces – as they shop, as they worship, as they take their children to and from school – they learn and they re-learn, very often without narrativizing, the commonsense of racial practice.

Conclusion

In this article, I have argued that narrative is one important form through which states teach and citizen-subjects learn identity: through civic education in the classroom, through public political addresses, and through public documents. But, I have emphasized, it is not the only form. States also teach, and citizens also learn identities practically. Actors, including state actors, teach identities by writing them into laws and other institutions, and by building them into spaces and other object forms. Individuals learn and re-learn identities when they are incentivized by such institutions, and when they experience such material forms with their bodies.

Much ink has been spilt – both in debates about civic education, and in social and political theory more generally – debating *what are the best identity stories for states to teach*. For some, the answer is 'civic nationalist' stories: identity narratives according to which 'who we are' is, not members of an ethnically or a racially defined group, but rather people who shared particular historical experiences and/or particular values and beliefs about the good life (Miller 1995, 2000, Canovan 1996, 2000). For others, 'constitutional patriotic' stories are best: stories according to which what unites 'us' and makes us a distinct people is our particular interpretation of liberal and democratic constitutional principles (see, especially, Habermas 1998, 2001a, 2001b; for an evaluation and critique, see Hayward 2007).

The argument sketched above, however, underscores that the solution to the problem of 'bad' identities is never simply 'tell better stories'. To be sure, telling better stories is often a crucial part of the process of building political support for change. But the point of intervention must be those institutions (those rules, laws, and policies), and also those material forms into which bad stories have been built. In the American case, the solution cannot be simply to teach people to explicate, interrogate, and revise the narratives from which 'race' was constructed. It cannot be simply to teach them to identify as 'American' for civic nationalist, for or constitutional patriotic reasons. Rather, it must be to change the institutions (including, importantly, the institutions of metropolitan governance) that incentivize people to act *as if* they endorse racial stories (Ford 1994, Frug 1999). It must be to change the urban and suburban spaces through which Americans learn and re-learn race corporeally.

Notes

1. This article is an abridged version of a chapter in my current book project, which is tentatively titled *Stories and Spaces: How Americans Make Race*. Early versions were presented at the Open University Symposium on the Pedagogical State in September, 2008, the annual meeting of the Western Political Science Association in March 2009, and the annual meeting of the International Political Science Association in July 2009. For helpful comments, I am grateful to participants in those sessions, as well as to Courtney Jung, Michael Neblo, and three anonymous referees for this journal.
2. There is a large and influential literature on narrative identity, on which I draw in this first section. Key works include Mitchell (1981), White (1981), Ricoeur (1984, 1988), Bruner (1986, 1987), Polkinghorne (1988), Kerby (1991), Freeman (1993), Somers (1994) and MacIntyre (2007). Claims that identity is inherently and inevitably narrative are not, however, undisputed. See, for example, Strawson (2004).
3. Hence, Hayden White's claim that 'every narrative, however seemingly "full", is constructed on the basis of a set of events which *might have been included but were left out*'. White (1981, p. 10), emphasis as in original.

4. This claim is consonant with, although not identical to, the view of Paul Ricoeur, for whom people select actions and interactions from their experience and relate those to one another in a specifically narrative form, because it is narrative that best captures what he calls the human experience of time (Ricoeur 1984, 1988). Although we often represent time in a linear fashion, the claim is (as a line linking points, much like a mathematical line links points in abstract space) we do not experience our lives-in-time that way. Instead, we experience the temporal progression of actions and interactions from the particular perspectives we occupy, relating differently to now, than to the past and future. As we construct events from our experiences, we link those events together to form a meaningful whole. '[N]arratives', according Ricoeur, 'are the modes of discourse appropriate to our experience of time' (Ricoeur 1979, p. 25).

5. Quoted in King (2000, p. 132). The quote continues '. . . who have fused into a national mosaic composed originally of European stocks (themselves mosaics) in rapidly descending proportion, as follows: primarily British, Irish, German, Scandinavian, French, and Dutch; secondarily, American Indian, Jewish, Spanish, Swiss, Italian, Austro-Hungarian, and Russian'. As for 'the negro', according to Laughlin, although 'he has, so far as he was able, adopted our institutions, our language, our religions, and essential laws and customs, . . . the contrast in blood between the northwestern European settlers and the African negroes is so great that racial assimilation is impossible'. Ibid.

6. This racial identity story represented a major revision of turn-of-the-century racial narratives. After the so-called 'Great Migration' of Southern blacks to northern and western cities, beginning with the first world war and continuing through the 1920s, established residents of those cities began to de-emphasize divisions among those whom eventually they would come to regard as '*white* ethnics', and to focus attention on what they increasingly characterized as a black/white racial divide. At the same time, they revised, in light of the conditions of industrial urbanism, the list of traits and behaviors they claimed biological race caused, and they began to tell a story the moral of which was that the proper relation between 'the races' was one of strict separation. See Hayward (2009).

7. Thus, according to one influential real estate text from that era: 'Among the traits and characteristics of people which influence land values, racial heritage and tendencies seem to be of paramount importance. The aspirations, energies, and abilities of various groups in the composition of the population will largely determine the extent to which they develop the potential value of land' (Babcock 1932, p. 86). The author went on to underscore that *racial* differences have a particularly powerful impact on real estate values: 'Most of the variations and differences between people are slight and value declines are, as a result, gradual. But there is one difference in people, namely race, which can result in a very rapid decline. Usually such declines can be partially avoided by segregation and this device has always been in common usage in the South where white and negro populations have been segregated'. Ibid, 91.

8. Our stories, to borrow Mark Freeman's (1993) language, do not simply reflect, so much as they 're-write' the selves they take as their subjects. Jerome Bruner (1987, p. 31) makes a similar point: 'You will ask whether . . . narrative forms and the language that go with them . . . are not simply expressions of . . . inner states . . . I believe that the ways of telling and the ways of conceptualizing that go with them . . . become recipes for structuring experience itself, for laying down routes into memory, for not only guiding the life narrative up to the present but directing it into the future'. Somers (1994, p. 614) emphasizes that '"[E]xperience" is constituted through narratives . . . people are guided to act in certain ways, and not others, on the basis of the projections, expectations, and memories derived from . . . social, public, and cultural narratives'. Ibid, p. 614.

9. Thus in its 1938 *Underwriting Manual*, the agency advised that neighborhood ratings should reflect the presence of what it termed 'Adverse Influences', including 'incompatible racial and social groups'. According to the manual: areas surrounding a location are investigated to determine whether incompatible racial and social groups are present, for the purpose of making a prediction regarding the probability of the location being invaded by such groups. If a neighborhood is to retain stability, it is necessary that properties shall continue to be occupied by the same social and racial classes. A change in social or racial occupancy generally contributes to instability and a decline in values (Federal Housing Administration 1938, par. 937).

10. Thus, the 1924 act (cited above) imposed quotas for legal immigration to the US based on would-be immigrants' nations of origin.

11. These indices include the black isolation index, which measures the extent to which persons identified as 'black' are isolated in predominantly 'black' areas, and the index of dissimilarity, which measures the evenness of the distribution of persons considered 'black' throughout a city. For detailed discussions of both measures, see Massey and Denton (1993, Chap. 2). Cutler *et al.* (1999) analysis of all American cities with 1000 or more black residents in 1890 shows that, for the nation as a whole, the index of dissimilarity was 46%, while the index of isolation was just 22%. Generally, a dissimilarity index must reach 60%, and an isolation index 30%, to be considered high. A half century later, in 1940, dissimilarity had increased to 71%, and black isolation had grown to 46% (Cutler *et al.* 1999).

12. Thus, Rogers Smith (2003, Chap. 2) stresses the role political struggles play in generating competition among those identity narratives he calls 'stories of peoplehood'. Would-be leaders want individuals to consider themselves part of a particular kind of political community, Smith's argument is: a community circumscribed in certain ways, and defined by certain constitutive traditions, values, and attributes. More specifically, they want people to consider themselves part of political communities for which *they* would make good leaders.

13. This definition is not meant to be exhaustive. There are other characteristics that can make identity stories good or bad. Good stories, for example, are intelligible, coherent, and internally consistent. Hence, people might reject as 'bad' those stories the basic elements contradict one another. See, for instance, Appiah's (2002) claim that black racial identities in the United States are bad stories because they are incoherent, in the sense that conforming to some of the norms that comprise them militates against conforming to others. One might argue, however, that narrative accommodates incoherence more easily than do many other discursive forms. Still, minimally, it seems plausible to suggest agents are unlikely to incorporate in their personal identity narratives collective identity narratives that violate their empirical beliefs and/or their deeply held principles.

14. See Hayward (2009), on which this paragraph and the one that follows draw.

15. To be sure, there were still some biological accounts of race after mid-century in some scientific realms. In the wake of the Human Genome Project in the early 2000s, the debate was revisited when several studies found patterned differences between African and non-African population groups in the structure of the DNA sequence. Most participants in the scientific debate agree, however, that there is a nontrivial gap between patterns of human genetic variation, and 'race' understood as biological type. Thus, the National Human Genome Center emphasizes that 'race' as traditionally understood is a flawed concept. Summing up the research presented at the inaugural *Human Genome Variation and 'Race'* meeting in 2004, Charmaine Royal and Georgia Dunston write, '... there seems to be consensus that "race", whether imposed or self-identified, is a weak surrogate for various genetic and nongenetic factors in correlations with health status' (Royal and Dunston 2004, p. 7).

16. (Commission to Study the Organization of the Peace 1973 [1944], p. 181.) Established by the League of Nations in 1939, CSOP published a series of reports over the course of the war years, lobbied the State Department and the White House, and conducted an ambitious public relations campaign, all with a view to promoting policy changes it claimed were necessary for a lasting international peace. For an historical overview of the Commission, see Mitoma (2008).

17. These were laws the purpose of which was to segregate by racial type. In 1910, Baltimore was the first American city to pass a racial zoning law. A host of other cities – including Atlanta, St. Louis, and Dallas – followed suit. The practice spread, but only until 1917, when the US Supreme Court ruled racial zoning in violation of the Fourteenth Amendment. *Buchanan v. Warley*, 245 US 60 (1917).

18. Legally enforced restrictions written into the deeds of private properties, restrictive covenants had been employed prior to the turn of the century, to limit what were regarded as 'noxious' uses, tanneries being one common instance, and another slaughterhouses. It was not until the first half of the last century, however, that legal prohibitions on the purchase, lease, rental, and/or occupancy by blacks (and often by other racialized groups, especially Jews) were written into the deeds of countless properties in American cities and in their growing suburbs (Fogelson 2005).

19. From the start of the FHA program in the mid-1930s, and for nearly 30 years after, through the early 1960s – a period during which the agency insured mortgages on close to a third of new housing in the United States – it awarded African-Americans less than 2% of state-insured mortgages (Squires 1994). Even these it allotted disproportionately to segregated areas in the American South.

20. See Hayward (2004), on which this paragraph draws.
21. On gender as performance, see Butler (1999). Although her account is more psychoanalytic than Bourdieuian, there are important affinities between her view and mine. See also Zerilli (1998) on the performance of 'rationally repudiated' identities.
22. The Fair Housing Act of 1968 prohibited racial discrimination in housing sales and rentals, but major housing audit studies in 1979 and 1989 documented widespread discrimination against minority home buyers and renters (Wienk *et al.* 1979, Turner *et al.* 1991). Noncompliance is largely a product of ineffective enforcement. Even after the 1988 Fair Housing Amendment Act, which strengthened the Department of Housing and Urban Development's (HUD) powers of enforcement, investigations are triggered only in response to complaints filed by people who experience discrimination. As critics note, this system grossly undermines effectiveness, given that many commonly employed discriminatory tactics are difficult for private individuals to detect. See Feagin (1994) and Reed (1994).

References

Abrams, C., 1955. *Forbidden neighbors: a study of prejudice in housing.* New York: Kennikat Press.

Appiah, K.A., 2002. The state and the shaping of identity. *In*: Grethe B. Peterson, ed. *Tanner lectures on human values.* Salt Lake City: University of Utah Press, 235–297.

Babcock, F., 1932. *The valuation of real estate.* New York: McGraw.

Banton, M., 1998. *Racial theories.* 2nd ed. Cambridge: Cambridge University Press.

Benhabib, S., 1999. Sexual difference and collective identities: the new global constellation. *Signs*, 24 (2), 335–361.

Bourdieu, P., 1977. *Outline of a theory of practice.* Trans. R. Nice. Cambridge: Cambridge University Press.

Bourdieu, P., 1990. Fieldwork in philosophy. In: *In other words: essays towards a reflexive sociology.* Trans. Matthew Adamson. Stanford, CA: Stanford University Press, 3–33.

Bruner, J., 1986. *Actual minds, possible worlds.* Cambridge, MA: Harvard University Press.

Bruner, J., 1987. Life as narrative. *Social research*, 54 (1), 11–32.

Buchanan v. Warley, 245 US 60 (1917).

Butler, J., 1999. *Gender trouble: feminism and the subversion of identity.* New York: Routledge.

Canovan, M., 1996. *Nationhood and political theory.* Cheltenham: Edward Elgar.

Canovan, M., 2000. Patriotism is not enough. *British journal of political science*, 30 (3), 413–432.

Commission to Study the Organization of the Peace, 1973 [1944]. Fourth Report, Part III, "International Safeguard of Human Rights", 163–84 in *Building Peace: Reports of the Commission to Study the Organization of Peace 1939–1972.* Metuchen, NJ: Scarecrow Press.

Cutler, D., Glaeser, E. and Vigdor, J., 1999. The rise and decline of the American Ghetto. *Journal of political economy*, 107 (3), 455–506.

Feagin, J., 1994. A house is not a home: White Racism and US Housing Practices. *In*: R. Bullard, J.E. Grigsby, III and C. Lee, eds. *Residential apartheid: the American legacy.* Los Angeles, CA: CAAS Publications, 17–48.

Federal Housing Administration, 1938. *Underwriting manual: underwriting and valuation procedure under title II of the National Housing Act.* Washington, DC: US Government Printing Office.

Fogelson, R., 2005. *Bourgeois Nightmares: Suburbia 1870–1930.* New Haven, CT: Yale University Press.

Ford, R.T., 1994. The boundaries of race: political geography in legal analysis. *Harvard law review*, 107 (June), 1843–1921.

Freeman, M., 1993. *Rewriting the self: history, memory, narrative.* New York: Routledge.

Frug, G., 1999. *City making: building communities without building walls.* Princeton, NJ: Princeton University Press.

Habermas, J., 1998. Appendix II: citizenship and national identity. *In*: J. Habermas, ed. *Between facts and norms: contributions to a discourse theory of law and democracy.* Trans. W. Rehg. Cambridge, MA: The MIT Press, 491–515.

Habermas, J., 2001a. The European Nation-State: on the past and future of sovereignty and citizenship. *In*: C. Cronin and P. De Greiff, eds. *The inclusion of the other: studies in political theory.* Cambridge, MA: The MIT Press, 105–127.

Habermas, J., 2001b. The postnational constellation and the future of democracy. *In: The postnational constellation: political essays*. Trans. and ed. M. Pensky. Cambridge, MA: MIT Press, 58–112.

Hayward, C., 2004. Doxa and deliberation. *Critical review of international social and political philosophy*, 7 (1), 1–24.

Hayward, C., 2007. Democracy's identity problem: is 'Constitutional Patriotism' the answer? *Constellations*, 14 (2), 182–196.

Hayward, C., 2009. Black places. *Theory and event*, 12 (4).

Helper, R., 1969. *Racial policies and practices of real estate brokers*. Minneapolis, MN: University of Minnesota Press.

Hirsch, A., 1998. *Making the second Ghetto: race and housing in Chicago, 1940–1960*. Chicago, IL: University of Chicago Press.

Jackson, K., 1985. *Crabgrass frontier: the suburbanization of America*. New York: Oxford University Press.

Kerby, P., 1991. *Narrative and the self*. Bloomington, IN: Indiana University Press.

King, D., 2000. *Making Americans: immigration, race, and the origins of the diverse democracy*. Cambridge, MA: Harvard University Press.

MacIntyre, A., 1997. Epistemological crises, dramatic narrative, and the philosophy of science. *The Monist*, 60 (4), 453–472.

MacIntyre, A., 2007. *After virtue: a study in moral theory*. 3rd ed. Notre Dame, IN: University of Notre Dame Press.

Massey, D. and Denton, N., 1993. *American apartheid: segregation and the making of the underclass*. Cambridge, MA: Harvard University Press.

McPherson, L. and Shelby, S., 2004. Blackness and blood: interpreting African–American identity. *Philosophy and public affairs*, 32 (2), 171–191.

Miller, D., 1995. *On nationality*. New York: Oxford University Press.

Miller, D., 2000. *Citizenship and national identity*. Cambridge: Polity Press.

Mitchell, W.J.T., 1981. *On narrative*. Chicago, IL: University of Chicago Press.

Mitoma, Glenn, 2008. Civic society and international human rights: the commission to study the organization of the peace and the origins of the UN Human Rights Regime. *Human rights quarterly*, 30, 607–630.

Myrdal, G., 1944. *An American dilemma: the Negro problem and modern democracy*. New York: Harper and Row.

Polkinghorne, D.E., 1988. *Narrative knowing and the human sciences*. Albany: State University of New York Press.

Reed, V., 1994. Fair housing enforcement: is the current system adequate? *In*: R. Bullard, J.E. Grigsby, III and C. Lee, eds. *Residential apartheid: the American legacy*. Los Angeles, CA: CAAS Publications, 222–236.

Ricoeur, P., 1979. The human experience of time and narrative. *Research in phenomenology*, IX, 17–34.

Ricoeur, P., 1984. *Time and narrative*. Trans. K. McLaughlin and D. Pellauer. Vol. 1. Chicago, IL: University of Chicago Press.

Ricoeur, P., 1988. *Time and narrative*. Trans. K. Blamey. Vol. 3. Chicago, IL: University of Chicago Press.

Royal, C.D.M. and Dunston, G.M., 2004. Changing the paradigm from "Race" to human genome variation. *Nature genetics supplement*, 36 (11), 5–7.

Shelley v. Kraemer, 334 US 1 (1948).

Smith, R., 2003. *Stories of peoplehood: the politics and morals of political membership*. New York: Cambridge University Press.

Somers, M., 1994. The narrative constitution of identity: a relational and network approach. *Theory and society*, 23, 605–649.

Squires, G., 1994. Community reinvestment: the privatization of Fair Lending Law Enforcement. *In*: R. Bullard, J.E. Grigsby, III and C. Lee, eds. *Residential apartheid: the American legacy*. Los Angeles, CA: CAAS, 257–286.

Strawson, G., 2004. Against narrativity. *Ratio*, XVII (4), 428–452.

Turner, M., Struyk, R. and Yinger, J., 1991. *Housing discrimination study: synthesis*. Washington, DC: U.S. Department of Housing and Urban Development.

White, H., 1981. The value of narrativity in the representation of reality. *In*: W.J.T. Mitchell, ed. *On narrative*. Chicago, IL: University of Chicago Press, 1–23.

Wienk, R., Reid, C., Simonson, J. and Eggers, F., 1979. *Housing markets practices survey*. Washington, DC: U.S. Department of Housing and Urban Development.

Zerilli, L., 1998. Doing without knowing: feminism's political of the ordinary. *Political theory*, 26 (4), 435–458.

Educating the new national citizen: education, political subjectivity and divided societies

Lynn A. Staeheli[a] and Daniel Hammett[b]

[a]Science Laboratories, Department of Geography, Durham University, South Road, Durham DH1 3LE, UK; [b]Department of Geography, The University of Sheffield, Sheffield, UK and School of Geography, University of the Free State, Bloemfontein, South Africa

This paper explores the ways in which citizenship education is used in an effort to create particular kinds of citizens as part of a larger effort at nation- and polity-building. This paper addresses the purpose of citizenship education and its role in creating political subjectivities for citizens. We argue that policies and programmes often attempt to heal social divisions by fostering a common linkage between citizens and nation, but in ways that may be ineffective, and in some cases, deeply problematic. This argument is developed through a consideration of the ways in which different agents involved in citizenship education use their own experiences to develop and interpret citizenship education programmes. Through this, both the meaning and the teaching of citizenship may be reworked. This conceptual argument is supplemented through a consideration of citizenship education programmes in South Africa.

In 2007, an adaptation of the play *Class Enemy* premiered in Sarajevo. The original, 1978 version of the play by Nigel Williams is set in a classroom in Brixton, an area of London that had a large Afro-Caribbean population. In the play, the teachers fail to appear one day, and while waiting, the students gradually organise themselves and create a classroom that reflects their experiences of the dysfunctional society that has cast them off. They barricade themselves into their room and teach 'lessons' of brutality and tragedy. The adaptation in Sarajevo focuses on the violence that permeates the city and schools, and then on attitudes shaped by ethnic cleansing, war and massacre. In preparation, actors and the director spent time in Bosnian schools, picking up stories and language to insert into the adaptation. The result is a reflection of the horror that has infused Bosnian life and culture and of the experiences of young people who do not recall life before the war. An article about the play in *The Guardian* quotes a man from Tuzla who was 10 years old when the war began:

'Lots of families have someone whose bones were never found. I went to a psychologist to ask what I could do about my anxiety attacks − I see pictures in my head of the war, the bloody bodies. She said I would just have to live with it.' He brought his mother, a secondary school teacher, to see the play. 'My ma was shocked by the rudeness of it and said she couldn't feel her legs after. But what most shocked her was how close to her experience of the classroom it was.' (Connolly 2008, p. 27)

This example illustrates what is at stake in citizenship education in the context of divided societies. What seems to be rather straightforward – teaching basics of civics, democracy, and the values and behaviours associated with citizenship – inevitably has to confront the histories that children, parents and teachers have lived. Many traditions of democracy implicitly assume that democracy and citizenship are built around core elements or core principles that are unchanging from place to place and from context to context. But how would students in Brixton, the original setting of the play, interpret and make sense of lessons about equality, confronting as they do racism and material inequality? How would students in Sarajevo make sense of lessons about respect and deliberation after living through a brutal war and the ongoing difficulties of forging a sense of mutuality and community?

Our focus in this article is on divided societies and the ways in which citizenship education is used – and perhaps manipulated – in an effort to create particular kinds of citizens who suit the national stories and imaginations that governments and other agents hope to foster. In this way, citizenship education should be seen as a tool in nation- and polity-building; it is one component of a suite of practices associated with social reproduction and citizenship formation (Marston and Mitchell 2004). This paper begins with a discussion of the purpose of citizenship education and its role in creating political subjectivities for citizens. We then address the relationships between citizens and states as they are often conceptualised in and mobilised by citizenship education theory and programmes. Policies and programmes often use citizenship education in an attempt to heal social divisions by fostering a common linkage between citizens and nation, or in Rogers Smith's (2003) terms, to tell 'stories of peoplehood.' These stories, however, may be deeply problematic in divided societies. We explore this possibility through a consideration of the ways in which different people involved in citizenship education – policymakers, non-governmental organisations, communities and young people – use their own experiences as citizens and as members of society to interpret and shape citizenship education programmes. Through this, we argue that while education may be intended as a means of moulding national citizens, individual citizens and communities will bring their own capacities, experiences and subjectivities to the education process and, in so doing, may contest or rework both the teaching of citizenship education and the ways in which it is received. Our argument is primarily conceptual, but we also draw on preliminary research on citizenship education programmes in South Africa. By way of conclusion, this paper addresses a set of issues that pose challenges for citizenship education in divided societies.

Why citizenship education?

Citizenship education is delivered in a variety of ways. In some countries, it is an explicit part of the curriculum and there is a subject or content area with that label. In other countries, there might not be a specific content area, but policies direct schools to teach certain principles. In still other circumstances, educational practices are justified in terms of the things citizens (including youth and adults) should know; in these circumstances, it is sometimes easier to think about education *for* citizenship, rather than to conceptualise citizenship education as being about government and politics. Two characteristics unite these diverse practices. The first is the central role that education broadly understood is held to play in the construction of citizenship and of a citizenry. The second is the ways that citizenship education provides an insight into the negotiations between abstract theories and ideals about democracy and the nitty-gritty of fostering citizenship in real places, with real histories of division and with real problems.

This section explores these issues through a discussion of the role of citizenship education programmes in creating political subjects with the skills and the sense of solidarity required to form an effective citizenry at a given moment. As the latter implies, citizenship education must be understood as reflecting particular temporal and national contexts. Yet, citizenship education is not something that is simply 'delivered' or taught to abstract (and perhaps passive) students. It is actively reworked and sometimes challenged as teachers, parents, communities and students match what is supposed to be taught against their lives and experiences, including social inequality, division and conflict. In the acts of receiving and contesting what is taught, the implications or the meaning of citizenship education can diverge from what states and others might have intended, and the kind of citizenry that emerges may be contrary to what was envisioned.

Education, nation-building and citizenship formation

The importance of education in fostering a democratic citizenry is hard to overstate. If, as many would argue, the goals of democracy are self-development, well-being and the good life (Young 2000, Gould 2004), then education is critical (see Gutmann 1987, Dewey 1916/1997, Osler and Starkey 2005, Bridgehouse 2006, Crick 2008). Yet, states have more than a normative interest in an individual citizen's well-being; they also seek to shape and maintain a political community capable of being governed. In divided societies, this may involve creating a national story of peoplehood that minimises, or even overlooks, division and conflict in order to promote a form of association in which the claims of 'the people' or nation take primacy over the claims of groups or over histories that might divide the people (Smith 2003). While such stories may be a powerful tool in providing a new basis for thinking about political membership that is not based on domination and oppression, Goldberg (2009) argues that there is a tendency to leave residues of oppression unexamined, and so to bury division and conflict, rather than address them directly.[1] Burying conflict, however, does not eliminate ongoing problems; it only makes the political grounds for addressing them more difficult to identify, as the politics of memory erases the memory of politics (Edkins 2003, Oglesby 2007). As such, lofty goals of creating political subjectivities as citizens are, in practice, combined with efforts to resolve needs and problems from across the society; actual programmes reflect negotiations between conflicting claims and are often internally inconsistent as a result. In short, relationships between economic, political and social contexts influence the meaning of and potential for citizenship and the kinds of polities that educational systems are intended to shape (Mitchell 2003).

We can see this argument in the development of American and South African citizenships at different historical moments. American education was from the very beginning part of a project that linked citizenship formation and the development of the polity to individual self-development and nation-building (although those terms would not have been used). The goal was to ensure that a new kind of political subject capable of functioning as a democratic citizen would be formed through an educational system open to all (or at least all white males). The most important skills for these subjects did not involve political and moral philosophy, however, so much as they involved animal husbandry, the ability to do sums and other skills that would enable Americans to function as autonomous subjects (Shklar 1998). Moral values were not completely ignored, of course, as moral and character education have been linked to citizenship in one way or other since Confucius and Aristotle. The intent of the system of public education was to create a citizenry with the requisite skills to behave according to a particular vision of democracy and a shared public morality (Dewey 1916/1997; on the importance of a shared morality, see also Callan 1997, Althof and Berkowitz 2006, Bull 2006).

Over time, and as the USA began to be populated with people from a wider range of backgrounds, and as former slaves, Native Americans and women gained more of the rights of formal citizenship, new 'political' skills were required for a diverse and divided citizenry, including those related to how one lives *as* an American citizen. The educational programmes of the Americanisation movement, for instance, included classes in hygiene, cooking, child-rearing, and so forth with the argument that fitting into – assimilating into – the American community was a component of citizenship (Hoy 1995, Spain 2001). While some of these programmes were comparatively benign, there was an element of coercion in many.

Yet for all of this, there have always been tensions in American education policy as a tool for overcoming difference and creating social solidarity. When the Americanisation movement was taking hold early in the twentieth century, there were also advocates for cultural pluralism and a certain kind of cosmopolitanism in education. A notable – and very contemporary sounding – intervention came in Randal Bourne's 1916 article 'Transnational America.' Shunning what he called the 'romantic gilding of the past' (p. 97), he argued that recognising the ideas and voices of new immigrants was not a threat to America, but rather an opportunity to explore what Americanism means and to build a stronger, more democratic America. Three decades later and ignoring the internment of Japanese citizens, the country experienced a resurgent American nationalism in which the greatness of the country was argued to rest on its foundation on universal principles of democracy that were somehow uniquely American (Adamic 1945). Impulses towards both pluralism and nationalism rested easily amongst many. For example, in an early call for cosmopolitanism, Bourne ended his 1916 article with the claim that 'Only America, by reason of the unique liberty of opportunity and traditional isolation for which she seems to stand, can lead this cosmopolitan enterprise' (p. 96). What may seem to be contradictions were nevertheless accepted as unremarkable in the formation of an American citizenship that met the changing needs of a nation.

Just as the vision of American citizenship has changed through history, so too have official conceptions of South African citizenship. The ideals of citizenship during the colonial and apartheid periods were broadly premised upon the development of white citizens and black subjects; these imperatives were evident in colonial government education projects, which sought to balance the need to 'civilise' the 'non-white' populations with the necessity to maintain a separate and superior 'white' identity and privilege (Keto 1990). Subsequent development of Mission-based education in the eighteenth century emphasised conversion and moral development of black populations, which meant the mission schools were often at odds with government policy. The colonial and religious authorities were caught in a contradiction, as they promoted citizenship and civilisation while also entrenching subjecthood and subjugation in a racially hierarchical society (Cross and Chisholm 1990, Comaroff 2001).

Legislation in the nineteenth and the early twentieth centuries introduced *de jure* racial segregation in schooling, separate curricula and differential educational expenditure. The rationale for these developments was that education should be 'for one's position in society,' which positioned whites as citizens and blacks as un- and semi-skilled subjects (Verwoerd 1954). Policies in the 1950s and the 1960s provided for racially differentiated education that reproduced class and racialised positions: a liberal education that promoted national belonging was provided to white students, while 'non-white' education emphasised vocational skills (Chisholm 1987). Attempts to paper over these contradictions through the introduction of Afrikaans as the compulsory medium of instruction in 1976 were met with riots in black schools, whose learners and teachers resented the imposition of the 'language of the oppressor' upon them.

Education policy anticipated the ending of apartheid, with gestures toward a democratic, non-racist, non-sexist, equitable education being made from 1990 onwards. The democratic transition extended the status of a new citizenship to all South Africans, with attendant imperatives to develop the skills of citizenship, both among the populations previously denied citizenship *and* those whose understandings of citizenship did not match the demands of the transformed nation. Education policy provided the 'pedagogical blueprint' and was grounded in the constitutional values of social justice, equality, egalitarianism and respect for human rights (Soudien 2007). While education policy documents contained elements of different theorisations of citizenship (Swartz 2006), they generally reflected broader nation-building imperatives that expanded citizenship to all South Africans and attempted to build a coherent nation from a divided society (Asmal 2003).

Contexts of citizenship formation

As the above examples demonstrate, citizenship is not some enduring category or status constructed to reflect universal ideals. Rather, citizenship is formed in relation to political, economic and social processes that operate within particular geographical and temporal contexts. Marston and Mitchell (2004) argue, therefore, that we should conceptualise citizenship through the processes by which it is formed and given meaning and not simply focus on the ways it is reified through law or theory. From this perspective, procedural and substantive aspects of citizenship become meaningful in light of the contexts and processes through which they are animated.

Returning to the example of American citizenship formation, we can reinterpret the potted history just provided in terms of the specific challenges to and competing visions of citizenship that the country seemed to face and the state's response to them. Whereas initially, providing productive skills and a common set of values that would constitute an American identity may have seemed the primary need, political and economic leaders later came to fear the break down of social solidarity caused by massive immigration and urbanisation; the primary task changed to one of making people learn and conform to the day-to-day practices of being an American. Contemporary debates over immigration and the promotion of ethos related to work and self-sufficiency in constructing a citizenry need to be similarly contextualised in terms of concerns over shared values and the ability of citizens to rise to contemporary economic and geopolitical challenges (see Sandel 1996, Rose 1999). Similarly, the educational system in South Africa both reflected and reinforced ideas about how the nation was constituted and the role of racialised populations within it. Yet, the history is different to (and more recent than) that of the USA.[2] For a considerable period in South Africa, national solidarity was defined in racially exclusionary terms, and a complex legal and education system was designed to sustain it. As the legal and political systems have changed in the post-apartheid period, the legacy of racial oppression continues and is manifested in the extreme poverty and inequality of the country. Contemporary education policy confronts the obvious divisions in the country, while still narrating a national story of peoplehood based on respect, international norms of human rights and equality (Enslin 2003).

Lest this argument seems to be too functionalist (i.e. the 'optimal' form of citizenship at any time or any place is directly related to the needs of the state and economy), it is important to remember that citizenship formation is itself an outcome and a reflection of struggles regarding the very meaning of citizenship and what a 'good' citizen would be. Furthermore, processes of citizenship formation reflect gaps between philosophical arguments and the requisites of governance at particular moments, in particular contexts, and in support of particular goals. Thus, while they perhaps rely on moral and political philosophy as guides in imagining citizenship, various institutions and agents associated with governing and ruling (whether in the state, economy or civil society) may have their own interests in governing in particular ways and in furtherance of particular ends. These interests are as likely to be implicated in ideas about citizenship and education as are the more abstract goals and ideals articulated through theory and philosophy; this is what Ranciere (2006) talks about as the School and its use by elites in closing down impulses and mobilisations that might otherwise challenge the structures and relations of power. In the gap between philosophy and practice, therefore, we find agonism and politics.

Subjects of citizenship formation

The discussion to this point has raised the possibility that institutions and powerful agents might have different ideas, politics and strategies regarding citizenship, and also different resources to effect citizenship formation. But the powerful agents and the institutions are not the only political agents who intervene in struggles over education and citizenship formation. Perhaps because education is such a fundamental element of social reproduction, a wide variety of agents are involved with and affected by educational practices. In the USA and the UK, debates over education policies and outcomes are only partly about test scores and league tables; they are also about structural inequalities, about the role of institutional and cultural racism and how (or whether) they should be overcome, about the role of state in mitigating inequality and racism, and over the kind of knowledge that should be valued and taught. In countries such as France, the UK and the USA, there are also debates over the roles of different rationalities in the production of knowledge and about the role of faith and religion in public life. In these debates, parents, teachers, students and communities often play as influential a role as do government officials, corporate leaders and the educational bureaucracy. These swirling debates and the processes of citizenship formation are complex, because individuals are shaped not just by what is taught in the classroom but also by what they learn as they move through the world. Students are not just taught by teachers but are also taught by peers, parents, communities and the world around them. As such, and as seen in *Class Enemy,* philosophical debates, policy initiatives and the best intentions of teachers can all be turned upside down in the face of broad social and political currents. Moreover, while educational systems may be tools to regulate and discipline future citizens, the process of regulation is not one that is uncontested and in which the outcome is foreordained.

Conceptualising citizenship education in divided societies

The processes by which citizenship education is formulated and the processes that shape its reception are complex and contested. Given education's role in shaping social solidarity, national imaginations and political subjectivities, nothing less should be expected. It is telling that concerns about citizenship and the roles of educational systems in promoting it often surface at moments when solidarity and the need to reinforce national norms and stories are in doubt. In Britain, for example, the emphasis on 'Britishness' and the development of a new citizenship test occurred in the context of what seemed to be a fragmenting society that had lost its sense of itself, as witnessed in racial conflicts in the early 2000s, fears of social breakdown as a result of new immigration and the perceived rise of extremism on the part of nationalist parties and Islamists. In light of what were interpreted as 'new' divisions, British values and citizenship had to be inculcated in a new generation of citizens (see Pykett 2007). In other countries, divisions may be firmly entrenched in societies through law and custom or may have been the source of conflict and war. In those cases, creating an identity as a national citizen may be a fraught process. Models of how to create national citizens abound, filling the pages of education journals. They are also evident in documents and programmatic statements issued by politicians and policymakers. In this section, we explore one model developed by two influential theorists and practitioners of citizenship education. We selected this model – which is one of several that might have been selected – due to the prominence of the authors and because it so clearly collects or assembles ideas from many different theoretical arguments about citizenship. As such, the model provides a clear linkage between theories of citizenship, a recognition of political and social imperatives and a guidance for educational practise.

In *Changing Citizenship*, Osler and Starkey (2005) proposed a model that describes the interrelationships between elements of citizenship. They argue that citizenship can be understood as involving three elements or dimensions: status, feeling and practice (see Figure 1). Citizenship as status is rooted in constitutions and jurisprudence and involves the legal conditions of citizenship, including who can be a citizen and the rights and responsibilities they carry. Citizenship as a *feeling* reflects the importance of an affective sense of belonging to a political community and the sense of solidarity that comes from citizenship (or what is often discussed in developmental discourses as the bonds of social capital (e.g. Muck 2004)). The *practice* of citizenship draws on the awareness that people have of their relationships with other citizens, which draws them into collective activities. These three elements of citizenship are presented as mutually reinforcing. A legal standing not only enhances the feeling of belonging, but also provides the basis for claims against exclusion. A feeling of belonging makes people more likely to participate in civic affairs as active citizens, while participation tends to reinforce the feeling of belonging. Also, holding a legal status often subtly compels people to behave in certain ways *as citizens*. As the above implies, this model of citizenship draws from a wide range of literatures, encompassing debates over liberal and republican theories, procedural and substantive citizenship, and the importance of individuals with respect to the communities and nations in which they are situated. Perhaps, most importantly, it provides a guide for teaching about citizenship and is suggestive of different strategies for developing subjectivities as citizens and thereby overcoming division.

Significantly, each of the elements can be 'located' in the sites and institutions with which the elements of citizenship are most closely attached, suggesting both a set of issues to be taught and a set of strategies for adapting to particular stresses and changes.[3] As such, these are sites in which debate and conflict might emerge over the ways citizenship should be formed through education; they are also sites in which one could anticipate that different experiences would affect the ways education programmes are received and

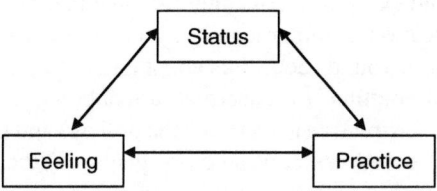

Figure 1. Elements of citizenship.

interpreted. One could imagine, for instance, that legal status would be associated with the state, indicating the need to teach about government and how to interact with the government as a citizen. Feeling is often discussed in the academic literature and in policy with respect to the political community and/or nation; it could, therefore, be assumed that enhancing feeling would be accomplished through the teaching of history and, in some cases, reconciliation. Finally, practice is often associated with localities, as the teaching of active citizenship encourages participation in community life, voluntarism, and so forth. Yet, such associations could be difficult in the context of deep divisions within a society and could reinforce the tendency to promote national identities and conceptualisations of citizenship that might be counterproductive in a globalising world. Many educators and philosophers of education worry that promotion of national identities and citizenships will hinder the development of a global consciousness or will denigrate the multiple identities and feelings of membership that youth may hold. In response, scholars such as Osler and Starkey advocate efforts to foster cosmopolitanism as a way of healing rifts or divisions between citizens within a country and to create citizens who will recognise the humanity of all people, regardless of their nationality or background. In this view, cosmopolitanism is a sensibility that links the elements of citizenship such that individuals can imagine themselves as citizens at local, national and global levels. As such, cosmopolitanism can help students process their identities and experiences in ways that do not dwell on differences, but rather highlight their connections to other students, to people who might have different racial backgrounds or religious beliefs and to see them as humans with shared aspirations (see also Gutmann 1987, Turner 2002, Bridgehouse 2006, Benhabib 2007, Kiwan 2008). These connections should provide a way to work together in a 'learning society' (Jarvis 2000) and perhaps a global citizenship (Roman 2003). Significantly, these practices may lead to selective decisions as to what should be taught (Stradling 2003), which may ultimately constrain the ability to change social foundations (Goldberg 2009). In the near term, however, cosmopolitanism offers a way to promote the *practice* of citizenship in localities, but while also emphasising the global level in teaching about *status* (e.g. would talk about human rights) and *feeling*.

This is, in many ways, an optimistic account of citizenship and how it can be fostered, and it carries an assumption that the state, or perhaps international organisations, can effect meaningful – and perhaps uncontested – change in national stories. The promotion of cosmopolitanism, however, would seem to be at odds with another state goal for citizenship education: to instil a national story and identity. History, for example, is commonly included as one of the subject areas comprising citizenship education, because it is a way to highlight the shared history that shapes the political subjectivity of citizens. From a practical perspective, it is not clear why governments would want to promote a post-national or non-national form of citizenship associated with cosmopolitanism, where allegiance to the state is downplayed.[4] In unravelling this puzzle, it is worth remembering that governments are fragmented, rarely consistent and have multiple goals that *are* contradictory. These contradictions may be seen in the variety of ways that citizenship is promoted in educational systems; there should be no expectation of coherence in either government's goals or in the ways that citizenship education is implemented or received. The broader point, however, is that there is a *politics* that surrounds decisions about citizenship education, curriculum and practice. Rather than attempting to construct a coherent, seamless narrative about citizenship education, it is instructive to examine the policies and practices in the classroom to identify multiple and sometimes contradictory goals. Furthermore, it is important to examine citizenship education as it is implemented, not just conceptualised, and as it is received and internalised. Policy statements and curricula, in this perspective, may be important, but do not comprise the totality – or even the most important parts – of education (Bridgehouse 2006). The processes by which the curriculum is implemented and received are laden with politics, as the gap between educational philosophy and practice is a site in which political subjectivities and meanings are formed. In the next section, we develop this argument based on the research in South Africa.[5]

Citizenship formation, education and the new South African citizen

As we have intimated, South Africa presents many of the difficulties that countries encounter as they attempt to use the educational system to foster a new kind of citizen. The post-apartheid government heralded a new kind of citizen and a new democratic nation that would move beyond the racialist policies and laws of the past. The educational system had many responsibilities, not least of which was developing a programme for citizenship education (Unterhalter 2002, Enslin 2003). But as should be anticipated from the argument presented above, the goals expressed by the government do not necessarily match what is taught in different schools.

The education policies developed at the national level are intended to create citizens who embody particular goals, including citizens with a sense of social justice, productive citizens with skills for a global economy, healthy citizens who embody (literally) values and behaviours that will stem the onslaught of HIV/AIDS (Department of Education 2001a, 2001b). The policy documents promote a vision of 'unity in diversity' and of citizenship rooted in human rights for all. Race and the racialised history of the country are not as prominent in policy documents as might be expected, although they are implicitly acknowledged in the opening statements of goals and values in many documents. Rather, the vision is forward-looking and emphasises the potential of a country in which all citizens can lead fulfilling lives. This strategy, and the passage of time, have meant that many students do not understand the full implications of the country's racialised history, and so the meaning of South African citizenship may seem unmoored. In this respect, the incorporation of citizenship education into all areas of the curriculum, but particularly into the 'Life Orientation' subject area is significant. As one teacher explained, this reflects a belief that citizenship is relevant to all aspects of life.

The policies can easily be seen as promoting a kind of cosmopolitanism; the critical issues, as Mitchell (2007) has argued, are whose cosmopolitanism and for what ends. The policies are intended to foster a citizenry capable of functioning in a global economy and that will see itself as bound to a framework of universal human rights. Business interests are pleased with the emphasis on skills for the international economy and have lobbied hard against policies that would redress historical disadvantage through affirmation action. The emphasis on human rights is consistent with the rhetoric of the anti-apartheid struggle that highlighted the responsibility of the international community to take action. This history may be one reason that the South African government promotes what, on the face of things, seems to support cosmopolitanism: the recognition of human rights of all people was the basis of their claim to be reintegrated into international organisations and the global community. Given this history, a discourse of human, as compared to national, rights is inextricable from the national story and identity. Indeed, government officials and teachers argued that human rights are essential to South African citizenship and are written into the South African constitution and thus are at the core of the nation, with the implication that they are built into the very status of 'citizen.' Nevertheless, none of the teachers talked about human rights or anything that might be associated with cosmopolitanism when they defined citizenship, and the idea of training students to be competitive in a global economy seemed very distant from the reality of grinding poverty in which many of the students from the townships lived. In the poorest high school, for instance, there were no posters on the walls alerting students to opportunities for further education in universities or in technical institutes. For these students, passing matriculation examinations seemed to be the most that anyone hoped they would achieve; given the challenges many learners and schools face, matriculation is itself a major accomplishment. Yet, in a country with an estimated unemployment rate of 22% and where 50% of the population lives below the country's poverty line (World Factbook 2009), the idea that these students would become part of a globally competitive labour force seems very remote.

Rather than cosmopolitanism, teachers typically discussed citizenship in terms of practice: knowing rights, obeying the laws of the country, acting responsibly and being a good member of the community. The country's history of racial division and its current reality of socio-economic inequality make it important – yet difficult – to instil a sense a meaningful citizenship, commonality or community. But that history and current reality also mean that it is necessary to remind some students that they do have rights and responsibilities *as equal citizens* and that they needed to know the structure of government in order to make claims upon it. As such, some teachers told learners where and how they could protest. Yet, teachers conceded that there was a large gap between what they were teaching and what students experienced. The disjuncture between education policy and practice in different contexts has emerged as a key challenge to educational reform. For one education NGO, the challenges are so great as to lead the director to comment that communities, teachers and learners were not 'ready' for citizenship education and that other issues should take priority. He commented on the poor training of many teachers, the difficulty of providing textbooks in the 11 languages of instruction and the lack of family and community support in sending learners to school ready for instruction. In this context, he felt citizenship education was a luxury that most schools could not afford.

Some aspects of the citizenship education curriculum could simply not be implemented. While the policy documents call upon teachers to promote the practice of active citizenship, in which students would engage in projects in their own communities and across different communities, this was nearly impossible to implement. As in many countries, active citizenship is promoted, in part, as a way to bridge divisions between communities by bringing students from different backgrounds into contact with each other. Yet, active citizenship was implemented in ways that might reinforce social distance, rather than bridge it. Two of the schools that charged high fees (including the private school) engaged in school-based community service activities intended to assist students from disadvantaged schools. Students in one school brought in books that were donated to children in the informal settlements surrounding Cape Town, and students in another school made lunches for AIDS orphans. In neither case did students come into direct contact with other students, as the books and lunches were picked up by staff from the beneficiary schools. At least one teacher was worried about the way these acts were interpreted by students, believing that these were acts of condescension rather than acts of citizenship rooted in equality and shared purpose. While believing that the activities were inadequate, however, teachers believed any effort to bring students in direct contact with students from disadvantaged backgrounds would be opposed by parents who were worried about the safety of their children; one teacher confessed that she would not have allowed her daughter to go into the townships while she was a high school student. Despite a commitment to active citizenship as a way of bridging social division, it is hard to see how the way active citizenship is practiced would create a meaningful sense of citizenship that could overcome the divisions within South African society.

The different situations and contexts of education and of participants make clear the difficulty of instilling a national sense of 'unity through diversity' in the curriculum. In one township high school, many of the windows were broken (and had been broken for a long time); feral dogs roamed through the school grounds; there was no custodial staff; some classes had over 50 students and there were not enough teachers, textbooks or even tables and chairs for all the students. 'Passing periods' involved more than the movement of students from room to room. They also involved the movement of tables and chairs through the hallways, as late-arriving students had to find and then move furniture. The educational landscape, thus, was not the one that matched the discourse of equality promoted in the curriculum and in human rights discourses. While these students were living the effects of apartheid, other students seemed not to have much knowledge about it. In a school in which most of the students came from middle- and upper-income backgrounds but who would have been classified as 'coloured,' students did not know that their parents and grandparents would have been unable to vote for the national government. For these learners, teaching about rights as though they were something special was a curious thing to do. That they could assume that they had equal rights is both an indication of the advances that have been made and an indication that class and economic privilege (which do not map directly onto race, although there remains a strong correlation between race and class) have supplanted the racialised privilege of the past; the history of apartheid may seem irrelevant to the current situation they experience. Struggles around the meanings of race and class are, however, addressed in the schooling environment and continue to frame young people's experiences, and, in part, reflect the experiences of teachers. Many teachers were involved in anti-apartheid struggles, and they negotiate their own histories as they teach South African history and as they prepare learners for a different future (Hammett 2007). In this context, it is hard to imagine a national story that links learners and teachers to each other and to the broader world that builds connections across difference, or that confronts – never mind heals – the challenges of the past and future.

Rather, citizenship education – as all education – is affected by the broad social contexts, personal histories and communal histories in which it is delivered and received. Education policies may have a goal of fostering new kinds of subjectivities, but as in the play *Class Enemy*, they may sometimes reproduce the status quo. Whether intentionally as Ranciere (2006) implies, or just by virtue of the scale of problems affecting South Africa, School and the educational system may be sites of agonism, but they are not at this point sites of mobilisation or radical change. Instead, the interplay between citizenship's constituent elements – status, feeling and meaning – seems incapable of providing the foundation for a new kind of citizenship in South Africa that will redress the divisions of the past. Whether a post-racial vision of the nation is capable of ever doing so, is an open question.

Conclusions

All transitions are complex and fraught, but transitions that involve attempts to overcome division through promotion of a new national story and a citizenry may be particularly difficult. Histories and geographies are implicated in the problems transitions confront and affect the resources that individuals, communities and nations can bring to the process. Citizenship education can be thought of as an attempt to remake those histories by teaching students new stories of peoplehood and giving them the tools to live as a new kind of citizen. But as the example from South Africa demonstrates, this is a difficult process with an uncertain outcome. There are three issues, in particular, that contribute to both the difficulty and uncertainty in creating new citizens.

The first issue revolves around the role that memory and history play. Programmes to make a new kind of citizen cannot simply wipe away the memory of conflict and oppression in divided societies. Truth and reconciliation commissions and memorialisations have been the common strategies to recognise suffering, but their effects are not clear. Furthermore, many educators worry about the efficacy of those strategies for young people, whom it is hoped will be raised without the burden of past conflicts. Yet, as the two versions of *Class Enemy* and the audience reception to them suggest, youth have their own experiences of conflict and the aftermath of conflict. Those experiences are further interpreted by their parents and teachers, and by interactions in their communities and daily lives. To be effective, calls to cosmopolitanism, active citizenship and a new national identity have to be reconciled with the experiences and subjectivities of youth.

Second, but related, citizenship education programmes in and of themselves are not sufficient to overcome the inequalities and processes of marginalisation that seem endemic to all countries and that limit inclusion in the democratic public (Lister 2008). The bases of inequality and for the feelings of exclusion that often accompany inequality are many, including poverty, gender, religion, sexuality and processes of racialisation. Furthermore, the bases of marginalisation are interlinked, positioning subjects in webs of relative privilege and marginalisation within a complex public sphere (Fraser 1990, Warner 2002). Adding another layer of complexity to this, however, are the different ways of understanding both marginalisation and inclusion. This issue is particularly important as non-governmental organisations, community leaders and other agents work with governments as they try to conceptualise and consolidate citizenships that reflect the histories, cultures and needs of different countries and as they respect the human rights and well-being of differently positioned citizen subjects (Gould 2004, Benhabib 2007, Phillips 2007).

Finally, and coming full circle, it remains to be seen whether cosmopolitanism provides the antidote to nationalism or to deeply rooted social divisions, and can therefore be the basis for a new democratic identity. Sears and Hughes (2006) argued that simply promoting citizenship in the educational system without providing evidence that it can be transformative or meaningful reduces citizenship education to a form of indoctrination. This may be particularly ominous in the context of societies where students need to see and to believe in democratic citizenship, if the society is to make fundamental moves to a more just future. Teaching patriotism and national identity easily slides into nationalism (Bridgehouse 2006), and there is some evidence that promoting ideas about global citizenship actually reinforces nationalism in students (Roman 2003). Yet, it is difficult to see how any of the different forms of cosmopolitanism can, on their own, counteract the experiences of violence and inequality that students and communities in divided societies have confronted. Both versions of *Class Enemy* point to the linkage between what is experienced and what is learned, as distinct from what is taught. Citizenship and citizenship education programmes seem unlikely to be meaningful if they do not provide a framework for reconciling experience and philosophy. That framework is crucial for the sustainability of democracy and new citizenship in societies marked by histories – and current realities – of social division.

Acknowledgements

This research was partially supported by a grant from the Economic and Social Research Council (RES-000-22-2841). We are grateful for the comments of participants in the workshop, The Pedagogical State: Education, Citizenship, Governing, and to Jessica Pykett and the

Centre for Citizenship, Identities and Governance at the Open University for including us in that workshop.

Notes

1. This is an explicit element of some subject-specific teaching guides in post-conflict Bosnia, for example. See Stradling (2003).
2. The USA has its own history of racialised oppression, of course.
3. It should be noted that this is not something Osler and Starkey do, however.
4. It should be noted that Osler and Starkey state that there is no necessary contradiction between fostering a sense of cosmopolitanism and national citizenship.
5. This research is based on national policy documents, interviews with government officials and educators, and classroom observations in five high schools in the Western Cape in February and March, 2009. The schools included a mix of public schools, most of which charged additional fees and one that did not; one independent school was also included. Regardless of revenue streams, all schools follow the national curriculum. This is part of a larger study that will include Eastern Cape and KwaZulu-Natal.

References

Adamic, L., 1945. *A nation of nations*. New York: Harper.

Althof, W. and Berkowitz, M., 2006. Moral education and character education: their relationship and roles in citizenship education. *Journal of moral education*, 34 (5), 495–518.

Asmal, K., 2003. *Preface to revised national curriculum statement, grades R-9*. Government of South Africa, Department of Education. Pretoria: Government Printers.

Benhabib, S., 2007. Twilight of sovereignty or the emergence of cosmopolitan norms? Rethinking citizenship in volatile times. *Citizenship studies*, 11 (1), 19–36.

Bourne, R., 1916. Transnational America. *Atlantic monthly*, 118 (July), 86–97.

Bridgehouse, H., 2006. *On education*. London: Routledge.

Bull, B., 2006. Can civic and moral education be distinguished? *In*: D. Warren and J. Patrick, eds. *Civic and moral learning in America*. New York: Palgrave, 21–31.

Callan, E., 1997. *Creating citizens: political education and liberal democracy*. Oxford: Clarendon.

Chisholm, L., 1987. Class and colour in South African youth policy: the Witwatersrand, 1886–1910. *History of education quarterly*, 27 (1), 1–27.

Comaroff, J., 2001. Reflections on the colonial state in South Africa and elsewhere. *In*: A. Zegeye, ed. *Social identities in the new South Africa*. Cape Town: Kwela Books, 37–80.

Connolly, K., 2008. And the lesson today is how to shoot. *The Guardian*, G2, 7 July, 26–27.

Crick, B., 2008. Democracy. *In*: J. Arthur, I. Davies and C. Hahn, eds. *Education for citizenship and democracy*. London: Sage, 13–19.

Cross, M. and Chisholm, L., 1990. The roots of segregated schooling in twentieth-century South Africa. *In*: M. Nkomo, ed. *Pedagogy of domination*. Trenton, NJ: Africa World Press, 44–74.

Department of Education, 2001a. *Human resource development strategy for South Africa: a nation at work for a better life for all*. Pretoria: Government Printers.

Department of Education, 2001b. *Manifesto on values, education and democracy*. Pretorial: Government Printers.

Dewey, J., 1916/1997. *Democracy and education*. New York: Free Press.

Edkins, J., 2003. *Trauma and the memory of politics*. Cambridge: Cambridge University Press.

Enslin, P., 2003. Citizenship education in post-apartheid South Africa. *Cambridge journal of education*, 33 (1), 73–83.

Fraser, N., 1990. Rethinking the public sphere: a contribution to actually existing democracy. *Social text*, 25/26, 56–79.

Goldberg, D., 2009. *The threat of race*. Malden, MA: Blackwell.

Gould, C., 2004. *Globalizing democracy and human rights*. New York: Cambridge University Press.

Gutmann, A., 1987. *Democratic education*. Princeton, NJ: Princeton University Press.

Hammett, D., 2007. Disrespecting teacher: the decline in social standing of teachers in Cape Town, South Africa. *International journal of educational development*, 28 (3), 340–347.

Hoy, S., 1995. *Chasing dirt: the American pursuit of cleanliness*. Oxford: Oxford University Press.

Jarvis, P., 2000. Globalisation, the learning society and comparative education. *Comparative education*, 36 (3), 343–355.

Keto, C., 1990. Pre-industrial education policies and practices in South Africa. *In*: M. Nkomo, ed. *Pedagogy of dominattpdelion*. Trenton, NJ: Africa World Press, 19–42.

Kiwan, D., 2008. *Education for inclusive citizenship*. London: Routledge.

Lister, R., 2008. Inclusive citizenship, gender and poverty: some implications for teaching for citizenship. *Citizenship teaching and learning*, 4 (1), 3–19.

Marston, S. and Mitchell, K., 2004. Citizens and the state: citizenship formation in space and time. *In*: C. Barnett and M. Low, eds. *Spaces of democracy: geographical perspectives on citizenship, participation and representation*. London: Sage, 93–112.

Mitchell, K., 2003. Educating the national citizen in neoliberal times: from the multicultural self to the strategic cosmopolitan. *Transactions of the Institute of British Geographers*, 28 (4), 387–403.

Mitchell, K., 2007. Geographies of identity: the intimate cosmopolitan. *Progress in human geography*, 31 (5), 706–720.

Muck, W., 2004. Global institutions and the creation of social capital. *In*: J. O'Loughlin, L. Staeheli and E. Greenberg, eds. *Globalisation and its outcomes*. New York: Guilford, 337–360.

Oglesby, E., 2007. Educating citizens in postwar Guatemala: historical memory, genocide, and the culture of peace. *Radical history review*, 27, 77–98.

Osler, A. and Starkey, H., 2005. *Changing citizenship: democracy and inclusion in education*. London: Palgrave Macmillan.

Phillips, A., 2007. *Multiculturalism without culture*. Princeton, NJ: Princeton University Press.

Pykett, J., 2007. Making citizens governable? The crick report as a governmental technology. *Journal of education policy*, 22 (3), 301–319.

Ranciere, J., 2006. *Hatred of democracy*. Trans. S. Corcoran. London: Verso.

Roman, L., 2003. Education and the contested meanings of 'global citizenship.' *Journal of educational change*, 4, 269–293.

Rose, N., 1999. *Powers of freedom*. London: Routledge.

Sandel, M., 1996. *Democracy's discontent: America in search of a public philosophy*. Cambridge, MA: Belknap Press.

Sears, A. and Hughes, A., 2006. Citizenship: education or indoctrination? *Citizenship and teacher education*, 2 (1), 3–17.

Shklar, J., 1998. An education for America: Tocqueville, Hawthorne, Emerson. *In*: S. Hoffmann and D. Thompson, eds. *Redeeming American political thought*. Chicago: University of Chicago Press.

Smith, R., 2003. *Stories of peoplehood: the politics and morals of political membership*. Cambridge: Cambridge University Press.

Soudien, C., 2007. *Youth identity in contemporary South Africa*. Cape Town: New Africa Books.

Spain, D., 2001. *How women saved the city*. Minneapolis, MN: University of Minnesota Press.

Stradling, R., 2003. *Multiperspectivity in history teaching: a guide for teachers*. Council of Europe.

Swartz, S., 2006. A long walk to citizenship: morality, justice and faith in the aftermath of apartheid. *Journal of moral education*, 35 (4), 551–570.

Turner, B., 2002. Cosmopolitan virtue, globalization and patriotism. *Theory, culture and society*, 19 (2), 45–63.

Unterhalter, E., 2002. Education, citizenship and difference in the South African transition: policy, politics and practice. *The curriculum journal*, 11 (1), 551–570.

Verwoerd, H., 1954. *Bantu education: policy for the immediate future*. Pretoria: Information Service of the Department of Native Affairs.

Warner, M., 2002. *Publics and counterpublics*. Brooklyn, NY: Zed Books.

World Factbook, 2009. South Africa. Available from: www.cia.gov/library/publications/the-world-factbook/print/sf.html [Accessed 2 March 2009].

Young, I.M., 2000. *Inclusion and democracy*. Oxford: Oxford University Press.

'A broadcasting university': educated citizenship and civil prudence

The Department of Sociology, University of Essex, Wivenhoe Park, Colchester, UK

This paper explores the political rationalities and discursive practices that epitomised adult education broadcasts in 1920's Britain. Taking as its keywords 'citizenship' and 'educated democracy', and its key practices as the dispassionate concern for truth and open debate, the paper will argue that early twentieth-century adult education, particularly as articulated in and through the BBC, was less concerned with the dissemination of knowledge than it was with endowing adult learners with new capacities for self-regulation so that they might better fulfil their newly acquired civic responsibilities following the long-awaited arrival of universal adult suffrage in 1918, whence adult learners were increasingly subjected to a series of self-governing, ethical obligations that are best characterised as 'civil prudence'.

The idea for a 'broadcasting university' is most commonly associated with the founding of the Open University (OU). Established in 1969, the OU's use of television to facilitate the delivery of degree programmes has made it the UK's main distance learning university, particularly for non-traditional students, many of whom are mature and in full-time work. Whilst the OU is to be commended for its open entry policy and promotion of democratic scholarship, its teaching methods can in fact be traced back to the eighteenth century, since when there have been constant efforts to realise an educational apparatus suitable for instructing adult men and women – in particular working-class adults – in matters deemed to be educational. Furthermore, the use of broadcast media for educational purposes dates back to the 1920s, a period during which the adult education movement sought to domesticate 'educated citizenship' in and through the emergence of public service broadcasting – under the aegis of the BBC – and its deployment as an apparatus of educative recreation.

Briggs (1965, p. 186) suggests that the roots for educational broadcasting 'were hidden in new soil', referring to a widespread concern during and after the First World War that the country had failed 'to conceive the full meaning and purpose of education as a whole', particularly in terms of creating an 'educated democracy'. However, Briggs' analysis is based on, and is largely sympathetic with, the then prevailing contemporary belief that education and broadcasting offered a solution to many of the country's social ills, particularly fears about the dangers of an uneducated citizenry. His line of argument implicitly assumes the public service utilities of education and broadcasting to be the achievement of a progressive democratic politics, capable of realising the complete development of the self-forming citizen, which necessarily presumes the perfectibility of human nature.

The argument I wish to pursue, in contrast, is one which refutes this type of liberal analysis and attempts to understand the formation of adult educational broadcasting as an apparatus for moral and cultural regulation. Drawing on the work of Foucault and cognate studies (for example, Donald 1992, Hunter 1988, 1994, Bennett 1998, Dean 1999, Rose 1999), I mean to demonstrate how the listening public were impelled into undertaking an ethical self-labour, so that they might better fulfil their civic responsibilities. But not so that they might contribute to the strengthening of the democratic process (even though it could be argued that this is what did actually happen).[1] Rather, it was more to do with training adult listeners in matters of conduct and social mores, so as to make them more governable. Understood thus, I want to argue that broadcast adult education was less concerned with educating adult men and women than it was with endowing adult listeners with a capacity for effecting techniques of self-regulation.

More than this, I argue that the early BBC and its educational ethos are better reconsidered as an extension of Christian pastoral pedagogy: insofar as it was constituted by normative cultural values deemed to be edifying and morally uplifting, there was a direct link between culture and self-improvement on the one hand, and religion and morality on the other (see Bailey 2007).[2] What was relatively new about the BBC's pastoral guidance, however, was that it was largely for secular purposes, that is to say, though some of the BBC's internal terms of reference were explicitly religious, its *raison d'être* was more properly concerned with moral training as a practical remedy, an everyday ethical practice, rather than a theology for the salvation of souls.[3] In short, just as other quasi and non-state agencies (the 'psy' disciplines, social welfare, education and medicine, for example) were deployed as pedagogical technologies during this period – which can and should be understood as a governmental response to the attendant secularisation and bureaucratic rationalisation of modern society – so too was the BBC entrusted with 'governing through pedagogy'.[4]

I shall also propose that broadcast education, in cooperation with other adult education agencies, was a means of enabling 'government by numbers' in the sense that government can also be understood as the 'will to know' (see Hacking 1990, Poovey 1998, Rose 1999, among others). This was especially so in the context of early twentieth-century Britain, a period characterised by a series of social and political disjunctures that radically altered many late Victorian and Edwardian civic and political institutions (for example, individualism, the family, constitution and the nation). For the state to maintain social order amidst these changing social relations, it was necessary for it to realise a new technique of social regulation that enabled government to better understand the specificity of individual social problems and act upon them (see Hall and Schwarz 1988). One such governmental technology was the statistical and sociological survey. Moreover, whilst there was a nexus of new discursive objects and targets for social enquiries and government intervention (for example, unemployment, public health, housing, sexual and juvenile delinquency, among others), there was a pronounced proliferation in public discourses which postulated that advancements in the provision of adult education and educative recreation were of utmost importance for post-war reconstruction.

First, however, it is necessary to provide a cursory history from which one can vaguely discern broad developments in modern adult education, so as to identify the available discourses and practices in relation to which the BBC had to position itself. I, especially, want to analyse the political rationalities which informed the administrative programmes of the liberal adult education movement that begins to emerge in the historical milieu of the early twentieth century, taking as its keywords 'citizenship' and 'educated democracy', and its key practices as the dispassionate concern for truth and open debate.

Educating the masses

The bulk of early adult education was undertaken by voluntary movements and religious bodies (e.g. Society for the Promotion of Christian Knowledge, the Adult School movement, The Society for the Diffusion of Useful Knowledge, the Mechanics' Institutes, among others). This changes, however, in 1851, when the state makes available for the first time public funding for Adult Evening Schools. Though the object of the evening schools was to assist elementary education, and whilst state aid was still minimal, the Committee of Council on Education's decision to aid evening schools was a significant watershed. From here on, the deployment of an adult education apparatus was to be more closely aligned with the art of liberal government, both in the narrowest and broadest sense of the term. In the narrowest sense, modern adult education was increasingly governmentalised, that is to say, elaborated, rationalised and centralised under the auspices of state-approved agencies. In the broadest sense, the emergence of modern adult education formed part of a complex machinery of government located in the whole social body.

Undoubtedly, the most significant development in the emergence of liberal adult education was the establishment of the Workers' Educational Association (WEA) in 1903. The organisation immediately sought cooperation with other educational agencies, not least the University Extension Movement (founded by a University of Cambridge Syndicate in 1873) and the Board of Education. In doing so, it soon became a state approved 'Responsible Body' and was, therefore, eligible for public funding, provided it continued to fulfil certain criteria stipulated by the Board of Education Regulations for further education. The main criterion was that the appointed Responsible Bodies provide a non-vocational education with an emphasis on objectivity and standards. Thus, students were divided into a hierarchy of different types of classes and courses: terminal courses, 1-year classes, university tutorial classes and university extension courses (see Mansbridge 1913, pp. 136–141, HMSO 1927, pp. 4–10, Peers 1934, pp. 94–107). Of the different types of classes and courses, the three year tutorial class represented the pinnacle of achievement, since they were required to 'approximate in quality to a University Honours standard' (Peers 1934, p. 101).

The initiative for the tutorial class system was provided by a conference convened by the WEA and the University of Oxford in the summer of 1907. The specific purpose of the conference was to consider 'what Oxford could do for working people' (Stocks 1953, pp. 40–41). The conference proceedings were published as a report, *Oxford and Working Class Education* (reprinted in Harrop 1987, pp. 79–269). What the report reveals was that much of the impetus for modern adult education came from a sense of change in the political presence of the working classes and the dangers which might follow their estrangement from the middle classes. The report was insistent, however, that educated workpeople remain in the class in which they are born and in doing so raise its level from within. 'To those who do this their education will be a means, not only of developing their own powers of enjoyment, but of enabling them to exercise an influence for good in the social life of their factory and town' (quoted in Harrop 1987, p. 176). What the report articulated was a governmental rationality whose *raison d'être* was to train useful workpeople, so that they might penetrate working-class communities and disseminate hegemonic cultural practices through their exemplary conduct. In short, adult learners became agents with which to regulate the conduct of others:

> If a class is formed under the control of members of the working-class societies, its influence filters through a hundred different channels, and may leaven a whole town. Every member of it is a missionary of education in a continually expanding field, and spreads habits of criticism and reflection among his fellows in a way that is impossible if education is organised from above. (quoted in Harrop 1987, p. 152)

Hence, the emphasis the WEA placed upon cooperation between tutors and students. Rather than the tutors deciding what the students should study, syllabuses were decided by both tutors and students. More crucially, modern adult education was less concerned with the dissemination of knowledge than it was with endowing individuals with new capacities for self-development and self-regulation.[5] As the WEAs founder, Mansbridge (1913, pp. 8–9), put it: 'Tutorial classes are less than nothing if they concern themselves merely with the acquisition or dissemination of knowledge. They are in reality concerned with the complete development of those who compose them'. It is probably for this reason that the WEAs precept was teaching adults 'how to think and not what to think'.

Educationalists as 'good shepherds'

One further – though perhaps less obvious – characteristic of the tutorial class was that tutors were deployed as pastoral pedagogues. Following Foucault (2002) and his analysis of the development of pastoral techniques of government in Christianity, we can see the mobilisation of modern adult educationalists as being in some way analogous to the ancient Hebraic conceptions of pastoral power modelled on the 'shepherd-flock' relation (cf. Dean 1999, pp. 73–83). Just as the pastoral relationship in Christianity is between God, the pastor and the pastorate, one can trace a similar 'shepherd-flock' relationship in the provision of adult education in early twentieth-century Britain. Particularly important was the responsibility of the tutor to devote his time and energy to knowing each of his tutees' particular needs and activities; like the 'good shepherd', tutors were responsible for guiding and caring for their flock of learners, to improve the lives of each and every one of them, in order to ensure their salvation.

Robert Peers, the first university Professor in adult education, provides us with what is undoubtedly one of the most lucid expositions from this period of the kind of pastoral methods that were to be utilised and it is worth quoting at length:

> The modern tendency in all forms of education is to stress the necessity of developing the individual as an individual ... The centre of gravity is placed in the living, active pupil rather than in the subject taught, and this attitude clearly implies that the teacher must seek to know his individual pupils as closely as he knows the subjects he professes to teach ... the tutor should set about getting to know his students as intimately as possible – the details of their occupations, their interests and hobbies, the political and religious opinions which form the background of their thinking, their home conditions, their ambitions ... Once the tutor has grasped the special meaning which the movement has for his students, he will realise that his responsibilities are by no means confined to the weekly meeting of the class ... If the subject of study is to have any real meaning, it must be built into the personal background of the student and brought into relation to the experience which has shaped and is shaping his life. Thus it is important that the tutor should learn, by informal contacts, to appreciate the temperament and the relevant circumstances of each student. (Peers 1934, pp. 119 & 157)

It was imperative that the tutor knows as much about his students as was possible, that is to render them knowable. Hence, some adult educationalists started to live in close proximity to their students; and those that did not were encouraged to take an active interest and participate in the communities in which they taught. Students were encouraged to reveal to their tutors and one another their experiences and consciousness. In doing so, it was possible for government to have a more accurate understanding of the mass of adult learners and their multiplicity of individual elements and social relations. Moreover, whilst there were limits to this technique inasmuch meeting places were varied and often *ad hoc,* what was striking about modern adult education was its attempts to penetrate the private cultural spheres of the home and entire communities.

In other words, modern adult education was inextricably entwined with the history of Christian morality and pedagogy, in the sense that adult learners were subjects of pastorship, albeit of a secular kind. The crucial difference between earlier forms of pastoral government and that operationalised by the various functionaries of modern adult education was that citizenship was the principal disciplinary objective driving pastoral guidance in the early twentieth century. Hence, the intertwining of civic duty with the idea of religious salvation, requiring adult learners to renounce any cultural practices that detract from the realisation of a political rationality best characterised as 'civil prudence' (see Dean 1999, pp. 84–88), a kind of Stoic asceticism that required its subjects adhered to self-mastery, meditation, obedience and abstinence. In short, the flock were expected to voluntarily comply with the shepherd's will, and in doing so, pledge their obedience and not to stray from the path of righteousness.

Revolting students

Of course, the reality of adult education was more agonistic. Diametrically opposed to so-called cooperative adult education was the movement for Independent Working-Class Education, which emerged with the founding of Ruskin College in 1899. The aim of the college was, in the words of one of its founders, Mrs Walter Vrooman, to 'take men who have been merely condemning our institutions and to teach them, instead, to transform these institutions so that in place of talking against the world they will begin methodically and scientifically to possess the world' (cited in Mansbridge 1920, pp. 7–8). What this involved, in fact, were endless attempts to 'sandpaper' the rougher characteristics of the students, proposals for closer links with the University of Oxford and interference with academic policy.

Not surprisingly, the college's early history was thus marked by much student dissent (see Jennings 1977). Two of the more significant events to arise from this malcontent were the setting up of the 'Plebs League' in 1908 and the infamous student strike of 1909. Several of the students were expelled and, subsequently, formed the Central Labour College in August 1909, later renamed as the National Council of Labour Colleges in January 1922. Unlike cooperative adult education providers, the Labour Colleges were, in the words of one of the dissident Ruskin students, Craik (1964, p. 86), committed to 'knowledge for action' rather than 'knowledge for its own sake'. In other words, the Labour Colleges properly championed independent working-class education, whilst state-approved adult education associations offered its students a liberal education. Furthermore, the Labour Colleges never sought recognition from the Board of Education, relying instead on the Trades Union Congress for its funding. Nor were the Labour Colleges afraid of engaging in polemic through their monthly left-wing newspaper, *Plebs*, which endlessly attacked liberal adult education as a ruling class stratagem. For example, an editorial published in October 1929 suggested that,

> ... the British governing class has never lacked representatives who appreciate how vital it is to control the education of the workers. As the demand for education grew in the working-class ranks, the governing class has not hesitated to spend large sums of money ... to inculcate in the minds of the workers the social theories necessary to ensure the continuance of

the present order of society. It is true that with its growth, the working-class movement becomes more and more sceptical of the governing-class's direct methods of education. With an adaptation that does it credit, the governing class, however, has surmounted this difficulty for the time being by retiring into the background and, by means of grants and through its trained educationalists from the universities, has maintained control over the education provided by bodies that have the appearance of being purely working-class ... With a class cunning that is difficult to beat, the governing-class has not made the mistake of keeping too tight a reign on such educational bodies ...

The capacity for state-approved adult education to effect governance from a distance is not in doubt. However, the manner in which the Labour Colleges sought to efface cooperative adult education was misplaced. Though the likes of the WEA were funded by the state, this does not mean they were first and foremost an ideological state apparatus. It was not just a straight forward case of who pays the piper calls the tune. More than this, adult education's *raison d'être* was not social control, but rather as a means for forming an adult working-class population with useful habits. It existed as a discipline rather than as an ideology. It was also an apparatus for regulating the relations between the different social classes of the nation's populace as a whole (cf. Jones and Williamson 1979). Understood thus, the deployment of adult education was not so much an attempt to contain and regulate the emerging power of the labour movement, but rather an effect of a whole economy of cultural and educational technologies whose rationality was to ensure the well-being and prosperity of the populace as a whole. Its source of power was founded upon a new solidarity and universal relation between the educated and uneducated.

Learning over the air

To this point, this paper has sought to demonstrate the 'bureaucratic-pastoral' character of modern adult education. I would now like to turn my attention to what is the more substantive theme of this paper: the emergence of public service broadcasting and its deployment as an apparatus of educative recreation, particularly for adult listeners.

The first systematic provision for broadcast adult education started in October 1924, shortly after educational broadcasting had been established as an administrative department in July 1924. The appointment of its first Director, J.C. Stobart, seconded from His Majesty's Inspectorate for Education, was reported on the front page on the *Radio Times* (13 June 1924) under the heading 'A Broadcasting University'.[6] The peculiarity and significance of a civil servant being loaned to what was still then a business organisation did not go unnoticed and was 'taken as evidence of the Government's realisation of the national importance of broadcasting'.

For Stobart, broadcast education was as much about uplifting public tastes as it was disseminating knowledge: ' ... it was early recognised that wireless would exercise a powerful influence, for better or for worse, on the public taste. The British Broadcasting Company has aimed at making their influence raise the standards in this respect' (*The Daily Chronicle,* 11 November 1926). Stobart also saw entertainment and education as synonymous: entertainment ought to have a rational purpose and education ought to be enjoyable. How to effect this synthesis was expanded upon by John Reith – the first Director General of the BBC – who advocated broadening the meaning of both terms.

> We must try to make the word 'education' sound a little less formal, and perhaps somebody will some day produce a better term. Let us also, however, make the word 'entertainment' a little less narrow in its significance than some would have it. No one here disputes that among the function of broadcasting is to entertain; but if we were only to 'entertain', and if the word were to be used in its narrow sense, it would be quite impossible to fill up all the hours of transmission agreeably. (*The Listener,* 30 April 1930)

This problem of the relationship between an entertainment medium and the process of education was a dilemma specific to the BBC. No previous model or discourse but adult education had been obliged to think through whether education should be entertaining or entertainment educational. The mass nature of the wireless as a medium raised this dilemma in acute form and much of the debate around adult education in the BBC would focus upon it.

New ventures in adult education

Of the various inter-war reports directly concerned with broadcast adult education, by far the most significant was *New Ventures in Broadcasting* (1928). The report was the outcome of a joint committee of enquiry between the British Institute for adult education and the BBC into the educational possibilities of broadcasting. The tone of the report was overwhelmingly optimistic. 'The educational possibilities of [wireless] are almost incalculable. Even if no single item labelled educational ever appeared in the programmes, broadcasting would still be a great educational influence' (BBC 1928, p. 1). The report also considered the bureaucratic advantages afforded by wireless: it was cheap and ubiquitous. 'Unlike the lecturer, it can be everywhere at once. It is the perfect method by which to conduct what has been described as "insidious education"' (ibid.). More than this, the report recommended an expanded concept of education, one which took measure of the ordinary person's everyday commitments to their work and their family vis-à-vis hours available for the use of leisure. It was acknowledged that a thirst for education might not be a priority for the average working adult.

Among the report's main recommendations were: (1) the establishing of wireless listening groups; (2) the setting up of a Central Council for Broadcast Adult Education comprised of representatives from important national bodies concerned with adult education and Area Councils representing local educational interests; and (3) the launching of a weekly educational broadcasting journal to supplement the aids-to-study pamphlets (BBC 1928, pp. 69 & 75–79). The report also recommended that broadcast adult education should supplement not displace existing adult education agencies. The objective was thus one of cooperation and mutual goal sharing.

The Central Council for Broadcast Adult Education was formally brought into existence in November 1928. Its membership was wide ranging and representative of the various adult learning agencies. The Council based its policy on its belief 'in the unique and decisive influence of wireless on the future of civilisation' (WAC R14/124). Two key objectives were identified. First, it aimed 'at inducing among listeners a high standard of intellectual curiosity, of critical ability and of tolerance to all views held and expressed with a sincerity and a regard for truth'. This required 'a respect, even a reverence for truth in all its aspects and a desire for knowledge unfettered by dogmas of any kind'. Second came 'the more particular and tangible objective': to educate listeners in 'an appreciation of the forces of transformation and change in the world about them', especially 'the developments of science, the enlargement of knowledge and the evolution of social custom and practices'.

Here, we see the general goals of culture, civilisation and democracy being translated into educational principles: the reverence for 'truth' (as opposed to 'dogma') and the understanding of 'science', 'knowledge' and 'custom'. Note the neutrality of the discourse: not a single truth we can tell them but a respect for truth; not a subservience to the natural order but an understanding of scientific and social change. It verges on advocacy of a kind of sociology but one clearly oriented to a dispassionate understanding which might well produce an urge to reform but not to revolution.

Wireless listening groups

Though always a minority, the main focus of broadcast adult education was the organisation and development of wireless listening groups (see WAC A/261, Williams and Hill 1941).[7] The stated object of listening groups was to develop 'the capacity to listen to other people's ideas even when they are unpalatable, and to follow up by discussion and calm analysis' (*The Listener*, 23 January 1929). Each group had a designated leader whose role was to 'guide and shape the discussion and know sufficient about the subject to take a lead with confidence'. A Board of Education inquiry (HMSO 1933, p. 9) considered group leaders to be 'the keystone of the listening group'. Peers (1934, p. 86) thought that the person chosen as leader should not only 'be competent to guide the discussion', but also 'have the ability to restrain his own and others' garrulity' (see also Williams and Hill 1941, pp. 240–243). Group leaders were not necessarily required to have specialist knowledge but should be 'educated' and 'respectable' persons from business and the professions.

Just as the tutorial class system was concerned with effecting disciplinary practices of self-regulation, the principal *raison d'être* for listening groups was to inculcate listeners in self-regulatory practices that were concurrent with the art of governance, that is rational discussion, tolerance, restraint and impartiality. It was important that the popular masses be taught how to think for themselves and how to imitate exemplary conduct. Understood thus, listening groups were as much to do with contact between conduct and conduct as they were with contact between mind and mind.[8]

Many of the committees of inquiry into the educative potentialities of broadcasting affirm this. For example, a Board of Education inquiry (HMSO 1933, p. 30) into Wireless Listening Groups thought that 'the value of real discussion lies in being able to take a particular topic out of a partisan or highly controversial atmosphere into an atmosphere, detached, disinterested and scholarly'. The report went onto state that 'insofar as the Listening Groups can help build up this dispassionate and critical outlook, they are performing a useful service for the community; but this can only be done if the members are willing to undergo the discipline which real discussion entails' (ibid.). Similarly, an article to appear in *The Listener* (8 August 1934) reiterated that the discourse of educated citizenship was as much about disciplining citizens in the art of self-government, so as to have a deeper sense 'of social responsibility, of sympathy and of the willingness to help in working for a common purpose' as it was with equipping them with abstract rights and freedom. Yet again, we can see the recurrence of a discursive practice that sought to de-politicise the discussion of social issues likely to cause conflict of public opinion. Such differences were to be suppressed in the interests of the community at large, the nation.

The art of listening

A further characteristic of broadcast adult education was the way in which the listening public was constituted according to a hierarchy of listening subjectivities. By the 1930s, the BBC began to differentiate between the casual and the serious listener. A.C. Cameron, then Secretary of the Central Committee for Group Listening, described those listeners who did not wish to commit to being members of approved adult education agencies as 'the Second XI of adult education' (*The Highway*, November 1937). In other words, there was an order of discourse in which the serious listener was deemed to be culturally superior and something the casual listener should therefore aspire to. Casual listeners, that is listeners who lay outside the scope of discussion groups, presented a special difficulty inasmuch as their cultural habits and comportment were unknowable. Consequently, they were not as easily subjectable to techniques of individualisation and normalisation. This was problematic from a governmentality point of view, since it presented an affront to the order of proper conduct necessary for ensuring social solidarity and civility. Converting casual listeners into serious listeners was thus crucial to the construction of an informed and ordered listening public, as the Central Council for Broadcast Adult Education Executive Committee recognised:

> The welfare of our nation depends upon a rapid increase in the number of those who were ready to think for themselves and ready to exercise individual judgement, ready to enter into a real relationship pooling their own mental resources with others in order that all together, as each gained some glimpse of the whole variety of truth, they might shape their policy as a people with reference to the whole of it. (WAC R14/120/4)

The Council was particularly anxious to curtail 'that element in contemporary life' whose qualities were deemed to be 'a certain pugnacity of temper with a herd mentality' (WAC R14/120/1). Such an unknowable mass was potentially unruly and liable to rebel. It was essential, therefore, that as much as possible be known about the many facets of the listening public: its social composition, cultural habits, tastes and preferences; especially that element of the adult listening public which remained untouched by educational broadcasting. Hence, listener research became a vital administrative feature from the late thirties onwards, whereupon Silvey (1977) was recruited to the BBC to establish audience research on a systematic basis. Also, whilst many in the BBC were sceptical about audience research, not least Reith, it soon became an indispensable diagnostic instrument for calibrating and quantifying popular opinion and ascertaining the demographics of its multifaceted audience (see Scannell and Cardiff 1991, pp. 234 & 375–380). Indeed, it was integral to the wider emergence and development of what I earlier referred to as 'government by numbers', particularly in the context of post-war reconstruction.

Enquiries into the extent of educational listening

Two relatively early and influential attempts at listener research were carried out by W.E. Williams (Williams and Heath 1936, Williams and Hill 1941), then secretary of the British Institute of Adult Education and editor of *The Highway*, the WEA monthly journal. *Learn and Live* (1936) was largely concerned with the consumer's view of adult education and surveyed the 'educational life-histories' of over 500 adult learners. This yielded a vast amount of quantitative and qualitative information covering every facet of adult education. *Radio Listening Groups* (1941) provided a comparative analysis of listening groups in the United States and Europe, Great Britain especially. The second study was based upon the testimony of more than 300 witnesses, mostly listening group participants. However, unlike the earlier enquiries into broadcast adult education, the tones of both reports were both cautious and agnostic about the efficacy of group listening as a means of education.

It was at about the same time that both the BBC and the adult education movement generally started to recognise that broadcast adult education had hitherto only appealed to a minority of adult listeners. One of the obstacles inhibiting the development of broadcast adult education and the practice of structured group listening as a pioneering activity was to do with the medium itself: radio was a domestically located medium listened to casually by families in their homes. As R.S. Lambert, the editor of *The Listener* pointed out, the success of group listening rested upon the assumption that, 'listeners would be eager to leave their comfortable firesides on wintry nights and go out to some local hall or schoolroom to sit round a loudspeaker and discuss the words of wisdom let fall by the invisible broadcaster in their midst' (cited in Robinson 1982, p. 61). Furthermore, for many adult learners, broadcasting was an informal alternative to the more formal tutorial classes and organised listening groups. Hence, Llewellyn-Smith thought that whilst 'broadcasting is an immensely powerful instrument for the diffusion of popular cultural entertainment ... as a means of education it is handicapped by the inevitable lack of personal contact between teacher and taught' (1935, p. 8). In short, the problem facing the BBC was thus how to convert radio's everyday familiarity into an instructional medium in the atmosphere of the classroom.

A supplement to direct investigation of listeners was to seek feedback from others strategically placed to gauge the effects of educational broadcasts. Library staff were such a group. An example was the BBC issuing a questionnaire to about 700 public librarians throughout the country in May 1927. Its object was stated in a memorandum on 'Adult Educational Broadcasting and Public Libraries' prepared by Lambert:

> One of the principal difficulties at present facing the development of adult educational broadcasting is the lack of knowledge concerning the constituency with which we have to deal, and the effects which our work is having upon it. Any piece of evidence which contributes to throw light on this problem is therefore of great importance. (WAC R14/145/1)

Two of the questions asked were: (1) 'Did you notice any effect of broadcasting on the demand for books in the last three months? Which talks, if any, were particularly successful in this way'? (2) 'Can you suggest any further lines of cooperation between your library and the BBC for the promotion of reading in your area'? (see BBC 1928, p. 51, WAC R14/145/1). Of the reported 75 libraries which replied to the questionnaire (see WAC, Newspaper Cuttings: Education, 1926–1928), 44 reported an increase in the issue of books referred to in the adult education talks. The *Morning Post* (19 August 1927) reported that many librarians from provincial libraries were 'being overwhelmed with requests for books that have never been stocked or ever before required'. The chief librarian of the Sheffield Library reported that group listening 'composed of a variety of personality, belief, opinion and outlook, could blend together and discuss questions of importance without any distinctions of bias or feeling'; and that 'the Library was indeed a 'Public House' for the free, open and sympathetic exchange of views' (WAC R14/120/1). The amount of information provided by librarians did not go unnoticed, prompting the *Yorkshire Post* (24 August 1927) to comment that 'every librarian is a statistician'.

Not only access to books was to be encouraged. The British Institute of Adult Education also experimented with exhibitions of loan collection of pictures 'in centres where there has hitherto been little chance for the ordinary man to see anything of the sort' (see *The Listener*, 13 February & 3 April 1935). The declared object of the experiment was to breach 'the gulf between art and men's ordinary activities' and in doing so 'expose' people to 'the novel experience of looking at good works of art'. At each exhibition, there were a number of 'observers' who, as well answering any questions, were also 'to instigate impromptu discussions with visitors'. Visitors were encouraged to answer a 'form of inquiry' consisting of four questions: (1) Which pictures do you like best? (2) Why do you like them best? (3) What opportunities do you get to visit Art Galleries or Exhibitions? (4) In what ways do you think these opportunities could be increased or improved? Whilst all four questions were clearly aimed at eliciting information about cultural tastes and preferences, questions (3) and (4) were particularly pertinent inasmuch as they required the interviewee to say something about how their social conditions affect their use of leisure. In other words, the experiment was clearly yet another attempt to render the problem of leisure more knowable by extracting information from working-class populations. This knowledge could then be acted on and incorporated into future governmental programmes of cultural management aimed at cultivating particular habits and capacities, whilst also maintaining certain cultural hierarchies. The above also demonstrates how the BBC closely identified with extant agencies with their own mission towards culture and civilisation: not only adult education groups but libraries and art exhibitions. The new medium was grafted onto some longstanding routes to cultured citizenship.

Educative leisure

Before concluding, I want to briefly consider some further examples of how leisure itself was problematised during this historical conjuncture – especially in and through the BBC – not least because it was felt by many early twentieth century social progressives that education would facilitate the proper use of leisure. For example, Ernest Barker, Principal of King's College, London, thought that, 'education is a necessity if men are to gain the faculty of using leisure easily, happily, and fruitfully' (Barker 1926, p. 32). More than this, he feared that,

> Leisure without faculty for its use may even be a mother of mischief; men may dissipate themselves in frivolities, and worse than frivolities, because they do not know how to concentrate themselves upon better things. A society which guarantees leisure is guaranteeing something which may be useless, and even dangerous, unless it adds, or at any rate encourages its members to add, the one thing which will enable the gift to be used – a continuous process of education (Barker 1926, p. 32).

Of the adult educational broadcasts which specially addressed the problem of leisure, probably the most interesting was *The Changing World* (see WAC, BBC Talks and Lectures, Vol. 6, September 1931–July 1932 & R129/3/1, BBC 1932, Briggs 1965, pp. 220–221, HMSO 1933, Robinson 1982, pp. 53–54, Williams and Hill 1941, pp. 181–183). The scope and aim of the series was to 'provide a survey of the many changes in outward circumstance, and in the evolution of thought and of values, which have brought into being the world as it is today'. Though each series of talks differed in subject matter, all centred around three key questions, one of which concerned itself with asking the listeners to reconsider their civic responsibilities in the light of certain prevailing forces of change to 'remodel our ways of life' and 'the machinery of government'.

One of the talks, *The Modern State*, was introduced by J. A. Hobson in a study-to-aid pamphlet. As well as outlining the desirability of broadcasting being a public utility, Hobson also expounded the educative potentialities of broadcasting:

> ... if, as may hold, the time has come for applying a conscious art of Government to the ordering of public affairs, in local, national, and international spheres, the all-important question of the part which the ordinary citizen shall play in this great new enterprise will depend upon the reliability of this new instrument [i.e. broadcasting] of popular education, more than upon any other fact or force. Not merely, or mainly, as the provider of sound information, but as the chief stimulus and irritant of thought and feeling, broadcasting must come to rank as the 'popular educator' .... (WAC R129/3/1)

Another of the talks was *Education and Leisure*. Listeners were exhorted to form discussion groups and to consider such questions as: (1) 'How do you think leisure ought to be employed'? (2) 'How far is it necessary to educate people in the proper use of leisure'? (3) 'In what ways would education need to be altered if this were to be regarded as an essential part of it'? (4) 'Has the cinema in your district made any difference to the popularity of the public houses'? (5) 'Do people stay at home more or less than they did in 1900'? (6) 'Can there be a civilised community without a leisure class'? (WAC R129/3/1). What we see here is yet another attempt to elicit quantifiable information from a public who will then become the object of its own confessional discourse.

The accompanying study-aid pamphlet, entitled *Learning to Live*, specified how education and leisure should be harnessed towards the same goals.

> We have to envisage education and leisure as forces of transformation ... we are not permitted to put education or leisure in watertight compartments. We are not concerned with education merely as education or with leisure merely as leisure. We are concerned rather with the whole nexus of our social life, and with education and leisure as forces within which are continuously at work changing and altering its character and its quality. (MacMurray 1932, p. 1)

Leisure was taken to be an index of: 'the quality of our humanity' since 'leisure ... is the condition of culture, for culture is merely the expression of free human activity' (MacMurray 1932, pp. 38 & 25). Hence, the pedagogical imperative that we 'learn to live', 'to be trained to use our freedom, and to employ our leisure to the best advantage' (ibid., p. 25). Not surprisingly, the main condition for the proper use of leisure 'is the possession of a spontaneous, self-controlling, self-directing mind' (ibid., p. 39). Rationality becomes the pre-eminence of the mind over emotions and the body. The idea of civilisation is one where the mind controls our baser natures. Note also the prominence of culture here and the way in which it was reinterpreted as encompassing leisure. In other words, the dilemma of the relationship between education and entertainment was inserted into a new problematic of the uses of leisure. In this way, the BBC positioned itself as both provider of leisure and arbiter as to how to best use leisure. Here then, was a kind of solution to the tension between education and entertainment.

Conclusions

The early years of the twentieth century were marked by a concerted effort to deploy a pedagogical apparatus that would train the adult population in the social, economic and political capacities required for an educated citizenry. The positive effect of this was that many previously uneducated working-class adults were to be given the opportunity to broaden their intellectual and cultural horizons and in doing so realise a fuller way of life. However, to say that adult education was concerned with the educational completion of its subjects is questionable. Rather, the governmental rationality was the inculcating of the adult working-class population in matters of culture and morality; and was made possible by a complex machinery of social investigation and administration that rendered the adult working-class population as both subjects and objects of government.

Understood thus, modern adult education was less to do with supplying the needs and demand of the working-class populace than it was to do with supplying a useful working-class populace who would discharge their democratic rights in the newly established, post-war mass democracy. Crucial to this project was that adult education was constructed as a self-acting imperative which the popular classes voluntarily followed in pursuing the abstract rhetoric of 'educated-democracy'. In order to secure governance from a distance, it was necessary for individuals to translate the values of a higher and distant authority into their own terms, such that they provided both totalising and individualising normative standards for conduct. It was essential that the populace both in its entirety and as individuals cared more about its civil responsibilities.

This said, there is some evidence to suggest that large sections of the working-class population still remained outside any serious educational influence. More specifically, though adult educational broadcasting was widely perceived as a technology of pedagogy *par excellence*, one of the problems faced by the BBC was the spatial and temporal 'distanciated' nature of broadcasting, which meant that many of its pedagogical strategies were liable to a certain indeterminacy. Yet another difficulty was that, in spite of the BBC's repeated efforts to promote educative recreation, the majority of the listening public experienced broadcasting as a form of popular entertainment rather than as a conventional teaching medium. Consequently, the importance initially accorded to adult education and listening groups steadily diminished, their eventual cessation being announced in June 1938. Hereafter, the educational emphasis was on the general audience, not the adult education audience.

Whilst the BBC's abandonment of its inter-war policy of cultural uplift and the ostensible practice of mutual learning may have been disappointing for those actively involved in the adult education movement, what it reveals is that, as well as seeking to discipline everyday conduct, pedagogical modes of governing must also bear some relation to the public they constitute if they are to be effective. That is, rather than merely imposing techniques of government, pedagogical functionaries also need to acknowledge actually existing social relations and, thus, be representative of the public they seek to govern. More crucially, this dialectic involves a degree of risk and uncertainty insofar as it opens up a space for ordinary citizens to challenge governing practices. In doing so, it has the potential to radically alter the intention and efficacy of governmental strategies and techniques. Such an agonism may also result in what Foucault (1980, p. 81, cf. Giroux 1992) described as an 'insurrection of subjugated knowledges', that is forms of comprehension that have been previously 'disqualified as inadequate' and 'low ranking' when compared to officially sanctioned knowledges.

The relevance of the above in terms of its bearing upon the present is that the governmental rationalities of educated citizenship need not necessarily be restricted to a set of protocols and discursive practices that require obedient and civic subjects; there will always be scope for unruly and dissenting citizens to advocate their own particular cultural tastes, ethical practices and forms of subjectivity, ones that facilitate the possibility of pedagogical technologies being transformed into creative technologies of the self, less concerned with didactic self-improvement and more encouraging of types of cultural politics and self-identity whose productive capacities are more properly expressions of the self as well as a diversity of different cultural values and practices. Conceived in this way, the pedagogical state should be understood as a site of political struggle and contestation in which both pedagogues and citizens continually enact and negotiate pedagogical subjectivities – albeit within particular historical and social contexts. Most of all, it means that the exercise of pedagogical power, insofar as it is contingent and indeterminate, necessarily implies a 'pedagogy of possibility' and 'hope' as much as it does a pedagogy tied to reasons of state and spiritual discipline.

Notes

1. For a more celebratory reading of autodidactism and adult education, not least its transformative and liberating effects, see Rose (2002).
2. Indeed, the word *broadcasting* has its origins in the iconography of the sower, a well-known parable from the New Testament (see Peters 2000). For just as Jesus told his disciples that the farmer goes out to sow his seed in order to yield a crop, similarly, the early BBC was an agency for casting abroad ideals of righteousness and good conduct in order that, 'He who has ears to hear, let him hear'.
3. The transformation of Christian pedagogy into a secular technique of governance is more fully explored by Hunter (1994) in the historical context of popular education and the emergence of the school.
4. That religion should become one of the BBC's core broadcasting activities only accentuated this process inasmuch as the church was seen to be actively consenting to the relegation of religion to the level of an essentially secular-based medium, that is, one far removed from the pulpit and pew. This is not to say that the church no longer figured in public life in the early twentieth century. Rather, Christian pastorship was deritualised and reinvented, thus transforming it into a

more accessible, everyday social phenomenon. Moreover, whilst previous media had served as intermediaries for pastoralism, broadcasting was particularly suited to extending, renewing and re-embedding Christian pedagogical traditions in temporal and spatial contexts on a scale that was previously unimaginable.

5. A summary report of the proposals made by the Adult Education Committee for the Ministry of Reconstruction reiterates this broader conception of governance: 'non-vocational adult education must be conducted in an atmosphere of cooperation, and with a large measure of "self-determination" on the part of the students. An adult class must, in other words, be a self-governing community' (Greenwood 1920, p. 16).

6. Stobart anticipated the possibilities of learning over the air in the form of what he envisaged to be a 'wireless university'. In a memo to Reith, Stobart stated that one of its main objectives 'would aim at a very broad culture, and would always have in mind the equipping of its pupils for good citizenship and cultured home life, as distinct from training for a particular profession or group of professions' (WAC R14/145/1; see Briggs 1965, p. 188).

7. Wireless listening groups were seen by many to be a new tutorial scheme. Indeed, the *Westminster Gazette* (12 October 1926) described group listening as 'Oxford and Cambridge by wireless'.

8. Public libraries were particularly favoured as venues for wireless discussion groups. They were ideal as disciplinary public spaces, as they were supervised by highly skilled cultural technicians in the form of librarians.

References

Bailey, M., 2007. 'He who has ears to hear, let him hear': Christian pedagogy and religious broadcasting during the inter-war period. *Westminster papers in communications and culture*, 4 (1), 4–25.

Barker, E., 1926. The uses of leisure. *The journal of adult education*, 1 (1), 27–35.

BBC, 1928. *New ventures in broadcasting*. London: BBC.

BBC, 1932. *Wireless discussion groups: what they are and how to run them*. London: BBC.

Bennett, T., 1998. *Culture: a reformer's science*. London: SAGE.

Briggs, A., 1965. *The history of broadcasting in the United Kingdom, volume two: the golden age of wireless*. London: Oxford University Press.

Craik, W.W., 1964. *The central labour college, 1909–29*. London: Lawrence & Wishart.

Dean, M., 1999. *Governmentality: power and rule in modern society*. London: SAGE.

Donald, J., 1992. *Sentimental education: schooling, popular culture and the regulation of liberty*. London: Verso.

Foucault, M., 1980. Two lectures. *In*: C. Gordon, ed. *Power/knowledge: selected interviews & other writings, 1972–1977*. New York: Pantheon Books, 78–108.

Foucault, M., 2002. "Omnes et singulatim": towards a critique of political reason. *In*: J.D. Faubion, ed. *Essential works of Foucault, 1954–1984, volume three: power*. London: Penguin Books, 298–325.

Giroux, H., 1992. The discourse of critical pedagogy. *In*: L. Grossberg, C. Nelson and P. Triechler, eds. *Cultural studies*. London: Routledge, 199–212.

Greenwood, A., 1920. *The education of the citizen*. London: Workers' Educational Association.

Hacking, I., 1990. *The taming of chance*. Cambridge: Cambridge University Press.

Hall, S. and Schwarz, B., 1988. State and society, 1880–1930. *In*: S. Hall, ed. *The hard road to renewal: Thatcherism and the crisis of the left*. London: Verso, 95–122.

Harrop, S., ed., 1987. *Oxford and working-class education*. Nottingham: Nottingham University Press.

HMSO, 1927. *Pioneer work and other developments in adult education*. Paper No. 9 of the Adult Education Committee. London: HMSO.

HMSO, 1933. *Board of education educational pamphlets, No. 92: adult education wireless listening groups*. London: HMSO.

Hunter, I., 1988. *Culture and government: the emergence of literary education*. London: Macmillan Press.

Hunter, I., 1994. *Rethinking the school: subjectivity, bureaucracy, criticism*. Australia: Allen & Unwin.

Jennings, B., 1977. Revolting students: the Ruskin college dispute, 1908–1909'. *Studies in adult education*, 9 (1), 1–16.

Jones, K. and Williamson, K., 1979. The birth of the schoolroom. *Ideology and consciousness*, 6, 59–110.

MacMurray, J., 1932. *Learning to live*. London: BBC.

Mansbridge, A., 1913. *University tutorial classes: a study in the development of higher education among working men and women*. London: Longmans, Green & Co.

Mansbridge, A., 1920. *An adventure in working-class education: being the story of the workers' educational association, 1903–1915*. London: Longmans, Green & Co.

Peers, R., ed., 1934. *Adult education in practice*. London: Macmillan & Co.

Peters, J.D., 2000. *Speaking into the air: a history of the idea of communication*. Chicago: University of Chicago Press.

Poovey, M., 1998. *A history of the modern fact: problems of knowledge in the sciences of wealth and society*. Chicago: Chicago University Press.

Robinson, J., 1982. *Learning over the air: 60 years in adult learning*. London: BBC.

Rose, J., 2002. *The intellectual life of the British working classes*. London: Yale University Press.

Rose, N., 1999. *Powers of freedom: reframing political thought*. Cambridge: Cambridge University Press.

Scannell, P. and Cardiff, D., 1991. *A social history of broadcasting: volume one 1922–1939. Serving the nation*. Oxford: Basil Blackwell.

Silvey, R., 1977. *Who's listening? The story of BBC audience research*. London: Allen & Unwin.

Stocks, M., 1953. *The workers educational association: the first fifty years*. London: George Allen & Unwin.

Williams, W.E. and Heath, A.E., 1936. *Learn and live: the consumer's view of adult education*. London: Methuen & Co.

Williams, W.E. and Hill, F.E., 1941. *Radio listening groups: the United States and Great Britain*. New York: Columbia University Press.

BBC Written Archives Centre (WAC), Caversham

WAC A/261, Broadcasting and Adult Education, 1934.

WAC R14/120/1–5, Central Council for Broadcast Adult Education, Executive Committee Papers, 1928–1932, Files 1–5.

WAC R14/124, Central Council for Broadcast Adult Education: Programmes and Publications Sub-Committee Papers, 1928–1934.

WAC R14/145/1, Adult Education: Papers and Reports 1924–1934, File 1a.

WAC R129/3/1, Adult Education Pamphlets.

Supernanny, parenting and a pedagogical state

Richenda Gambles

Department of Social Policy, Faculty of Social Sciences, The Open University, Walton Hall, Milton Keynes, UK

This paper explores the messages and assumptions relating to parenting that are promoted through *Supernanny* and how this connects with the policy expectation or hope of New Labour – that parents should take responsibility for being skilled educators and developers of their children. In exploring these state and non-state governance discourses and what these suggest about contemporary ideals and expectations relating to parenting, I make use of Raymond Williams' structure of feeling approach and draw on this to develop the definition and reach the idea of a pedagogical state. I argue that a pedagogical state can be seen as a state of mind or way of being that is produced through and producing of a particular sort of mood and set of sensibilities, in this case relating to contemporary understandings and experiences of parenting. In considering various viewer responses to *Supernanny*, some resistance to and scepticism of these discourses can, however, be detected. In this context, I further explore the idea of a pedagogical state as a disposition and mood relating to parenting which is disrupted – but also deepened – through people's evaluative reflexivity and (healthy) scepticism.

Parenting, particularly the first few years of parenting, is a time of deep personal transition and significance with Wetherell arguing that 'to become a mother or father in whatever type of family context is to acquire a new set of experiences, a new set of relationships and a new sense of self' (1995, p. 215). These personal changes and transitions occur, however, in the context of much contemporary policy attention relating to parenting. Indeed, parenting, including the first few years of parenting, has become a site of intense Government intervention in the UK in recent years. This is evident through extensive policy activity such as the development of parental leave, parental rights to request flexible working, 'affordable' child care and Sure Start initiatives, and the extension of midwife and health visitor services (Home Office 1998, DCSF 2007, DfES 2007). This recent policy outpouring can be seen to promote two sets of expectations or hopes relating to parenting: the idea that parents have economic and moral responsibilities to be active in paid work so as to provide financially for themselves and their child as well as being a role model for their child; and the idea that parents will display particular parenting styles, approaches and skills deemed appropriate for the nurturance and development of their child (Featherstone 2004, MacLeod 2004, Gillies 2005, 2007, Williams 2005, Lister 2006).

These expectations – seen by New Labour as essential for the well-being of children and wider society more generally – can be linked, more generally, to what Furedi (2002) has called 'parental determinism' in which parenting is increasingly seen as the key determinant in the behaviour and development of children (see also Gillies 2007). This idea of 'parental determinism' can be seen, too, in the range of popular cultural genres focused on and geared at parenting. Indeed, parenting is the subject of much contemporary public discussion in the UK news media as well as other forms of popular culture such as parenting books, magazines, websites and television shows (MacLeod 2004, Hardyment 2007). One such television show is *Supernanny*, a well-known reality TV programme similar to *Little Angels, The House of Tiny Tearaways* and *Nanny 911,* which focuses on the education and training of parents to enable them to deal more effectively with their children.

In this paper, I explore the messages and assumptions relating to parenting that are promoted through *Supernanny* and how these connect with the policy expectation or hope of New Labour – that parents should take responsibility for being skilled nurturers and developers of their children. In exploring these state and non-state governance discourses and what these suggest about contemporary ideals and expectations relating to parenting, I make use of Raymond Williams' (1961, 1977) structure of feeling approach. Structure of feeling is a concept and approach that seeks to capture a 'mood, sensibility or atmosphere associated with a specific period or generation' (Lewis and Fink 2004, p. 58). It refers to the 'actual living sense of a culture' where 'official consciousness of a period, as codified in legislation and doctrine, interacts with the lived experiences of that period, and defines the set of perceptions and values common to a generation' (Macey 2000, p. 366). For Williams, structure of feeling is a theoretical concept and a methodological approach in which legislation or policy can be read alongside popular cultural texts so as to get a nuanced and dynamic reading of a mood or sensibility of a period (Williams 1961, p. 70). This mood is the one that contains multiple forces – dominant, residual and emergent – which jostle together to create a living and potentially moving structure of feeling. For Williams, the dominant is a 'lived system of meanings and values' and 'a sense of reality for most people in the society . . . beyond which it is very difficult for most members of the society to move' (Williams 1977, p. 110). Yet, he argues that there will always be alternative movements and ideas – residual and emergent – within and beyond the dominant, which highlight this more nuanced and dynamic mood or sensibility.

Supernanny – and New Labour policy developments relating to parenting skills – can be said to constitute, in part, a mood or disposition relating to parenting in which the importance placed on parenting skills and practices in popular culture and policy is emphasised, because particular pedagogical dispositions and behaviours of parents are seen as critical for child well-being and development. Yet, as people respond to these ideas in a variety of ways, these ideas are subjected, in part, to challenge, resistance and potential change. Indeed, as Lewis and Fink (2004, p. 55) have suggested, while people are called upon to 'identify with, and make their own, a set of normalised and subject positions and practices of everyday living' that correspond with dominant ideas found within a structure of feeling, there are always alternative ideals and ways of being available and this highlights and opens up contestation (Lewis and Fink 2004, p. 60). My interest in these dynamics has been informed by the idea that ' . . . people are not just addressed or summoned by dominant discourses – but also "answer back" in reflexive, critical and sometimes unexpected ways' (see also Clarke 2005, Clarke *et al.* 2007, p. 142). Indeed, while people are deeply influenced by and constituted through governance discourses of both state and non-state kinds, in offering varied responses, they are also active in the making and the development of these governance discourses. How parents respond to governance discourses and strategies, in this case of those found in *Supernanny* as well as certain New Labour texts, is thus a critical dimension to consider in the location of a structure of feeling relating to parenting.

In the research that this paper draws on, in which I sought to locate a contemporary structure of feeling relating to parenting, I made use of three distinct data sources. The first was selected New Labour policy documents relating to the first few years of parenting. The second was a selection of media and popular cultural representations geared at parents including parenting manuals, the interactive parenting website mumsnet.com and the reality television show *Supernanny*. The third was a collection of 23 interviews I carried out with a socially and economically diverse set of first-time parents of children aged between 9 months and 3 years who were recruited through various parent and child care networks in the Oxford area. Through the collection and analysis of these different data sources, I worked to (a) capture something of a mood or sensibility relating to contemporary understandings and experiences of becoming and being a parent and (b) make more visible the ways in which personal experiences and dispositions are shaped and shaping of cultural and political sensibilities.

In reflecting on these different data sources, I noticed that the focus, techniques and strategies that were encouraged in *Supernanny* – which link with New Labour policy – appeared to resonate, in part, with parents I interviewed who watched the show. Yet, parental resistances and scepticism could also be detected. In considering such responses to *Supernanny*, I develop my argument in this paper by suggesting that the idea of a pedagogical state can be seen as a particular sort of mood or disposition in relation to expectations of parenting that is disrupted – but also deepened – through parent's evaluative reflexivity and (healthy) scepticism. In developing this claim, I draw on examples of the *Supernanny* show with particular reference to three episodes from the 2005 series[1] alongside a recent book by *Supernanny*, Jo Frost, *Supernanny: How to Get the Best from Your Children*, published in 2005. I consider these in relation to New Labour policy texts that take up similar issues and concerns raised in *Supernanny* programme and extracts from some of my interviews in which parents talk about the show.

Introducing Supernanny

The philosophy behind the TV show *Supernanny* is summed up by Jo Frost in her book as follows:

> I don't think there's such a thing as a "bad" child. I believe that every child has the potential to behave as expected. By that I don't mean Goody Two Shoes. I mean happy, relaxed children who have their own individual characters but who know where the limits are. Everything I've seen and experienced convinces me that children need boundaries. And to keep those boundaries in place, there needs to be discipline. Discipline is not about harsh punishment. A key part of it, in fact, is praise. But it does mean setting rules and backing up the rules with firm and fair control. (Frost 2005, pp. 11–12)

In this statement, Frost might say there is no such thing as 'a bad child' but her comments in her book and her TV programmes suggest that there is such a thing as 'bad parenting'. The show and her book focus on changing this 'bad parenting' by encouraging parents to reflect on the problems they are facing in relation to their children's behaviour, to take responsibility – if necessary – for taking up *Supernanny's* 'tried-and-tested' rules and techniques for improving this and to take responsibility for putting in the hard work necessary to achieve the promised results.

In considering the content and format of the show and the sentiments or sensibilities relating to parenting that are carried and created, at least two sets of ideas are suggested.

The first is the idea that parents, themselves, often need to learn expertise about how to parent, that parenting does not always come 'naturally', but that parents should take personal responsibility for developing parenting skills and expertise with the help of experts like *Supernanny*. The second is the idea that parents must work – if this has not come 'naturally' – to develop particular parenting strategies and approaches. The desire or hope for such parenting taps into a range of concerns relating to 'bad' parenting that is linked with widespread contemporary concerns about 'unruly' children and teenagers and their anti-social behaviour and the negative implications for these children as well as wider society more generally (see Butler and Margo 2007).

Learning to parent from **Supernanny,** *the 'expert'*

Supernanny works to promote the idea that Jo Frost, as a particular sort of expert who has had years of experience as a nanny, can change and transform the lives of parents who are experiencing problems with their children. The presence of Frost and the 'success' of her approach as portrayed through the TV show support and promote the idea that parents can and should, if necessary, learn from experts.

The issue of expertise in relation to parenting is, however, a fraught one. This can be seen more generally, for example, in contemporary parenting manuals in which detached medical expertise is dismissed, in part, for an emphasis on 'real' or hands-on experience. Indeed in Gina Ford's bestselling *The New Contented Little Baby Book* (2002), Ford acknowledges that she is neither a doctor nor psychologist and goes onto claim her own expert status *because of this*:

> What is so different about my book is that it comes from years of hands-on experience. I have lived with and cared for hundreds of different babies. I offer real and practical advice on how to establish a good feeding and sleeping pattern from day one, thus avoiding months of sleepless nights, colic, feeding difficulties, and many of the other problems that the experts convince us are a normal part of parenting. (Ford 2002, p. xii)

The emphasis on – and virtue made of – hands-on experience chimes, in part, with the idea that doctors and psychologists might be somewhat detached basing their claims on observation rather than direct experience. Similar sentiments are offered, too, by Jo Frost in her *Supernanny* book in which she explains how her expertise has built up through working as a nanny for many years,

> I'm not a parent. That's true. I'm not a paediatrician, either, or a child psychologist. I've had no formal training to do what I do. Which puts me in much the same position as most parents, without the intense emotional attachment (although us nannies have feelings too!). (Frost 2005, p. 11)

Here, Frost positions herself as an expert but in a way that is more aligned with parents and because of her lack of scientific training, she is 'in much the same position as most parents'.

This positioning corresponds with something of a backlash from parents about the role of distant and detached expert (see Furedi 2002, Foster *et al.* 2003). Frost (in both the TV programme and especially the book) acknowledges this mistrust and scepticism of experts, particularly if these 'experts' are not parents themselves, yet she also, simultaneously, has to work up her own claims of expertise in relation to parenting. Although she is not a parent, she highlights years of 'real life' rather than formally developed expertise and – like many parents– has learnt through her 'own gut instincts' (Frost 2005, p. 11). Yet, she claims she has a less intense emotional attachment than parents which puts her in a better place to advise parents: 'when many parents find themselves in difficulties they're too emotionally involved to see the bigger picture' (Frost 2005, p. 11). At the same time, she is at pains to suggest that she is not a completely detached and unfeeling person. Indeed, she suggests that, like other nannies, she has 'feelings too!'. These complicated sets of manoeuvres suggest the delicacy surrounding issues associated with expertise relating to parenting skills and practices which are seen, simultaneously, as private, personal and, as seen through the presence and popularity of shows such as *Supernanny*, also matters of much *public* concern.

The setting up of her own expertise in relation to parenting can be see in the TV show in which Frost, after spending the first day observing the family in action, delivers her damning verdict. In one particular episode, for example, Frost's diagnosis of the problems is met with tears from the mother and nods of recognition from the father and Frost works to seek reassurance from the parents that her diagnosis is correct. Frost asks the mother, Caroline, 'Am I lying with what I am saying?' Caroline, through her tears, replies, 'Not at all. You said everything that I would have said if I knew how, in the right way. You said it perfectly' (*Supernanny* 2005b). With the thorny issues of Frost's diagnosis – and expertise – now acknowledged and confirmed, she returns the next day and gets to work with her 'tried-and-tested' routines and techniques. In her book, Frost describes these techniques as 'common-sense ways of dealing with the type of ordinary challenges and problems most parents of children under five face most days' (Frost 2005, p. 10). She emphasises that she did not invent these techniques, but that,

> By and large I've simply followed my instincts and observed parents and kids to see what worked and what didn't work. What I've called the "Involvement Technique", for example, is just what many parents have done instinctively over the years when they have needed to get on with a household chore. The "Naughty Step Technique" – a way of enforcing a rule by getting a child to think about their behaviour – has probably been around for as long as stairs have had steps and rooms have had corners. (Frost 2005, p. 10)

In positioning herself as working with a set of common sense strategies for dealing with children, she works to hold up the idea that most parents already have this expertise but that some parents – including the ones she is working with on the show – need more intense instruction and support. For them, 'good' parenting does not, perhaps, come naturally or instinctively, yet the message of the show is that they have a responsibility to acknowledge this and work to develop such skills and attributes.

The promise of Supernanny*'s 'tried-and-tested' parenting strategies and approaches*

The TV show features parents who learn, with the help of *Supernanny*, how to be 'better' parents to their children. With this in mind, the show typically begins with chaotic scenes of children running riot, having tantrums and being rude or disrespectful to their parents who, in turn, are portrayed as being at their wits end or close to breaking point. In these opening scenes, viewers are told by a narrator of the particular problems facing the family that *Supernanny* will be working with in this particular episode. In episode 1 of series 2, for example, we are introduced to a family in which children are 'out of control'. We are also introduced to the mother, Karen, who is depicted as being too soft on her children and feeling drained and lacking in energy because of the chaos created through her softness. In contrast, father, Jason, takes a 'zero tolerance' approach in his parenting, shouting at and smacking the children when he gets home from work. We are thus told of relationship problems between the mother and father, because of their disagreements about parenting styles and approaches (*Supernanny* 2005a). Episode 3 of the same series starts in much the same way with viewers introduced to 'the youngest teenagers in town' who 'eat what they like, go to bed when they like and help themselves to everything. From using kitchen knives to hammering their dad's credit card, these kids are out of control!' (*Supernanny* 2005b). After general scenes of mayhem illustrating these observations and being introduced to the idea that the mother and father have different approaches to parenting, the narrator asks, 'Can Supernanny, Jo Frost, put the young Pandits [family name] in their place? Or will mum and dad's differences get in the way?' (*Supernanny* 2005b).

Once the 'problems' are introduced and viewers have watched Frost observing a 'typical' day and set of events, in which she frequently turns to the camera to make disapproving comments about what she is witnessing, Frost offers her critiques which are always linked to a lack of discipline, respect and routine that the parents have failed to provide for their children. Once her diagnosis of the problems is confirmed, she returns the next day to get to work on introducing new rules and techniques that she feels will transform the family's lives by restoring or creating happiness and harmony. This includes, for example, the Naughty Step Technique which works 'to remove the child from the scene for a few minutes' allowing them 'time to cool down, think about what [they've] done and get ready to apologise' (Frost 2005, p. 80). In her book, Frost gives the following example:

> Your jealous four year old has pushed his little sister and thrown a toy at her. She's fallen over and has started to wail. It's all going pear-shaped. You'll be furious; you might be worried and panicky too. Check first that your daughter is okay, resist the adrenalin surge that makes you want to yell at the top of your lungs and put the Naughty Step Technique into practice. (Frost 2005, p. 80)

The idea, then, is for the parent to get the child to sit on the step until she/he is calmed down and said sorry, keeping them there until this happens and remembering to praise the child when this does. Another example is her Involvement Technique, which works with the idea that small children want and need attention and that they like to feel part of things. She suggests that,

> Small children don't find tasks like cleaning, sorting, fetching and carrying as boring as their older brothers and sisters sometimes do. Small children love to help. Helping makes them feel responsible and gives them confidence. (Frost 2005, p. 77)

Through techniques stressing, for example, the importance of discipline and getting a child to reflect on their behaviour and say sorry, or the importance of involving a child so as to enable it to feel more responsible in life, we begin to see the use of a pedagogical set of strategies relating to parenting.

In the TV show, Frost works with the family for a few days to educate and support the parents in the deployment of her chosen techniques relating to her particular diagnosis. Although there are always teething problems of some sort, the chaos portrayed at the beginning of the show is soon replaced with calm, order and tranquillity. Through this, we see the confirmation of the effectiveness of her pedagogical approach – on the children, but also, crucially, on the parents. Frost then leaves the family to see if the parents can manage on their own, with Frost monitoring them remotely through video recordings, which she accesses on her laptop. She observes the parents struggling in their attempts to execute the techniques she has introduced and the inevitable return of the chaos and disorder she sought to change. As she observes such scenes, she makes her frustration very apparent and criticises the parents for failing to take up the strategies that she thinks will help them. Frost then returns to the house to ensure the parents *properly* apply her rules and techniques and that they understand exactly what they should be doing and why. Once this second round of technique training is over, she leaves having reinforced the power and importance of her approach to parenting. This brings the show to a close with images of a now happy (or happier) family coupled with reflections from the parents about the positive difference Frost has made to their lives. In episode 1 of series 2 father Jason says, 'I've always said you can't teach parents how to be parents. I think this proves you can teach parents how to be parents'. Mother Karen agrees with him, demonstrating a now united front and a healed marital relationship, telling viewers 'we're giving them proper guidelines' (*Supernanny* 2005a). In episode 4 of the same series, the mother says 'not everything is 100%. You know we still have a few hurdles to cross. But we'll carry on and we'll try the best we can to make this work . . . we have to make this work because I'm not going back to that old life before'. (*Supernanny* 2005c)

Supernanny and links with contemporary governance strategies

Working with a governmental approach, Ouellette and Hay (2008a) argued that reality TV shows such as *Supernanny* are important examples of 'social and cultural institutions that disseminate everyday techniques through which individuals and populations are expected to reflect upon, work on and organize' (p. 473; see also Lunt 2008). Ouellette and Hay (2008a, 2008b) further argued that the emphasis on techniques and approaches that encourage reflexivity and transformational work on the self have emerged out of recent developments in welfare discourses. Indeed, they noted that in 'chronicling the details and challenges of lifestyles and the outcomes of ordinary people's choices and behaviour . . . [and by] aligning TV viewers with a proliferating supply of techniques for shaping and guiding themselves and their private associations with others, reality TV has become the quintessential technology of advanced or "neo" liberal citizenship' (Ouellette and Hay 2008b, p. 4). Such links can be seen clearly with *Supernanny* and recent New Labour policy discourses that stress the importance of 'good' parenting and the enactment of particular parenting skills and dispositions for realising this (see DCSF 2007, DfES 2007). Indeed, as Dawn Butler MP, then Chair of the All Party Group on young people, and Margo have suggested, 'The single most important factor in the development and socialisation of young people is their immediate family. In this area, policy needs to recognise the importance of hard factors – such as income, poverty and time off work – and softer factors – such as parenting skills and experience, support and advice' (Butler and Margo 2007, p. 328).

An emphasis on the skilling of parents to be 'better', more 'skilled' and more 'effective' can be seen, for example, in the *Every Parent Matters* (DfES 2007) document – an approach which is justified with reference to an 'evidence-based' or 'what works' framework. Indeed as Alan Johnson MP, then Secretary of State for Education, in the foreword to the *Every Parent Matters* (DfES 2007) document states, 'Being a parent is – and should be – an intensely personal experience and parents can be effective in very different ways. However, we also have a growing understanding, evidenced from research, about the characteristics of effective parenting' (DfES 2007, p. 1). This focus, as well as being 'evidenced from research', is further justified in Johnson's foreword through acknowledgement of the interest that parents, themselves, are showing in popular culture relating to parental skills and attributes, 'parents are demonstrating a growing appetite for discussion, information and advice, as we see from the increasingly vibrant market in television programmes, magazines and websites' (DfES 2007, p. 1). Moreover, with direct reference to *Supernanny* in a speech about parenting, Beverley Hughes MP, then UK Minister for Children, Young People and Families suggested that 'Government too must extend the opportunities for parents to develop their expertise; the popularity of *Supernanny* exemplifies the hunger for information and for effective parenting programmes that parents often express to me' (Beverley Hughes, MP, keynote speech, IPPR, July 2006, cited in Gill and Jensen 2008).

It is perhaps no coincidence that reality TV shows, which emerged from the mid-1990s to the late 1990s, correspond with the growth of third way discourses and an emphasis on the active and personally responsible citizen who will be supported and encouraged in their attempts to better themselves through an 'enabling' and 'empowering' state (see Giddens 1998). Ouellette and Hay (2008b) argued that reality TV shows, including *Supernanny*, have taken up and regularised what they refer to as 'post-welfare' ideas of 'personal responsibility and self-empowerment'. Yet, a structure of feeling approach encourages attention, too, to the ways in which reality TV shows such as *Supernanny* have, themselves, also worked to shape, in part, these policy discourses and ideas. Indeed, the development of reality TV and a policy approach taking up ideas of personal empowerment and responsibility in relation to parenting skills can be seen as reflecting a particular sort of pedagogical mood that is mutually constituted by popular cultural and policy discourses in *dialogic interaction* (Holquist 1990, Holland and Lave 2001, Maybin 2001).

The emphasis on personal responsibility to work with and learn, if necessary, particular forms of parental expertise that are produced through *Supernanny*, which can also be seen in contemporary Government discourses, demonstrates the ways in which popular culture and policy discourses work to promote a mood or set of sentiments about appropriate behaviour and an appropriate disposition assumed or hoped of parents if they are to be considered responsible. Through these pedagogical sentiments, parents are called and expected to enact or take up particular educative strategies and to critically consider, evaluate and transform, if necessary, their parenting styles to ensure they – and the children they raise – become the reflexively evaluative and self-transforming citizens desired now as well as in the future (see Williams 2005, Lister 2006, Butler and Margo 2007). Through an emphasis on such pedagogical approaches and techniques, parents are encouraged and empowered to work on their parenting styles and family relationships in ways that, while difficult, promise positive and fulfilling outcomes (Ouellette and Hay 2008a, 2008b).

The focus on techniques and skills and the personal capacity and responsibility for developing these have been critiqued, however, for what it overlooks or silences. In particular, it silences difficulties (because of a lack of time, material or practical resources) or resistances (because of different cultural values and ideals associated with parenting) to taking up such ideas (Gewirtz 2001, Gillies 2005). In *Supernanny*, for example, the typical set of parents she works with are the ones where there is a mother and father present and where the mother is often a stay-at-home mom or someone who works short part-time hours (while the father, in contrast, works full time in paid work, often doing long hours). The techniques she introduces to the house need a lot of time and attention and this would not be possible without the constant presence of one of the parents (usually the mother). Moreover, on the television show, apart from *Supernanny*, there is never a nanny, granny, childminder or nursery featured giving the impression that it is just the parents (and mainly the mother) dealing with the behaviour and education of their young children. This emphasises the idea that mothers are – or should be – present with their children, working hard to educate and skill them, which is, of course, one of New Labour's key policy hopes or expectations. Yet, this focus silences or at least downplays tensions with New Labour's other key policy hope or expectation: the idea that parents (including mothers) can or should be active in paid work.

The show, rather than acknowledging or legitimising difficulties or resistances with *Supernanny*'s focus on parenting skills, features parents who are complicit with her approach. This suggests that responsible parents, if shown how, will see the importance and benefit of learning and adopting this pedagogical style of parenting and that if they have been shown this, any subsequent problems or failures relating to their children or their parenting must, by implication, be the parents' own fault. Such critiques can be made of *Supernanny* as well as New Labour policy approaches that place particular emphasis on the development of parenting skills and the positive outcomes such skills are associated with. Indeed, Gillies (2007) finds that recent New Labour policy has tended to take the form of guidance and education in relation to parenting rather than material help for parents. She suggests that such a focus, which can be seen in *Every Parent Matters* (DfES 2007) and *The Children's Plan* (DCSF 2007), is 'part of a creeping professionalisation of family life' in which the idea that 'parenting can be distilled into a series of detachable, universally applicable skills' is emphasised at the expense of material factors and dimensions (Gillies 2007, p. 7). Moreover, as Gillies argues, New Labour policy discourses of parenting skills can be seen to have a particularly gendered and classed address: it is not all parents but rather working-class mothers who are targeted by policy initiatives such as those promoting parenting skills and training because 'working class mothering practices are held up as the antithesis of good parenting, largely through their association with poor outcomes for children' (Gillies 2007, p. 2). Similar sentiments can be made, too, of reality TV parenting shows such as *Supernanny* which often feature working-class or lower-middle-class parents in which these parents (particularly the mothers) are the subject of voyeuristic ridicule and, through *Supernanny*, are encouraged to change and develop their behaviour in line with more pedagogically oriented middle-class approaches to parenting (see Walkerdine and Lucey 1989).

Resistance and scepticism: viewer responses to Supernanny

Ouellette and Hay (2008b) argued that reality television teaches viewers to monitor, improve and transform themselves in ways that emphasise and promote personal responsibility but, like much governmental scholarship, their assertion gives little attention to the various ways in which people – in this case, parents as viewers – might respond. This oversight can be critiqued for its 'textual determinism', which assumes audiences uncritically absorb media (as well as policy) messages (Clarke *et al.* 2007, p. 142, Gill 2007, p. 17). Such critiques have been informed by and have led to more consideration of the classed, gendered and/or racialised locations of viewer positioning, which are seen as generating a variety of responses (see Gill 2007, pp. 17–18). This is an important set of observations. While it has been suggested that middle-class norms and standards are promoted through reality TV as well as through policy, resistances to such norms and standards as well as awareness, the resources required to achieve these may be lacking, have been noted (on these claims, see Skeggs and Wood 2008, in relation to reality TV; Gillies 2007, in relation to New Labour parenting policy; and Gewirtz 2001, in relation to New Labour education policy).

In my own interviews, I saw a variety of responses – a few of which I discuss here. The examples I offer are all from mothers, mainly because mothers had more to say about *Supernanny* than the fathers I spoke with. This supports the idea that the programme – and New Labour's emphasis on parenting skills – has a particularly gendered address. But what about class? In an interview I carried out with a young working-class lone mother called Natasha, she appeared to enjoy and agree with the skills and strategies being promoted through *Supernanny*: 'She teaches how to do it right . . . I don't know, I seem to learn some things from there . . . It's really good for me. That's why I like to watch that programme'. Such a response suggests Natasha is responding in ways that Ouellette and Hay (2008b) suggested – that she appears to take up these messages and that she seeks to learn from them. In this context, the show – and the idea of parenting skills more generally – may have a classed address and this is taken up complicity by this working-class mother. Skeggs *et al.* (2008) in their own research on audience responses of reality TV shows found, however, that the interview encounter was limited in terms of what it can reveal about working-class responses to reality TV and through their own observation of working-class viewer responses, resistance and scepticism towards the 'expert' were revealed. This resistance, they claimed, not only included verbal and non-verbal displays of disagreement over appropriate ways of parenting, but also resistance in terms of what is seen as possible in the context of their own material resources and the practicalities of their daily lives. Such resistance did emerge in another interview I carried out with Tina, another young working-class lone mother who lives with her own parents, who spoke of the problems she encountered when she tried to adopt *Supernanny's* bedtime routine: 'Well I tried to, but obviously living in the house with other people, when they've got to get up in the morning, they don't want to listen to a baby screaming. So I go to bed with her and she does go to sleep'. This example, alongside claims made by Skeggs *et al.* (2008), suggests classed resistance and scepticism about the potential and promise offered through *Supernanny's* (but also, perhaps, New Labour's) parenting strategies.

Scepticism can also be identified, however, when considering more middle-class parental responses. Alison, a more affluent mother I spoke with discussed this directly:

Richenda: So um . . . have you seen Supernanny?

Alison: Yeah, a little bit

Richenda: What do you think of that?

Alison: I think, um, I haven't watched her enough actually, I'd like to watch her more. Er, I'm very sceptical of TV experts, do you know what I mean? I just think they have to be a certain type of personality, I just know what they're doing, they think they're brilliant at it but I just think they're in for a, not, not, like a TV producer will chose someone for great charisma, not good advice . . . I mean I thoroughly enjoy them but just like I would watch *Wifeswap*, you know what I mean?

Richenda: So more entertainment factor than anything else?

Alison: Yeah, definitely.

This scepticism, as well as resistance, is evident in an interview I carried out with another middle-class mother called Amy. Amy described *Supernanny* as 'awful' and was very scathing about an electronic naughty step she recently saw in a magazine: 'I mean talk about making punishment a game! The child's supposed to sit on there and I don't know, some little voice comes on and tells it when it can stand up or something . . . I was like, clearly all this is nonsense and we're going to have to develop our own methods'. So, despite such shows focusing on parenting skills and approaches, promoting what Skeggs and Wood (2008) refered to as middle-class norms and standards relating to parenting, my interviews suggest middle-class parents, themselves, are *also* deeply sceptical and somewhat resistant to such ideas – and seemingly more willing to articulate this in an interview format.

In this context, why do so many parents – and non-parents – watch shows such as *Supernanny*? This question feeds into the idea of pleasure that is offered through the 'spectacular entertainment' value of such shows (Gill 2007, p. 18, Gill and Jensen 2008). Pleasure, seen in audience responses to such shows, has been argued to open up possibilities for personal affirmation and that in judging and scrutinising others, many viewers can take reassurance in relation to their own styles and techniques of parenting which, they conclude are not too 'bad' or at least not as 'bad' as those presented on the shows (Gill and

Jensen 2008). This sort of response can be seen in an interview I carried out with a working-class mother called Sarah. She gets pleasure from *Supernanny* saying she finds it 'hilarious' because 'some parents on there are so dappy' and, for her, she finds reassurance in this: 'you realise, well actually there are other parents out there who can't cope. And we're just normal, just normal'. But she also gets pleasurable reassurance from the show because in comparing the parents on screen with her own experiences as a parent she concludes that she, herself, does an okay job: 'It's so nice to; its sounds horrible, but you do compare yourself to them [laughs]. Actually, you know, we're so much better than that'. The pleasure of judging others and, in the process, judging the self more favourably can also be seen in a response from a more middle-class mother I spoke to called Samantha: 'we did used to watch *Supernanny*, but that was more for an entertainment thing . . . it was just, again, shout at the telly and "my child's never gonna do that [laughs]". It is this pleasure through judging and the self-reassurance it affords that might explain, in part, why so many parents – regardless of their class location – watch shows such as *Supernanny*'.

This section has sought to highlight the ways in which viewer's responses to *Supernanny* are often the ones of pleasure in which the judging and scrutinising of other's works offer people reassurance about themselves. Viewers can enjoy a reassurance that their own styles and techniques of parenting are not as 'bad' as some others and in the process, they can construct and perceive themselves as more enabled, empowered and responsible. Yet, there is also suggestion of an awareness of the difficulties and/or resistances parents might have with taking up these ideas – because they go against their self-constructions of what constitutes good parenting, or the practicalities of daily life that might make the take up of these strategies more difficult. Just as critical commentators have argued that a focus or emphasis on the development of particular kinds of parenting skills as the main way of producing well-behaved and well-developed children is problematic, so parents, too, in all their diversity appear to share this sceptical view. Instead of taking up policy and popular cultural ideas relating to parenting in uncritical or unreflexive ways, the parents (particularly the mother) I spoke to appeared to reason through and evaluate these strategies in reflexive and sceptical ways. Such scepticism and evaluative reflexivity about the promise and potential of the development of parenting skills offer a more nuanced reading of the ways in which parents resist but – through the process of sceptical resistance – take up hopes and expectations for skilled, pedagogical and deeply reflexive parenting that are found in popular cultural and policy discourses.

Concluding thoughts

The presence of parental resistances and scepticism might, through one reading, disrupt the idea of a pedagogical mood or state of mind relating to parenting. Yet, another reading is that the presence of resistance and/or scepticism further emphasises it. Indeed, Pykett (this volume) argues that a pedagogical state is one which invites public scepticism and which promotes the capabilities of citizens to reflexively self-govern which subsequently contains the conditions for its own challenge. This paper has shown that parents, themselves, regardless of their classed location, display critical and reflexive responses to messages relating to parenting skills. Their responses might not correspond directly with the hopes and expectations suggested in *Supernanny* – or indeed, recent New Labour policy discourses emphasising parenting skills; but the presence of scepticism and resistance to these messages demonstrate the fluidity, flux and instability of state and non-state governance ideas and strategies. Attention to these dynamics offers a deeper and more situated reading of a structure of feeling relating to parenting in which parents are encouraged to display particular pedagogical attributes and skills. These pedagogical attributes and skills are seen as critical for the successful nurturance and development of their children – and this is a message which contains and carries a particularly gendered and classed address. As seen through my interview data, mothers respond, however, in ways that are not necessarily reducible to their class locations. Indeed most of the mothers, in their own ways, demonstrated resistance and scepticism of the techniques and approaches espoused by *Supernanny*. Through this, it is possible to see how parents demonstrate evaluative reflexivity and (healthy) scepticism, which, while disrupting the idea of a pedagogical mood or sensibility, actually works to deepen it.

Acknowledgements

I am very grateful to John Clarke, Janet Fink, Jessica Pykett and two anonymous reviewers for their helpful comments on earlier drafts which I have tried, as far as possible, to incorporate.

Note

1. These episodes were initially selected because of their availability, though in subsequent work I am extending my analysis to a selection of episodes spanning the four UK series screened in 2004, 2005, 2006 and 2007.

References

Butler, D. and Margo, J., 2007. Freedom's orphans: raising youth in a changing world. *In*: N. Pearce and J. Margo, eds. *Politics for a new generation: the progressive moment*. Basingstoke: Palgrave Macmillan.

Clarke, J., 2005. Merely rhetorical? Language, scepticism and governing, paper for Cultures of Consumption programme workshop on Interpretative Approaches to Governance, 20 July.

Clarke, J., Newman, J., Smith, N., Widler, E. and Westmarland, L., 2007. *Creating citizen-consumers: changing publics and changing public services*. London: Sage.

Department for Children, Schools and Families (DCSF), 2007. *The children's plan*. London: HMSO.

Department for Education and Skills (DfES), 2007. *Every parent matters*. London: HMSO.

Featherstone, B., 2004. *Family life and family support: a feminist analysis*. Basingstoke: Palgrave Macmillan.

Ford, G., 2002. *The new contented little baby book: the secret to calm and confident parenting*. London: Vermillion.

Foster, R., Longton, C. and Roberts, J., 2003. *Mums on babies: trade secrets from the real experts*. London: Cassell.

Frost, J., 2005. *Supernanny: how to get the best from your children*. London: Hodder and Stroughton.

Furedi, F., 2002. *Paranoid parenting: why ignoring the experts may be best for your child*. Chicago, IL: Chicago Review Press.

Gewirtz, S., 2001. Cloning the Blairs: New Labour's programme for the re-socialization of working-class parents. *Journal of education policy*, 16 (4), 365–378.

Giddens, A., 1998. *The third way*. Cambridge: Polity Press.

Gill, R., 2007. *Gender and the media*. Cambridge: Polity Press.

Gill, R. and Jensen, T., 2008. Public intimacies and intimate public: the personal, political and mediated intimacy, paper presented at the *Emergent Publics* seminar, 13th–14th March, The Open University, Milton Keynes.

Gillies, V., 2005. Meeting parents' needs? Discourses of 'support' and 'inclusion' in family policy. *Critical social policy*, 25 (1), 70–90.

Gillies, V., 2007. *Marginalised mothers: exploring working class experiences of parenting*. London: Routledge.

Hardyment, C., 2007. *Dream babies: childcare advice from John Locke to Gina Ford*. London: Frances Lincoln.

Holland, D. and Lave, J., 2001. History in person: an introduction. *In*: D. Holland and J. Lave, eds. *History in person: enduring struggles, contentious practices, intimate identities*. Oxford: James Curry.

Holquist, M., 1990. *Dialogism: Bakhtin and his world*. London: Routledge.

Home Office, 1998. *Supporting families*. London: HMSO.

Lewis, G. and Fink, J., 2004. 'All that heaven allows': the worker-citizen in the post war welfare state. *In*: G. Lewis, ed. *Citizenship: personal lives and social policy*. Bristol: Policy Press.

Lister, R., 2006. An agenda for children: investing in the future or promoting well-being in the present? *In*: J. Lewis, ed. *Children, changing families and welfare states*. Cheltenham: Edward Elgar.

Lunt, P., 2008. Little angels: the mediation of parenting. *Continuum: journal of media and cultural studies*, 22 (4), 537–546.

Macey, D., 2000. *Dictionary of critical theory*. Harmondsworth: Penguin.

MacLeod, M., 2004. The state and the family: can the Government get it right? *Rethinking care relations, family lives and policies: an international symposium*. School of Sociology and Social Policy. London: University of Leeds.

Maybin, J., 2001. Language, struggle and voice: The Bakhtin/Volosinov writings. *In*: M. Wetherell, S. Taylor and S.J. Yates, eds. *Discourse theory and practice: a reader*. London: Sage.

Ouellette, L. and Hay, J., 2008a. Makeover television, governmentality and the good citizen. *Continuum: journal of media and cultural studies*, 22 (4), 471–484.

Ouellette, L. and Hay, J., 2008b. *Better living through reality TV: television and post-welfare citizenship*. Oxford: Blackwell Publishing.

Skeggs, B. and Wood, H., 2008. The labour of transformation and circuits of value around 'reality' television. *Continuum: journal of media and cultural studies*, 22 (4), 339–572.

Skeggs, B., Thumin, N. and Wood, H., 2008. Oh goodness, I am watching 'reality TV': how methodology makes class in multi-method audience research. *European journal of cultural studies*, 11 (1), 5–24.

Supernanny, 2005a. Series 2, Episode 1, Accessed March 2008 from 4 on Demand through BT Vision on Demand.

Supernanny, 2005b. Series 2, Episode 3, Accessed March 2008 from 4 on Demand through BT Vision on Demand.

Supernanny, 2005c. Series 2, Episode 1, Accessed March 2008 from 4 on Demand through BT Vision on Demand.

Walkerdine, V. and Lucey, H., 1989. *Democracy in the kitchen*. London: Virago.

Wetherell, M., 1995. Social structure, ideology and family dynamics: the case of parenting. *In*: J. Muncie, M. Wetherell, R. Dallos and A. Cochrane, eds. *Understanding the family*. London: Sage.

Williams, R., 1961. *The long revolution*. London: Penguin.

Williams, R., 1977. *Marxism and literature*. New York: Oxford University Press.

Williams, F., 2005. New Labour's family policy. *In*: M. Powell, L. Bauld and K. Clarke, eds. *Analysis and debate in social policy*. Bristol: Policy Press.

Towards a pedagogical state? Summoning the 'empowered' citizen

Janet Newman

Department of Social Policy, Faculty of Social Sciences, The Open University, Walton Hall, Milton Keynes, UK

After critically reviewing the apparent 'turn' from welfare states to pedagogic states, I focus on forms of pedagogy evident in notions of citizen empowerment. Issues raised through documentary analysis of key UK policy texts are examined through frameworks offered by Aradhana Sharma's work on women's empowerment in India in order to widen the analytical lens, opening up issues and questions that might be helpful in analysing new configurations of governance in the UK. These include the problem of multiplicity in the identification of strategies and technologies; the idea of pedagogy as a gendered domain, both in terms of the subjects targeted and in those involved in pedagogical work; and the problem of conceptualising 'the state' in formulations such as the 'pedagogical state'. Although questioning the idea of a 'pedgagogic turn', I conclude by addressing the forms of politics and political subjects called forth by pedagogic projects. The paper was written before the 2010 election but the analysis has much to offer to the politics of Cameron's Big Society.

Across the global north and south, we can trace an increasing focus on pedagogic programmes of development and capacity building as responses to poverty and exclusion. This has been a dominant theme in the programmes of the World Bank since the mid-1990s, but has also become an increasingly significant governmental strategy in 'mature' welfare states. Such strategies are often associated with new forms of governmentality:

> Empowerment, self esteem and self help are the newest technologies, which help mold individuals into responsible citizen-subjects who fit the requirements of the prevalent governance regime and who participate in the project of rule by governing themselves. The neo-liberal doctrine of limited, small and participatory government is premised on de-centralising power and self-regulating citizens who are not coerced to follow certain regimens but voluntary submit to a "tutelary power" (Cruikshank 1996, p. 234), such as a social worker, a program or a therapist, because it is in their interest to do so (Sharma 2008, p. 17).

What Cruikshank (1999, p. 125) terms 'liberatory therapies' are conducted through the work of activists, organisers, educators, social service professionals and social scientists. My concern in this paper is with what insights might be gained from a study of emerging governmental strategies in the UK; in particular, how far we might be able to categorise the UK as a form of 'pedagogical state'.

When we survey the policy landscape of the UK towards the end of the particular period of governance innovation associated with 'new Labour', we can find examples of the focus on citizens as the objects of pedagogy everywhere: trained and retrained in the context of labour market activation and employment policies; developed to become active members of the polity and local community; subject to new governmental strategies on diet, exercise, smoking, parenting, recycling, volunteering and wellbeing in old age. They are brought into closer encounters with government actors through a range of co-production, participation and governance initiatives; initiatives through which citizens are tutored in the logics and rationalities of good governance. It is, then, tempting to suggest that we are witnessing a new form of 'post welfare' state, one involving a turn away from citizenship as a status and set of entitlements towards citizenship as a constellation of duties and responsibilities.

But what we are witnessing is not, I want to suggest, a single turn but a cluster of different reframings of public and social policy, such that to collapse them into a single overarching 'governmentality of the self' or new form of citizenship may obscure more than it illuminates. The nature of the 'turn' can also be contested, not least because of the ways in which apparently new pedagogies draw on or reinflect older forms of tutelage but also because of the diversity of strategies at stake in programmes of development, modernisation and reform. These questions are pursued in the first section of this paper. I then focus on one strand of UK policy, that of citizen empowerment, through an examination of four UK policy documents. The following sections set out to interrogate the issues raised in these documents, drawing on perspectives suggested by Sharma's (2008) work on a programme of women's empowerment in India. This is significant for at least two reasons. First, the literature on the global South has a much more explicit focus on the role of capacity building and citizen empowerment than does the European literature on welfare reform. Second, other attempts to open up conversations between North and South (e.g. Cornwall and Coelho 2007) have been highly productive. However, mine is not intended to be a comparative project; rather I draw on Sharma in order to widen the analytical lens, opening up issues and questions that might be helpful in analysing new configurations of governance in the UK. These include the problem of multiplicity in the identification of strategies and technologies, the idea of pedagogy as a gendered domain and the problem of conceptualising 'the state' in formulations such as the 'pedagogical state'.

One turn or many?

The idea of the state – and associated state bodies – engaging in a pedagogy of citizenship is not new. In Britain, we can trace different forms of pedagogical intervention in the seventeenth and eighteenth century attempts to school unruly populations (whether at home or in the expanding colonies); in the nineteenth century Workers Education movements and charitable endeavours to address poverty, in the twentieth century development of universal schooling, and in Blair's rallying cry of 'education, education, education' as the lynchpin of reform in the twenty-first century. Many commentators have suggested that we are currently witnessing a distinct policy 'turn' associated with the modernisation of welfare states and the elaboration of new governmental rationalities of citizenship. The character of this 'turn' is, however, differently inflected. Within one strand of welfare state literature, we can trace the idea of a turn from welfare state to social investment state. Here, governments are viewed as switching resources towards investment in the education of future generations and the retraining of current workers (and non-workers) in order to better position the nation in the changing global economy (Esping-Andersen 2002, Lister 2004). A second strand of literature focuses on the ways in which states are turning their attention from the provision of welfare to the building of capacities for self-provisioning and self-management. Citizens are encouraged to take greater responsibility for families and communities, being 'activated' to participate in governing bodies and deliberative forums on finding solution to 'local' problems, encouraged to stop smoking, to eat more healthily, to become better parents and so on:

> New Labour likes to see people being busy, and active citizens have been promoted across a variety of intersections between the state and members of society. Active citizens were a means of reducing cost and activity pressures on the National Health Service – becoming 'expert patients', taking on managing their own life styles and well being, and requiring less attention from hospitals and general practitioners. Active citizens 'volunteer' and create mutual self help as the basis for community activation and regeneration. They embrace the spirit of 'do-it-yourself', from staying active in old age to dealing with the annual tax returns for the Inland Revenue (Clarke 2005, p. 448).

This intersects with a third strand of literature on the 'moralisation' of welfare. For example, Rodger (2008) notes how state policies have become increasingly preoccupied by 'moral regulation', targeting social discipline rather than social justice:

> This is accomplished by a redirected social sphere in which policy is preoccupied with dysfunctional families (Sure Start) and the juvenile justice system is preoccupied with NEET status [not in education, employment or training] and anti-social behaviour among teenagers. ... The preferred solution to how to control personal behaviour in a liberal society has been the creation of a sphere of activity, here called the social sphere, to employ a range of techniques of intervention to manage problem populations in the language of *social therapism* or *social education*. (2008, pp. 199 and 201, emphasis as in original).

These in turn require particular forms of pedagogies of the self, albeit ones that have a more coercive and compulsory character.

Finally, a fourth strand of the literature on the reform of welfare states engages with the turn towards public participation and involvement. This itself has multiple origins (Barnes *et al.* 2007), bringing together a cluster of concerns about the health of civil society, the legitimacy of government institutions, the flexibility and responsiveness of service delivery organisations and the 'empowerment' of disadvantaged or excluded populations. While sometimes associated with a quasi-republican model of citizenship, in contrast to the liberal tendencies of consumerism (Hvinden and Johansson 2007), this has also been theorised in terms of neo-liberal rationalities that require citizens to be tutored to the needs and requirements of good governance and norms of 'good citizenship' (Abram 2007).

These different strands of thinking have each informed debates on the Left about the formation of a 'progressive' politics appropriate for future cycles of policymaking. For example, a collection titled 'Politics for a New Generation: the progressive moment' (Pearce and Margo 2007) includes contributions from Ed Balls on training and support; from Beverley Hughes on investment in children; and Ed Miliband on the need to empower communities, all at the time of writing members of the UK government. The think tank Compass has engaged positively with the policy discourse of 'co-production' that invites citizens to work with social agencies in the delivery of social and welfare services, the governance of communities and the renewal of the social fabric of civility, tolerance and respect (see Needham 2007, Gannon and Lawson 2009). Pearce and Margo argue for a 'civic liberalism', to be elicited through education for citizenship, through the cultivation of civic virtues, 'and a strengthening of the mechanisms for citizen involvement in democratic deliberation, in both civil society and the institutions of the state' (2007, p. 13). The notion of the Big Society has drawn – unevenly – on each of these strands.

We can, then, trace a number of different sources and origins for the idea that we are witnessing a pedagogic turn in state practices. As noted earlier in this paper, discourses of empowerment have long been associated with the policies of the World Bank and other development agencies. Such discourses – albeit differently inflected – are now appearing in the policy texts of 'mature' welfare states seeking strategies for survival and success in the global economy. Challenges to state welfare require, it seems, not only new forms of development to ensure that those inside and outside paid work are prepared – or preferably tutored into how to prepare themselves – to take their place in the globalising national economy. But welfare beyond the welfare state also depends on citizens taking greater responsibility for the health and wellbeing of themselves, their families and neighbours and their 'communities'. This in turn requires skills, capacities and orientations that need to be inculcated, whether it is on how to eat healthily, to be better parents, to make responsible lifestyle choices, to engage in the 'co-production ' of services or to participate in democratic spaces of decision making.

At the same time, we can trace the emergence of a new focus on the enhancement of 'capabilities' as the route to social justice. Here, the work of Sen (1999), Nussbaum (2006) and others has been invoked in policy shifts from substantive definitions of equality to more fluid – but arguably more holistic – conceptions of well being (DCLG 2007). Finally, we need to take account of the hegemonic status of 'choice' in contemporary policy discourse in the UK and beyond (Clarke *et al.* 2007). At first sight, this seems to offer something rather different from the paternalism associated with 'old' forms of service delivery and 'new' forms of pedagogy. Indeed, choice has been formulated as a claim on the part of disabled people's and other movements attempting to free themselves from state paternalism. However, the exercise of choice is deemed to require new capacities and skills on the part of consumers, and we have witnessed a very rapid expansion of information and advocacy services, websites and guidance documents to help develop the choice-making capacities of the responsible consumer.

Informing, tutoring, empowering and developing are, then, all part of the repertoire of modern governance and can be conceptualised as new governmentalities of the self (Cruikshank 1999, Rose 1999). However, the diversity of strategies and perspectives I have highlighted here lead me to suggest the need for some caution before announcing yet another new form of the state. Nor should the multiple political projects and governmental strategies be collapsed into each other in identifying a singular new form of governmentality. Such claims operate at a level of abstraction that can be challenged by a closer examination of specific policies and their enactment. In the next section, I explore the pedagogical strategies associated with a specific set of New Labour policies promoting citizen empowerment.

The paradoxes of pedagogy: developing the 'empowered' citizen

In 2006, the UK Office of the Deputy Prime Minister published Promoting Effective Citizenship and Community Empowerment: a guide for local authorities on enhancing capacity for public participation. This began:

> Relationships between local government and the public are changing. Effective governance requires an informed, engaged citizenry which votes in elections, participates in decisionmaking and works with service providers in designing, delivering and monitoring services. ... This guide provides advice on what local authorities can do to support *learning for effective citizenship*. By 'effective citizenship' we mean people having the knowledge, skills and sense of empowerment

to play a meaningful role in local decisionmaking. Thus, this guide builds on the work that many local authorities already do to widen participation, but suggests further ways that councils can support people in *learning how they can be more involved* (Office of the Deputy Prime Minister 2006, p. 6, my emphasis).

The language here is significant. We might note four points. First is the elision established between 'effective governance' and 'effective citizenship'. Effective governance, we might have assumed, is something which citizens should expect of their government; but here notions of effectiveness are displaced from the state onto citizens. Second, citizenship is defined not as a status, not an identity, nor even as a responsibility, but as set of practices ('votes', 'participates', 'works with') that together constitute the enactment or performance of effective citizenship. Third, such practices require a set of capacities (knowledge, skills and a 'sense of empowerment') that can be elicited and encouraged by local authorities. But fourth, local authorities are not summoned as teachers (of information) nor tutors (of skills), but as the 'supporters of learning'. The pedagogic strategies promoted by the guide are quite varied. Formal learning (through citizenship education in schools and courses for adults) takes a relatively minor place alongside informal and experiential learning. The local authority is viewed as engaging in a range of activities, including effective communication of information and knowledge about local decision-making processes, the development of capacity building programmes and the extension and improvement of public participation.

A second document published some two years later was intended to promote public and stakeholder engagement around a forthcoming white paper on local government. The *Community Power Pack* (DCLG: April 2008a) was written in conjunction with a not-for-profit organisation (Involve) 'to aid local groups organise and facilitate discussion on the topic of empowerment' (p. 5). It promised that feedback from such discussions would inform and shape empowerment activities, including what was at that point termed the Empowerment White Paper, though the short time period between the Pack and the White Paper itself – published in July 2008 – suggests that response to such feedback was likely to have been limited. The Pack itself is an interesting pedagogical tool, offering advice on the format and facilitation of participation events as well as substantive content on what are termed 'empowerment issues'.

The Pack has several points of interest in the context of this paper. First, the headline language shifts from citizens to communities, and from effectiveness to empowerment. This suggests a significant change of emphasis. However, the four thematic aims of the White Paper introduced in the Pack tell a different story. These themes are 'to encourage active citizenship, improve services, promote work and strengthen local accountability' (2008, p. 13). And in the first of these, active citizenship, notions of effectivity return:

'Government has an interest in promoting active citizenship across the spectrum because

(1) it will help people and communities find *common solutions to shared problems,*
(2) it can generate *social capital* – bridging and bonding,
(3) it can stimulate *collective efficacy* – social pressures on groups of people to behave responsibly and look after each others' interests,
(4) it can achieve *co-production* – government working alongside the third sector to achieve shared outcomes in public service and
(5) there can be clear *progression routes* along the spectrum into forms of civic involvement which support democratic and public service infrastructure' (DCLG 2008a, p. 15, emphasis in original).

Such forms of active citizenship, while undoubtedly bringing social benefits, imply the extension of citizen labour in community and civil society. This is a very different kind of labour from the extension of paid work set out in the third theme, 'Work and enterprise for all'. Here, we read that

> Getting a job is the best way out of poverty and the most effective way to empower people to take control over their own lives... Worklessness and a weak neighbourhood economy is personally damaging for the individuals involved, undermining personal confidence and their power to contribute to society, not just economically, but through decisionmaking and community activities (2008, p. 18).

What is interesting here is the way in which the apparent tensions between the extension of voluntary labour in community and civil society and of paid work in the formal economy are smoothed away: paid work, it suggests, enhances the capacity for civic involvement rather than reducing it (cf Newman 2005).

The White Paper itself formalised many of the responsibilities that local government was expected to undertake in terms of capacity building, information providing and fostering involvement – all, within the terms of this volume, pedagogic activities. But running beneath these duties and responsibilities of government is a continuous emphasis on the duties and responsibilities of citizens themselves to engage in a pedagogy of the self, learning how to 'get involved', to 'have a voice' and to 'take control'. The title *Communities in control: real people, real power* is itself interesting: the subtitle resonates with John Clarke's analysis of the valorisation of 'ordinary people' as the desired partners of government (this volume). And, unlike many government documents, citizens are addressed directly. The verso of the cover page is headed 'What can I do' and has bullet points such as 'Information is power', 'Gear up your group' and 'Take a stand', the latter going on to ask readers to 'find out about being a local councillor, a Young Advisor, a school governor or housing association representative. Your council should help you find out more'. The direct address is expressed not only through the text but also through the images of 'real' people looking direct to camera and holding up placards on which titles and text are displayed throughout the document.

Empowerment through participation and voice is, however, only one strand of the current policy direction. The final documents I want to refer to are produced not by DCLG but by the Department of Health and concern the modernisation of health and adult social care in the UK. These stress the need to shift from a paternalist relationship between service providers and users, one which encouraged dependency, to the fostering of 'adult' forms of citizenship. The 2005 White Paper on social care (DH 2005) aimed to 'foster independence and control' by transforming the role of service users such that they become active participants in the construction, production and management of their own care, whereas the 2006 White Paper on health aspired to 'shift the whole system towards the active, engaged citizen in his or her local community and away from monolithic, top down paternalism' (DH 2006, para 1.39). Policies introducing direct payments and individual budgets, well established in social care and promised for health services, are directed towards what Scourfield (2007, p. 112) terms the 'transformation of citizens into both managers and entrepreneurs'. Although some citizens have been more than ready to take on such roles, the transformation requires professionals and advocacy organisations to engage in new pedagogical practices in order to empower vulnerable groups and to build the capacities and skills for self-assessment, budgetary management and the consumption of a fragmented array of care services (Newman *et al.* 2008).

One might read such policy texts in a range of ways, highlighting contradictions, exploring ways in which new subjects are summoned and how new regimes of power are inscribed in and through discourse. Such readings are open to the charge of reifying the text and paying too little regard for how policy is both produced and enacted. They also overlook how processes of 'implementation' might be more troubled than policy documents suggest, involving processes of mediation and translation in which the text is imbued with meanings other than those intended (Newman and Vidler 2006, Lendvai and Stubbs 2007), and in which new spaces of agency might be opened up which have the capacity to challenge governmental logics (Barnes *et al.* 2007, Newman and Clarke 2009b).

But this is not my project here. Rather, I want to highlight how the governance innovations traced in the policy documents discussed above draw on a range of resources: on professional discourse, community activism, 'progressive' projects of decentralisation and democratic renewal, academic research, think tank activities and so on. The health and social care reforms draw on the discourses and projects of subaltern groups such as disabled people's movements, but also on radical reforms within the welfare professions based on notions of democratisation, voice and participation. The guide for local authorities on 'enhancing capacity for public participation' published by government (ODPM 2006) was authored by academics at the Centre for Local and Regional Government Research at Cardiff University, a group with a long tradition of involvement with, as well as research into, local government. This document, like the later Community power pack (DCLG 2008a) written in conjunction with 'INVOLVE', includes case studies and examples of projects whose intentions, and the purposes of their pedagogical practices, might be considered antithetical to – or at least different from – government modernisation programmes or neo-liberal rationalities. The 'local empowerment' theme of the White Paper on local government (DCLG 2008b) builds not only on the struggles of community activism but also on a specific policy lobby group – the New Local Government Network – that has championed the cause of local government in Whitehall, as well as offered its own ideas about democratic renewal. These capacities and resources are drawn into governmental projects in ways that seek to render them compatible with the modernising thrust of reform. This may be more or less successful; but the tensions and contradictions inherent in governmental projects, the fragility of some of the alignments on which they are based, suggest the need for caution in announcing yet another new form of the state.

In order to develop this argument, and to throw further light onto the pedagogic projects expressed through these and other UK documents, I want to turn to a different context in which governmental discourses of empowerment is deployed, drawing on the work of Aradhana Sharma on India. I do so with no intention of engaging in comparative analysis; rather my purpose is to see how Sharma's work might open up concepts and analytical framings which could further illuminate the analysis of the 'pedagogic turns' of UK policy.

Widening the analytical lens

Sharma sets out to analyse how far and in what ways the move away from *welfare style dependent development* towards *empowerment style self development* has manifested itself in the Gender and Development policy regime of the Indian state. She takes as her starting point the ways in which a regime of neo-liberal governmentality is associated with changed relationships between state and social actors, transforming development and reshaping citizenship and popular politics. But she shows how

> an inquiry into the 'particular' and 'peculiar' ... complicates neo-liberalism's so-called universal core and consequences and illuminates the cracks in its purported global hegemony ... I offer a situated look at how transnational neoliberal ideologies of development articulate and jostle with histories of state and subject formation and of popular

movements in India, producing a spatially uneven and ambiguous terrain of changes not easily captured by the rubric of dewelfarised states, depoliticised existence, and disciplined, consuming, individuated civic actors (2008, pp. xvii–xviii).

Sharma (2008, p. 22) points to four empowerment frames, which 'stem from different ideological perspectives and arose out of diverse spatial locations and historical moments'. In the Indian context, these included a feminist strategy to engender feminist social transformation, a Freirian liberatory struggle against oppression, a Gandhian order of moral self-rule and a neo-liberal project that fosters individualise conceptions of market empowerment in order to solve poverty and reduce big government. Sharma notes how the feminist frameworks on which the Gender and Development programme was based explicitly drew on Freire's radical ideas of pedagogy:

> Empowerment is a pedagogic process that facilitates a transformation of both the self and society... The oppressed, individually and collectively, needed to reflect upon and recognise their lived realities of alienation and oppression; they then had to collectively intervene in and transform these unjust realities. (2008, p. 8).

Such ideas were articulated with the ideas of Gandhi, who expounded 'a utopic and locally relevant ... vision of an ethical and just free society premised on the notion of swaraj (self rule) and attainable through the practice of satyagraha (the struggle for truth, or passive resistance)' (2008, pp. 11–12).

These two framings are aligned with the neo-liberal project of development, so giving neo-liberalism, and the World Bank itself, a 'social and ethical spin' (2008, p. 20). We can see, then, how empowerment strategies in India encompass both hegemonic and counter-hegemonic frames, but all seek to mould behaviour and so all must, Sharma argues, be viewed as governmental projects. Within the context of this paper, they might all also be viewed as pedagogic projects, even though only one – that drawn from Freire – explicitly uses the language of pedagogy. However, they diverge in terms of the social subjects they wish to create and the kind of society they seek to establish. These are not, however, determining of the subjects summoned to power:

> Even as development attempts to create and regulate disciplined individuals and collective bodies, it also breeds subversive tactics and unruly subjects who protest their subjectification and subjection, who test the state and unbound it from presumed limits, and who resignify development (2008, p. xxxv).

There are many insights we might derive from Sharma that we might miss from a simple reading of the British context, of which I want to highlight three: insights about multiplicity, about gender and about the state itself. These are developed in turn in the sections that follow.

Framings of 'empowerment'

The empowerment frames associated with the UK documents discussed earlier in this paper are different from those discussed by Sharma. But I want to develop her idea of multiple frames. Across the documents discussed, I think it is possible to trace at least three frames, each of which imagines the relationship between state and citizen differently, and each of which invokes different kinds of citizen-subject. The first is based on calls for the transformation of the professions; and in particular the dismantling of the 'knowledge-power knot' in which the professional is positioned as the guardian of expertise and the citizen as dependent supplicant of their specialist knowledge. A range of policies were set out to empower the citizen by freeing her from the paternalistic protection of professional decision making, offering independent control of individualised budgets and/or choice in the expanding marketplace of care and welfare services. In the field of health and social care, these policies have resulted from the action of social movements (e.g. of disabled people, of mental health service users, of people with learning disabilities) and pressure from patients' organisations, aligned somewhat uneasily with state strategies of modernisation which result in the 'responsibilisation' of individuals and communities. However, rather than the dismantling of professional power, we can see the rise of new forms of professional work oriented towards a pedagogy of personal lives: how to manage budgets, how to stay fit and healthy into old age, how to care for those dependent on the provision of informal labour in household and community and how to access and use information so as to be able to 'choose' appropriate services and service providers. Much of this work is associated with new configurations of professional power based on the 'co-production' of health and care outcomes, configurations which privilege professional conceptions of the purpose of empowerment – the self-managing patient, the well being of those in need of continuing care.

The second framing of empowerment traceable in the policy documents concerns freeing communities from an overweaning centralised state. This too draws on counter-hegemonic political pressures, not least from a New Local Government network that has been highly influential in reasserting the value of local governance, but also from successive generations of community workers and community activists, and from commentators concerned about the growing 'democratic deficit' and lack of trust between government and people. Following a period of state experimentation with local action projects, neighbourhood management schemes and other invocations of the 'local' in public policy, the local government white paper cited above (DCLG 2008b) sets out the new 'duties' of local government to empower local communities and to foster citizen participation in local decision making. Rather than a pedagogy of self-management in the first framing, the focus on collective self-governance requires a pedagogy of 'effective' citizenship, with citizens being tutored through the process of participation itself. Such pedagogies are themselves compound rather than singular, as might be expected from the varied political forces that underpin them. But each offers a pedagogy of participation. It is through the acts of participation in community project and local participation exercises that citizens are brought into closer relationships with state power and tutored in the logics and rationalities of governance itself. But it is also through such practices that local authorities are to be transformed, with the expectation that pressure 'from below' might succeed where 'top down' modernising reforms have failed.

Such practices appear very different from those fostered through the third framing of empowerment – that of participation as consumers in the marketplace of goods and services. The exercise of choice offers new routes to equality that transcend the failures and limitations of old, state-led universal policies, and it is through the market that citizens can be truly empowered and lifted out of poverty. But to exercise these market freedoms, citizens must contribute to economic growth through paid work; and it is the role of government to support and empower the worker citizen through the inculcation of skills, capacities and the fostering of new conceptions of the self. This takes us closer to conventional framings of empowerment as a neo-liberal strategy, but inflected through social democratic discourses of equality and fairness.

These multiple framings cannot, I suggest, be collapsed into a singular conception of neo-liberal governmentality seeking to produce responsibilised citizen-subjects. Nor do they suggest a conception of the state in which it surrenders power to the 'empowered' citizen.

Gendering empowerment

Sharma's work, like other analyses of development programmes in the global south, opens up questions about how empowerment pedagogies may be gendered. I want to highlight several possible ways in which empowerment might be considered as a gendered domain of governance. First, it is gendered in the sources on which it draws. The women's movement, in calling for a redrawing of the personal/private/political boundaries, arguably opened up a politics of personal lives that prefigured the new pedagogies of the self. Sharma suggests that 'The languages of empowerment, self help, and self esteem, which emerged out of social movements and critical feminist practices . . . , now function as neoliberal "liberation therapy" that fashions rights-bearing, entrepreneurial personhood' (Sharma 2008, p. 17). This resonates with other work on development that explores the relationship between women's movements and international relations (Braig and Wölte 2002). Many of the prefigurative pathways on which governance innovations draw were developed by women's groups, community activists and the female-dominated welfare professions. However, as Braig and Wölte argue, in the process of becoming mainstreamed, such projects may be regendered and radical projects depoliticised.

Empowerment is also gendered in the subjects called forth (women as economic agents, entrepreneurs, worker-citizens) and in the subjects charged with pedagogical forms of work. The idea of pedagogy as a gendered domain draws attention to the opening up by feminism of a politics of personal lives, and the role played by female-dominated welfare professions in shaping state interventions into parenting, childcare, domestic violence and other aspects of what were previously mapped as 'private' lives. The gendering of pedagogy, then, can be traced both in the populations to be 'developed' and in those who are charged with pedagogical work. The work of developing, teaching, capacity building and tutoring remains largely women's work. This might be seen as an extension of the female-dominated professions of social work and teaching, but is also linked to the feminisation of the management of 'dangerous' populations by police and prison services as strategies for the control of violence through force give way – in part – to strategies of communication, conflict resolution and the pedagogy of 'anger management'.

But the gendering of pedagogical work extends far beyond that of engaging in the practice of pedagogy itself. The governance strategies summon citizens as 'empowered' subjects do not rely on traditional conceptions of welfare professionals working in state bureaucracies. The new spaces of pedagogical governance have to be assembled from diverse resources, opening up the need for forms of work involving translation (working across different systems of meaning) and alignment (bringing together different political projects into a coherent programme). Sharma herself identifies several difficulties associated with translating Freire's ideas into a development programme, including the difficulty of 'achieving a workable balance between open-ended definitions and strategies, on the one hand, and installing measurable indicators of empowerment, which donors demand, that necessarily bring some closure and rigidity' (2008, p. 10) on the other. In the UK, community projects have to be aligned with funding regimes, new technologies of participation have to be aligned with traditional political spaces of representative government, local innovations have to be aligned with central government targets and evaluation regimes, politicised forms of agency have to be aligned with logics of governance that privilege managerialist conceptions of effectiveness and so on.

The problem of the state in the pedagogical state

Developments in governance theory over the last two decades have problematised equivalences between political projects and the state. The state, it is argued, has been decentred or hollowed out, and governmental power dispersed, devolved and decentralised. Although there continues to be a thriving academic industry in announcing 'new' formations of the state, work on governance and governmentality focus rather on how power is exercised beyond the formal machinery of state institutions. In the context of the UK, the policy documents discussed earlier suggest different kinds of relationship between state authority and that of quasi-autonomous agents of delivery, local government, professional bodies and, above all, 'communities' themselves. We can also trace a proliferation of hybrid organisations and public/private agencies with diverse relationships to governmental power (Newman and Clarke 2009a). In the Indian context, Sharma coins the term GONGOS – government organised non-governmental organisations. 'These do not necessarily imply a shrunken state but point to a multiplication of governmental bodies whose autonomy from the state remains questionable' (2008, p. 90). Although the GONGO status of MS, the programme analysed by Sharma, offered relative independence for its staff, and prevented direct government intervention, its relationship to government remained ambiguous. And such ambiguities open up questions about the reach and effectiveness of new formations of state power.

A further difficulty associated with the idea of a pedagogical state is the multiple framings I noted above. A focus on multiplicity draws attention not only to diverse political and governmental projects, but also to the multiple agents and actors who are involved in pedagogical work. The new governmentalities of pedagogy are, then, multiple, not singular. There is a temptation, in reviewing the British case, to find evidence of a neo-liberal tendency to substitute pedagogy for redistribution as the preferred route to social justice. Or we might look to the recent history of the British state to gain insights into the moral and quasi-paternalistic tendencies of new forms of pedagogy. However, as I hope I have shown, such formulations miss the ways in which multiple, sometimes antagonistic, projects are articulated into apparently coherent projects – projects in which, however, paradox and instability are all too evident. Turning once again to Sharma, we find a convincing account of the ways in which neo-liberalism is articulated with the history and politics of the Indian state: 'The usage and sway of grassroots empowerment and decentralised development and governance in contemporary India cannot be seen as simply a translation of transgenerational feminist ideas or a localisation of Frierian insights. They are, rather, a complex result of the articulation of these translocal forces with local historical trajectories and deployments of similar terms' (2008, p. 11).

In the British case, we are confronted with hegemonic projects of modernisation, activation and labour market flexibility, articulated with the complex strands of Labour party politics (Newman 2001). Both 'old' and 'new' Labour, and the 2010 Coalition government, draw on multiple sensibilities and projects and I cannot do justice to their complexity here, nor to the differences opening up between the ruling authorities of the different nations – or potential nations – within the UK. But I do want to highlight the problematic articulations of economic strands of activation, in which governments attempt to 'empower' citizens for the global market as both workers and consumers, with the moral sensibilities underpinning the activation of civic and community attachments.

Viewing these as articulations rather than single projects raises questions about the forms of politics and political subjects called forth by pedagogic projects. New forms of pedagogy, I want to suggest, have to be regarded as both politicising and depoliticising. They are politicising in that they summon populations as citizens, tutor them in the skills and capabilities of citizenship and address them through the language of empowerment. These summonings are of course highly differentiated, with migrant populations summoned to perform a particular formation of Britishness, disadvantaged citizens being summoned as empowered and agentic members of communities, activist or potentially disruptive citizens being summoned as partners in governance, dependent welfare clients summoned as independent, choice-making customers and school pupils summoned as the responsible citizens of the future. Each offers at least the possibility of politicised forms of agency or the mobilisation of political resources and capacities. But each also carries depoliticising tendencies. Activism is not erased but reframed, the spaces of participation are highly managed and subaltern forms of politics are subject to depoliticising tendencies through their alignment, in partnership bodies and governmental projects, with managerial and institutional logics.

Pedagogical practices, then, have to be understood as practices through which different forms of knowledge, power and agency are assembled, producing ambiguities and sites of strain. Such assemblages are complex, drawing on multiple framings of empowerment and assembling different political projects – including those of coercion and conditionality, choice and cohesion. Despite the significance of pedagogical work in state projects of modernisation and reform, this is a long way from the idea that we are witnessing a turn from a social democratic state to a new form of pedagogical state. As Sharma argues,

> state actors ... face the risk that their initiatives might produce results that are contrary to those that they had imagined – that empowerment programmes will not bring about the orderly and manageable transformations that officials seek but will generate an uncontrollable excess, bitter opposition, disruptive conduct, and imperfect subjects. These lurking dangers compel us to carefully scrutinise the forms of political action (whether banal or exceptional, individual or collective) that bureaucratised empowerment projects open up and foreclose (2008, p. xx).

References

Abram, S., 2007. Participatory depoliticisation: the bleeding heart of neo-liberalism'. *In*: C. Neveu, ed. *Cultures et practiques participative: perspectives comparatives*. Paris: L'Hartmann, 113–134.

Barnes, M., Newman, J. and Sullivan, H., 2007. *Power, participation and political renewal: case studies of public participation*. Bristol: Policy Press.

Braig, M. and Wölte, S., eds, 2002. *Common ground or mutual exclusion? women's movements and internatioal relations*. London: Zed Books.

Clarke, J., 2005. New labour's citizens: activated, empowered, responsbilised, abandoned? *Critical social policy*, 25 (4), 447–463.

Clarke, J., Newman, J., Smith, N., Vidler, E. and Westmarland, L., 2007. *Creating citizen consumers: changing publics and changing public services*. London: Sage.

Cornwall, A. and Coelho, V., eds, 2007. *Spaces for change: the politics of citizen participation in new democratic arenas*. London: Zed Books.

Cruikshank, B., 1999. *The will to empower*. Ithaca, NY: Cornell University Press.

Department for Communities and Local Government (DCLG), 2007. *Fairness and freedom: the final report of the equalities review*. London: DCLG.

Department for Communities and Local Government, 2008a. *The community power pack*. London: DCLG.

Department for Communities and Local Government, 2008b. *Communities in control: real people, real power* (Cm 7427). London: DCLG.

Department of Health (DH), 2005. *Independence, Well being and choice* (Cm 6499). London: DH.

Department of Health, 2006. *Our health, our care, our say* (Cm 6737). London: DH.

Esping-Andersen, G., 2002. *Why we need a new welfare state*. Oxford: Oxford University Press.

Gannon, G. and Lawson, N., 2009. *Co-production: the modernisation of public services by staff and users*. London: Compass.

Hvinden, B. and Johansson, H., eds, 2007. *Citizenship in the nordic welfare states: dynamics of choice, duties and participation in a changing Europe*. London: Routledge.

Lendvai, N. and Stubbs, P., 2007. Policies as translation: situating transnational social policies. *In*: S. Hodgson and K. Irving, eds. *Policy reconsidered: meanings, politics and practices*. Bristol: Policy Press.

Lister, R., 2004. The third way's social investment state. *In*: J. Lewis and R. Surrender, eds. *Welfare state change: towards a third way?* Oxford: Oxford University Press, 157–181.

Needham, C., 2007. *The reform of public services under New Labour: narratives of consumerism*. Basingstoke: Palgrave.

Newman, J., 2001. *Modernising governance: new labour, policy and society*. London: Sage.

Newman, J., 2005. Regendering governance. *In*: J. Newman, ed. *Remaking governance: peoples, politics and the public sphere*. Bristol: Policy Press, 81–100.

Newman, J. and Clarke, J., 2009a. *Publics, politics and power: remaking the public in public services*. London: Sage.

Newman, J. and Clarke, J., 2009b. Narrating subversion, assembling citizenship. *In*: M. Barnes and D. Prior, eds. *The subversive citizen*. Bristol: Policy Press.

Newman, J. and Vidler, E., 2006. Discriminating customers, responsible patients, empowered users: consumerism and the modernisation of health care. *Journal of social policy*, 35 (2), 193–209.

Newman, J., Glendinning, C. and Hughes, M., 2008. Beyond modernisation? Social care and the transformation of welfare governance. *Journal of social policy*, 37 (4), 531–558.

Nussbaum, M.C., 2006. *Frontiers of justice*. London: Belknap Press.

Office of the Deputy Prime Minister (ODPM), 2006. *Promoting effective citizenship and community empowerment*. London: ODPM.

Pearce, N. and Margo, J., 2007. Introduction. *In*: N. Pearce and J. Margo, eds. *Politics for a new generation: the progressive moment*. Basingstoke: Macmillan.

Rodger, J.J., 2008. *Criminalising social policy: anti-social behaviour and welfare in a decivilised society*. Cullompton: Willen.

Rose, N., 1999. *Powers of freedom: reframing political thought*. Cambridge: Cambridge University Press.

Scourfield, P., 2007. Social care and the modern citizen: client, consumer, service user, manager and entrepreneur. *British journal of social work*, 37, 107–122.

Sen, A.K., 1999. *Development as freedom*. Oxford: Oxford University Press.

Sharma, A., 2008. *Logics of empowerment: development, gender and governance in neoliberal India*. Minneapolis, MN: University of Minnesota Press.

Learning beyond the state: the pedagogical spaces of the CAB service

Rhys Jones

Institute of Geography and Earth Sciences, Aberystwyth University, Aberystwyth, UK

This paper discusses the role played by the Citizens Advice Bureau service in enabling British citizenship and the way in which such a project has been facilitated through two different processes of learning. First, the service has been part of a wider network of organisations within the UK, which have promoted a pedagogic process whereby citizens learn about their various rights. Second, the CAB service over the long term has sought to promote a second kind of learning, as individual bureaux seek to learn of the challenges facing their clients. The CAB service is particularly interesting because it seeks to further these two different kinds of learning – learning *about* and *by* the state – as part of the 'shadow state'. The paper uses this backdrop as a context within which to examine two specific instances of pedagogy within the contemporary CAB service. Drawing on documentary research and interviews with employees of the service, I explore, first of all, the *access strategy* that it has employed by in order to reach out to more clients. Second, I discuss the way in which the service – through its *social policy* work – enables the British state, in a variety of different contexts, to learn about its citizens and about the impacts of its policies on its citizens. Taken together, such themes illustrate the key role played by different kinds of learning as part of CAB service's broader project of facilitating citizen identities in the UK.

Since its inception at the outbreak of the Second World War, the Citizens Advice Bureaux service[1] [hereafter CAB service] has acted as an independent, membership-based organisation, which has provided support and guidance to British citizens facing all manner of welfare, financial or consumer difficulties. The central body of Citizens Advice, along with individual bureaux, has in many ways enabled a British citizenship. They have encouraged British citizens to access their welfare rights and, in this respect, have been crucial in the expansion of the social citizenship that was a central plank of British nation-building project during the second half of the twentieth century (Marshall 1950).

My main aim in this chapter is to examine the way in which the CAB service's role in forming citizens has been predicated upon different forms of learning; what I have termed learning *about* and *by* the state. The service's two key aims make clear these different forms of learning. Its aims are to 'ensure that individuals do not suffer through lack of knowledge of their rights and responsibilities' and to 'exercise a responsible influence on the development of social policies and services both locally and nationally' (Citizens Advice 2007a, p. 3). The first aim relates to the organisation's objective to enable individuals to learn, predominantly about their rights as citizens but also, to a large extent, about their responsibilities towards the state and their fellow citizens. The service to a large extent, therefore, can be viewed as a promoter of the so-called 'fourth right of citizenship'; namely the right to education and information, which can act as the basis of citizens' civil, political and [especially] social rights (NCC 1977, p. 6). As such, the CAB service is part of a broader range of organisations that seek to impart information to citizens about their rights and responsibilities within the UK state, including the education system, online services and search engines, and advice services such as NHS Direct. In addition to learning about the state, the CAB service has also sought to promote a second process of learning by the state. In order to 'exercise a responsible influence on the development of social policies', the organisation has had to facilitate a different kind of learning process as individual bureaux learn of the challenges facing their clients or of the failures of particular policies and transmit this knowledge to the Citizens Advice umbrella organisation and thence to various government departments.

The paper's secondary aim is to demonstrate how the dual pedagogic role carried out by the CAB service has been complicated by a number of tensions, which derive from its character as an organisation. These organisational traits require some explanation. First, we need to appreciate the tensions that derive from the CAB service's position within the so-called 'shadow state' (Wolch 1990), occupying as it does a place in the twilight zone between the state and civil society. Since its formation in 1939 'as an emergency service of free and unbiased information and advice *for* citizens and *by* citizens', individual CAB has been staffed by volunteers, with each bureau existing as a semi-autonomous charity (Brasnett 1964, p. 7, Citron 1989, p. 1, Richards 1989, pp. 1–2). Similarly, the National Committee of CAB and subsequently the National Association of CAB and latterly Citizens Advice, which have guided the actions of the various bureaux, have existed as independent charitable bodies. At the same time, there are strong links between the CAB service and the state at a number of different scales. Apart from a brief period during the 1950s, the majority of the grant received by the central CAB service has come from the UK state, with its largest current contributor being the Department of Business, Innovation and Skills (formerly the Department of Trade and Industry) (see Citron 1989, pp. 175–185). Similarly, individual bureaux throughout the UK have conventionally received most of their grant aid from local authorities of different kinds: county, district and town councils.

Second, the work conducted by the CAB service has also been associated with both passive and active forms of citizenship. As I have already noted, the CAB service has been crucial in enabling citizens to access their various social rights, particularly those associated with the welfare state. The majority of enquiries directed towards Citizens Advice in 2006–2007, for instance, focused on enabling clients to gain relief from issues relating to benefits and debt (Citizens Advice 2007a), and, given the current economic conditions, such queries are likely to have become even more dominant. In these terms, the creation of the CAB service can be viewed as something that has enabled the creation of passive citizens, who have been all too ready to accept the welfare rights to which they have been entitled. Conversely, the work of the CAB service has been predicated upon the contributions of volunteers within various localities (Citron 1989). Although the CAB service has sought increasingly to staff its bureaux using paid workers, the majority of advisers are still volunteers (Citizens Advice 2007a, p. 11). Through its dependence on volunteers, therefore, the CAB service reflects an active form of citizenship that exists beyond the orbit of state control.

Third, some confusion arises concerning the geographic scales over which the CAB service promotes its form of citizenship. The CAB service's main goal has been to enable the citizens of the *whole* of the UK to access their citizen rights. Although the national scale has informed the CAB service's policies and practices, it is also clear that other scales are implicated within its activities, most importantly the local scale. Citron's (1989, p. 15) history of the CAB service gives a clear account of the localised character of the organisation:

> Several official CAB directives are intended to ensure that the CAB is a service for the community by the community. The managers' handbook reminds managers that their bureau management committee members are 'your link with the community you serve'. Members should be 'well-informed about the needs of the community' and...an equal opportunity recruitment policy confirms that CAB staff should reflect the community.

In this regard, the form of citizen identity being promoted by the CAB service can be viewed as something that exists at a number of different scales and, in this way, echoes recent conceptual contributions to debates about the scales of citizenship (Yuval-Davis 1999, Painter 2000).

My goal in the following section is to position the CAB service within the literature on the emergence of a pedagogic state and the literature on the 'shadow state' (Wolch 1990). There then follow two sections in which I examine in more detail the two forms of learning which are central to Citizens Advice's role as an enabler of British citizenship. I begin by exploring the *access strategy* that has been employed by the CAB service in order to reach out to more clients. The access strategy is crucial, in this respect, because it lies at the heart of the organisation's efforts to 'help more people and [to ensure] that those in greatest need receive the most appropriate service' (Citizens Advice 2007b, p. 1). Second, I discuss the way in which the CAB service – through its *social policy* work – enables the British state, in a variety of different contexts, to learn about its citizens and about the impacts of its policies on its citizens. In doing so, I also seek to how these twin pedagogic roles have been complicated by aspects of the CAB service's organisational structure. The empirical discussion draws on documentary research and interviews conducted with employees of the CAB service.

Learning in the shadow of the state

Academics working throughout the social sciences in recent years have begun to examine the pedagogic processes associated with state governance. Although the majority of this work has engaged with state pedagogy in implicit ways, there is an increasing attempt to think through more explicitly its social and spatial aspects. The aims of the literature in this general area are numerous. First, work in this area has attempted to examine how the notion of pedagogy reflects the state's (neo-liberal) priorities. Even though it is not couched explicitly in terms of pedagogy, the research that has been conduced on the emergence of 'workfare' political agendas, for instance, seeks to understand the neo-liberal imperatives that underpin state efforts to teach citizens to act in different ways (Peck 2001). Workfare seeks to teach the unemployed to be 'employable' and increasingly job-ready through various job search training and education mechanisms (Mead 1997).

Second, researchers have also examined the different modes of learning which are associated with a pedagogic state. Workfare, for instance, is predicated upon paternalist and enforced methods of learning. Some of the more interesting contemporary research conducted in this area, however, has focused on the notion of soft or libertarian paternalism, which relates to the state's efforts to devise less formal and circumscribed ways of encouraging citizens to learn new kinds of behaviour. Referred popularly to as 'nudging' (Thaler and Sunstein 2008), the term soft paternalism draws on research in behavioural economics and behavioural psychology in order to find the most appropriate ways for the state and other organisations to promote behaviour that will be of most benefit to citizens. Recent policy developments in the UK in the fields of health (e.g. healthy eating campaigns), finance (e.g. pensions policy) and the environment (e.g. the use of public transport) testify to the increased effort being made by the state to think through the most effective ways of 'teaching' its population (Ereaut and Segnit 2006).

Finally, academics have also explicitly explored the way in which state pedagogies lead to the formation of new kinds of citizen identity. Kaplan (2006, p. 19), for instance, focuses his research on 'the pedagogical processes that constitute the relations between citizens and the state, as well as among citizens of th[e] state'. A range of pedagogic processes are employed by the state to encourage citizens to enact particular identities, including those associated with: the state education system (Bullen and Whitehead 2005, Pykett 2009), governmental publicity campaigns (see Ereaut and Segnit 2006) and a range of other voluntary and non-profit agencies (Fyfe 2005, Trudeau 2008). Of course, there is considerable scope for citizens to contest and contradict the identities that the state seeks to encourage them to learn. Pykett (2009), for instance, has shown how place-based identities complicate the kinds of identity being foisted on schoolchildren as part of the UK state's Citizenship Education programme.

Taken together, research in this area shows how the state seeks to encourage its citizens to understand their place within civil society and to learn about appropriate forms of behaviour. But in addition to enabling citizens to enact particular kinds of identity, it is evident that state pedagogies are also concerned with encouraging citizens to learn about the state itself or, as Corbridge *et al.* (2005) have put it, to 'see the state'. In effect, the state's pedagogic practices also draw attention to the way in which the state operates and the potential kinds of identity which are opened up to citizens in terms of their relation to the state. This is certainly true of the role played by the CAB service. It is an organisation that allows individuals to comprehend the character of the state and its agencies, particularly in the context of the way in which it affects their own lives. It also enables them to perform certain kinds of citizen identity with regard to the state and its organisations.

But in addition to recent work on the pedagogic state, there is, of course, a much longer academic tradition of studying the way in which the state seeks to learn about its citizens in different ways. The work of Foucault has been a source of considerable inspiration for academics working on these themes (Foucault 1998 [1976], 2007 [2004]). Two issues are of importance here. The first relates to the emergence within the modern state of territorialised bureaucracies, which have enabled the state to monitor, calculate and govern populations living and working under their control. Scott (1998), in his acclaimed *Seeing like a state*, has sought to elaborate on some of the visual and spatial techniques that have been associated with this kind of governmentality. He has drawn attention, for instance, to the process of abstraction and simplification that characterise a state's effort to make society and nature 'legible' (see also Hannah 2000). Second, Foucault's work has also drawn attention to the way in which individual members of a state's population have also taken on the responsibility of constituting themselves as governable citizens. Foucault's arguments concerning governmentality in particular show how citizens have been part of a process of monitoring their own activities on behalf of the state. Drawing on Foucault's (1990 [1984]) analysis of the care of the self, Rose (1999), for instance, has considered how different sciences of human subjectivity (particularly psychology and psychiatry) have facilitated the emergence of a modern governable subject, which self-governs itself according to the state's priorities and needs.

The significance of an organisation such as the CAB service, I would argue, is that it draws together these two pedagogic processes. As I will show in the following section, the CAB service is involved in making the UK state more legible to its citizens and contributes to the enactment of its clients' citizen identities. At the same time, it is an organisation that is part of the 'knowledge-acquisition apparatus' (Latour 2007, p. 4) of the UK state and enables it to learn about – or monitor – the effects of its policies on the UK population. As such, the twin pedagogic processes associated with the CAB service illustrates what Trudeau (2008, p. 685) refers to as the 'multiple directionalities [that are] involved in government-non-profit relationships'.

As noted in the introduction, part of the significance of the CAB service is the fact that it has played this dual pedagogic role as part of the 'shadow state' (Wolch 1990). The term 'shadow state' has become popular within the social sciences as a term used to refer to all voluntary, non-profit or third sector organisations. Popularised by Wolch (1990, p. xvi), the term specifically refers to the:

> para-state apparatus comprised of multiple voluntary sector organizations, administered outside of traditional democratic politics and charged with major collective service responsibilities previously shouldered by the public sector, yet remaining within the purview of state control.

There has been an increase in the significance of the shadow state in the UK in recent years. Fyfe (2005, p. 537), for instance, has shown how there has been an emphasis in the UK since the 1990s on a notion of 'neo-communitarianism' as a means of facilitating 'economic development and social cohesion (see also Jessop 2002). The election of the Labour government in 1997 and its initial emphasis on 'third-way politics' further invigorated the role to be played by the voluntary sector within UK governance (Kendall 2000). Some academics have noted the potential role that can be played by the third sector in leading to more progressive forms of politics. Brown *et al.* (2000, p. 57), for instance, argue that voluntary organisations can lead to the democratisation of politics. Others have sounded a more cautious note. Wolch (1990, p. 15), for instance, has argued that 'the increasing importance of state funding for many voluntary organisations has been accompanied by deepening penetration by the state into voluntary group organisation, management and goals'. Similarly, Trudeau (2008) has recently shown with regard to non-profit organisations working with immigrants in the US that the unequal power relationships between government agencies and voluntary organisations – not least in relation to funding – have the potential to undermine the latter's scope for promoting progressive forms of politics.

Two other important aspects of work on the 'shadow state' are worth stressing. The first is the emphasis that has been placed within this literature on the potential for voluntary and non-profit organisations to encourage more active forms of citizenship (e.g. Brown 1997). The organisation of 'neighbourhood watch' schemes that seek to guard against crime, community initiatives that attempt to provide or support education, social housing and welfare provision outside the state sector and the promotion of community-led action for economic regeneration (e.g. Kearns 1995, Edwards 1998), for example, all testify to the increasing significance of active forms of citizenship within the voluntary sector in the UK. The significance of the CAB service, I would argue, is that it has been predicated as an organisation on the long-term commitment to active citizenship displayed by its volunteers. At the same time, it has traditionally been involved in reproducing quite passive forms of citizenship for its clients as the recipients of benefits associated with the welfare state. Recent developments within the organisation, however, show how it has sought to extend the benefits of more active forms of citizenship to its clientele. I discuss these developments in the following sections.

Second, work on the 'shadow state' has examined the way in which it has been associated with a re-scaling of governance from the national scale to the local scale. There is a politics associated with this re-scaling (Swyngedouw 2003) as national governments seek to absolve responsibility for societal problems whose resolution becomes a matter for voluntary organisations operating within particular localities. For instance, Trudeau (2008, p. 685) has argued that voluntary organisations have been 'instrumental in state efforts in the US to restructure the social welfare system in a way that does not provoke crises of legitimacy'. If, as Marston and Mitchell (2004, p. 110) have maintained, 'geographical scale is centrally implicated in producing and sustaining citizenship formations', then the re-scaling of state governance that has been associated with the increased significance of voluntary sector organisations in recent years has the potential to lead to different scalar enactments of citizen identities by volunteers and clients alike.

The aims of the following two sections are to illustrate empirically the significance of these conceptual debates. As stated in the introduction, my main aim is to demonstrate the twin pedagogic process associated with the CAB service – learning about and by the state. Within this broad aim, I also seek to show how the CAB service's status as an organisation within the 'shadow state' impinges on this twin process of learning. Brief conclusions then follow.

Learning about the state: the CAB service's access strategy

The new access strategy lies at the heart of the CAB service's attempts to ensure that clients learn of remedies to the various problems that they face. It was adopted in 2005 as what one worker described as the organisation's 'number one priority'. Its current aim is to 'help more people and [to ensure] that those in greatest need receive the most appropriate service' (Citizens Advice 2007b, p. 1).[2] A number of different groups and places have been targeted, which are said to have been poorly served – in a relative sense – by the organisation in the past. The disadvantaged groups initiatives, for instance, have focused on increasing the use made of the CAB service by young people, prisoners and young offenders, rural dwellers and workers, migrants and settlers, gypsies and travellers, and deaf people (www.cablink.org.uk, accessed on 17 September 2008).

The access strategy represents for the CAB service a relatively novel approach to increasing access to knowledge about the state and its services. Whereas discussions in the organisation in the past have centred around physical access to bureaux, and thence to knowledge (e.g. Blacksell et al. 2007), the current access strategy, according to one interviewee, has 'moved away from saying that there has to be a bureau in every location' and centres more on the need to create a 'service in which people can contact a bureau or can contact an advice service and get advice at an appropriate level, quickly and easily'. What this means, in effect, is that clients are being asked to access knowledge (a) from a variety of advice organisations and (b) in more novel and unconventional ways.

For the remaining paragraphs of this section, I want to concentrate on two emerging trends within the access strategy, which are transforming the way in which the CAB service reaches out to its client base. First, there is an increasing use of new technologies – email, an internet advice service and, in future, a single telephone number for the CAB service – which are leading to new modes and scales of learning for the organisation's clients. Second, there is an additional emphasis on developing more active forms of learning among the CAB service's clients. The clearest instance of such a shift lies in the context of the 'Gateway Assessment Approach', which has become increasingly popular in bureaux in recent years.

New technologies and new forms of learning

The CAB service, for a number of years, has sought to develop the use of electronic means of accessing its services. For instance, it launched Advice Guide, its information and advice website, in 1999. The aim of the website is to act as 'the main public information service of

Citizens Advice, providing people with round-the-clock access to CAB information on their rights – including benefits, housing and employment, and on debt, consumer and legal issues' (www.adviceguide.org.uk, accessed 18 September 2008). This trend towards the use of non-traditional ways of accessing information was to receive further impetus with the implementation of the access strategy. The first access strategy Newsletter, published in August 2007, for instance, made clear that the CAB service was increasingly going to rely in coming years on using new technologies as a way of increasing the number of clients that it helped. Two of its three objectives stated as such, when it was maintained that the organisation should: 'work towards establishing a single telephone number for the CAB service, and; create an electronic advice service' (Citizens Advice 2007b, p. 1). The CAB service has moved forward with these plans. The single telephone number service, for instance, is currently being piloted and it is hoped that it will be launched as a bilingual Wales-wide service in 2009, before being rolled out in England in 2010 (interview). In shifting to using these new technologies, it has been argued that the CAB service can act as an important contributor to the e-government agenda (OPM 2002, p. vi).

The use of these technologies is significant, given the concerns of this paper, for two main reasons. First of all, it is clear that the development of these new technologies is leading to a re-scaling of sites of learning, as localised sites of learning – in other words, forms of learning that would have taken place within individual bureaux – are gradually being replaced by sites of learning which exist at the national scale. This is a potentially significant shift. It is a re-scaling that is, to a large extent, changing the ethos of the CAB service. As noted in the introduction to this paper, the original aim of the organisation was to act as a 'service for the community by the community' (Citron 1989, p. 15). And yet, as a highly placed individual within Citizens Advice said, the creation of new national ways of accessing information has the potential to undermine the link between bureaux and the communities that they serve. Of course, there is a broader conceptual significance to such a shift because it indicates the fluid scalar character of certain voluntary organisations. Although much has been made in the literature on the 'shadow state' concerning the increased emphasis within the contemporary state on using voluntary services that are largely localised in character (Kearns 1995, Edwards 1998), there is a suggestion that the use of new technologies of learning with the CAB service is actually reconfiguring sites of learning – and related sites of citizenship formation – away from the local to the national scale.

The second significant aspect of the use of new technologies is the fact that is associated with an attempt to promote a more active form of learning among its clients. The evidence for this shift comes most clearly in the material provided to explain the purpose of the Advice Guide website:

> We aim to empower people by providing them with the information they need to solve their own problems and to signpost them to appropriate advice when necessary. Advice Guide helps you to have a better understanding of your rights and entitlements, and also to take the first steps in resolving your problems (www.adviceguide.org.uk, accessed on 18 September 2008).

The emphasis placed on encouraging clients to become more active in their association with the CAB service is apparent in the above quote. In addition to being an organisation that has been based in large part on the commitment of a 'community of service providers' (Ilcan and Basok 2004); therefore, there is an emerging sense that the organisation is seeking to promote forms of active citizenship among its clientele. We witness here the way in which the sphere of active citizenship is extending outwards from a voluntary organisation into the society that it seeks to govern. This shift has also been apparent in the other major development that has taken place in the context of the organisation's access strategy; namely the Gateway Assessment Approach.

The Gateway Assessment Approach to accessing information

The Gateway Assessment Approach was advocated by the access strategy team in their first newsletter in August 2007 (Citizens Advice 2007b). The approach is similar to that of triage, in which clients' needs are initially assessed before being graded into different degrees of seriousness. Underlying this shift is an opinion that 'there are some people who can resolve their own problems providing they have access to quality-assured information' (ibid., p. 2). Three different categories of clients are identified in this approach, which require different methods of learning and teaching:

> There are some people who are able to resolve their own problems provided that key elements of information are identified and/or highlighted (assisted information);
>
> There are some people who are able to resolve their own problems following detailed advice or a brief intervention on their behalf (generalist advice);
>
> There are some people, those in greatest need, who at a particular point in their lives require a skilled adviser to act on their behalf (casework) (ibid).

What is significant in the above quote, of course, is that there is almost a presumption in this approach that clients, on the whole, have the ability to solve their own problems and, indeed, that they should be encouraged to do so. Even those clients who are in 'greatest need' are assumed to be in that situation for short periods – 'at a particular point in their lives'.

The adoption of the Gateway Assessment Approach by bureaux has increased gradually. In 2007, approximately 25% of bureaux had adopted some sort of Gateway Assessment Approach (ibid). Some initial resistance was demonstrated by CAB service staff towards the approach with some maintaining that it compromised their ability to identify fully the problems facing clients. Citizens Advice, nonetheless, following a period of consultation, has since made the approach mandatory and expect all bureaux to employ the system by October 2010.

Two main issues were identified by an individual involved in the access strategy as reasons for the adoption of the Gateway Assessment Approach. First of all, there was a clear need to increase the number of people being helped by the CAB service and the Gateway Assessment Approach was viewed as a means of increasing the efficiency of bureaux. An individual involved in promoting the approach stated that 'it really has made a difference. We're seeing fifty per cent more people . . . and waiting times have been reduced by fifty per cent'. There is a second perceived benefit arising from the adoption of the Gateway Assessment Approach, namely the way in which it seeks to enable individuals to learn themselves about their own rights and to find ways of solving their own problems. Individuals involved in promoting the approach viewed it as an important way of encouraging their clients to be more 'active' in resolving their own problems, as the following quote makes clear:

> There is a broader benefit. Our view is that if you do something for someone then [pause] this sounds terribly patronising, then they won't take responsibility for the position they're in. You know, 'give me all of that, don't worry, I'll sort it out for you'. They're much more likely to carry things through if they've been involved in the process themselves.

The above quote demonstrates the broader value of the Gateway Assessment Approach in promoting more client-centred forms of learning and, through that, more active forms of citizenship among the CAB service's clients. Indeed, clients are increasingly been encouraged to act not merely as passive citizens whose identities are configured by a remote and faceless state but rather as active citizens who play a key role in enacting their own citizen identities. In this way, the CAB service's clients may well be contributing to a fluid and contested process of citizenship formation, as described by Marston and Mitchell (2004, p. 110):

> Citizenship is not a monolithic social category that is determined by state edict and endures unchanged through time and across place. It is, instead, an actively created and negotiated status that is shifted and remodeled in response to large and small economic, social and cultural processes and movements.

The CAB service, through its access strategy, can be viewed as an organisation that is enabling such a process. Its contribution is significant, moreover, because it is targeted at enabling those individuals and groups that lie at the margins of the state's citizenship project to engage in more proactive ways in the process of citizenship formation (Isin 2002, Isin and Nielsen 2008).

Learning by the state: the social policy work of the CAB service

My aim in this section is to discuss empirically the way in which the CAB service – through its *social policy* work – enables the British state, in a variety of different contexts, to learn about its citizens and about the impacts of its policies on its citizens. As noted in the introduction, the CAB service (Citizens Advice 2007a, p. 3) has always attempted to 'exercise a responsible influence on the development of social policies and services both locally and nationally'. The key processes of learning that facilitate this aim are the ones by which individual bureaux learn of the problems facing their clients, how this information is fed up into the umbrella body of Citizens Advice and how this information is then used as a means of criticising and influencing state policies, whether at the national, regional or local scale.

The kinds of policies targeted by the CAB service as part of its work are wide ranging. A trawl through the Social Policy Bulletins published by the organisation over the vast year indicates a broad range of social policy agendas, which fall within its purview, such as providing evidence for the office of fair trading so that it could prosecute a test case against banks concerning the excessive use of bank charges (Citizens Advice 2007c, p. 11) and working with Age Concern in order to lobby the Department for Business, Enterprise and Regulatory Reform to change the laws on doorstep selling (Citizens Advice 2007d, p. 4).

I want to draw attention to four issues regarding the social policy work conducted by the CAB service. First, and in general terms, we need to appreciate how the CAB service's social policy work is undergirded by a process of learning. Various officials that I interviewed were keen to stress that the social policy work conducted by the CAB service was wholly dependent upon the evidence that it was able to collect from its clients. Research on Cyngor ar Bopeth – the semi-devolved branch of the CAB service in Wales – for instance, has shown that the plentiful sources of evidence available to Cyngor ar Bopeth have contributed directly to its effectiveness in influencing the policy agenda within Wales (Jones forthcoming). An individual involved in Cyngor ar Bopeth's social policy work in Wales, in this respect, argued that 'we know what we're talking about'. A Citizens Advice worker developed this theme when he argued that the CAB service's emphasis on using evidence gleaned through its bureaux brought an additional credibility to the organisation, especially when compared with other lobbying or campaigning groups. For this individual, the CAB service's insistence on basing its social policy work on evidence was its 'unique selling point'.

Second, there is an interesting scalar relationship that underpins the CAB service's social policy work. Material about the various clients seen in bureaux has, over the long term, been communicated to Citizens Advice so that it, in turn, can use it as a source of information both for monitoring the types of enquiry being brought to bureaux and for conducting policy campaigns. But in addition to this regular collection of qualitative information from clients, Citizens Advice also seeks to garner from bureaux information about key issues that they want to explore in more detail. Over two hundred bureaux responded to surveys in November 2006 and May 2007, for instance, which sought to chart the impact of the changing working practices of Jobcentre Plus on vulnerable individuals (Citizens Advice 2007c, p. 1). This is part of a broader pattern, as the following quote from an individual involved in the CAB service's social policy work makes clear:

> When we're studying something in particular or we may well have got a good idea from the evidence that's come in and the case records of what sort of issues but if we're wanting a bit more of a nuanced picture, then we will either do a ten per cent sample or approach a bureau where we know they deal a lot with that particular issue.

The information collected from bureaux is then used to inform national policy work in a variety of different contexts; through publications, seminars, policy fora and direct lobbying. Connections are made with government departments 'across the board' but most especially with the Department of Work and Pensions, the Home Office, Ministry of Justice and the Department of Health. In addition, the CAB service seeks to influence other national bodies that are part of the 'shadow state', such as the Council of Mortgage Lenders and the British Banking Association. The CAB service, therefore, is involved in ensuring that a variety of different organisations – governmental, quasi-governmental and private – learn about the impacts that their policies have on individuals.

And yet, national campaigns are never merely that. The CAB service also enrols local bureaux in order to promote a multi-pronged social policy campaign. The value of this coordinated approach between local bureaux and the national umbrella organisation was explained by one worker:

> Yes, perhaps if I give you an example. There's a proposal at the moment to change some benefit rules around the ability to back-date a benefit that you are entitled to claim . . . As well as lobbying the government department nationally . . . what we're asking bureaux to do – and we've provided them with a model letter and so on – is to lobby their MP and ask the MPs to lobby the Minister. And then you get a groundswell impact as well as a direct one. So we're working at the national level with the Department but also getting bureaux to feed it through their MP and we're getting a good influence that way.

This multi-pronged approach speaks of a more fluid connection between the national umbrella organisation of Citizens Advice and individual bureaux; in terms of the nature of the policy work that they conduct and with regard to the routes through which the state learns about various social policy issues. In broader terms, such evidence testifies to a sophisticated use of scalar connections by the CAB service as it seeks to promote a groundswell of support in favour of policy reforms (cf. Trudeau 2008).

The third issue echoes some of the themes raised in the previous section. A greater emphasis has been placed in recent years on encouraging clients to contribute to social policy campaigns, as made clear in the following quote:

> What we're increasingly trying to get bureaux to do is to tell clients about the campaigning work that we're doing, get their interest and engagement in that. For one thing we get better evidence if they understand what we're doing and why we're doing it, they tell us more of what we need to know. But also we think there are opportunities for them to engage in the campaign too.

Clients are recruited to this work in a variety of ways. For instance, they are asked to explain their situation on postcards, which are placed in bureaux waiting rooms. These life stories can then be used as snapshots of the problems facing individual clients. In addition, posters have been daubed on waiting room walls, which provide further information to clients about the CAB service's role in influencing social policy agendas. The significance of this development is evident. It shows the way in which clients themselves are being enrolled into the process of teaching the state about the problems that they face. In more conceptual terms, it is redolent of a process outlined by Chatterjee (2006) in which a more popular form of politics – practiced by 'ordinary' citizens – can reach back and influence the formal politics that is associated with the state.

Finally, one needs to realise the way in which the CAB service's success within its social policy campaigns can problematise its status as an independent voluntary organisation. Concerns have been raised recently, for instance, about the character of the relationship between the CAB service and the state and its potential to influence the way in which the service is perceived by its clients as well as by the public. An Office for Public Management review of the CAB service made this point clear when it stated that

> the service faces a dilemma in its interface with government...There are increasing opportunities and pressures from government for more input from the service. This is an opportunity to help clients. But in the field of social policy there is a danger that the service may become too closely associated with the policies it has helped to shape (OPM 2002, p. vi).

The report proceeds to argue that, unless properly managed, the service's interface with government has the potential to 'compromise the independence of the service and by so doing lessen its value to both clients and government' (ibid). The potentially problematic relationships between the CAB service and the UK state is symptomatic of a broader tension than can exist between voluntary organisations and the states within which they operate. Wolch (1990, p. 15) has argued that the funding relationships between states and voluntary organisations have the potential to problematise the latter's status. The evidence from the CAB service demonstrates that even the existence of a successful dialogue between such an organisation and the state can lead to the development of an equally problematic relationship between the two, which needs to be managed carefully.

Conclusions

My aim in this chapter has been to examine the way in which the CAB service has played a significant role in forming or enabling citizen identities in the UK. Different processes of learning have been key to this broader agenda. The organisation was originally formed as a way of enabling individuals to learn about their place within the state and most notably their citizen rights. The aim of enabling individuals to learn about the state has continued to this day. Recent initiatives with regard to the organisation's access strategy show that such concerns, although still present, are evolving in different ways. Key here has been the development of new technologies and mechanisms of accessing information about the state. In this regard, although the provision of information and advice may well still remain a 'fourth right of citizenship' (NCC 1977), it is clear that the emergence of different ways of gaining information and advice may well be re-configuring the social and spatial forms that that citizenship takes; whether through the emergence of more active citizen learners and citizen learners who's geographical frame of reference is becoming increasingly divorced from the locality within which they are based.

At the same time, the CAB service has also enabled the state to learn about the impacts of its policies on its citizens. Its long-term emphasis on collecting information about its clients has proved to be an invaluable source of evidence and a sign of its trustworthiness as a contributor to policy debates. Interesting aspects of this work include its multi-scalarity – with individual clients, local bureaux, county-wide coalitions of bureaux and the national umbrella organisation combining to affect policy change – and the increasing emphasis being placed on enrolling clients into social policy campaigns. But, although the

CAB service can be viewed as part of the UK state's efforts to make its society more governable or 'legible', it is possible that the form of legibility promoted by the CAB service is different from the one described by Scott (1998). Rather than being associated with a form of legibility that is based upon abstraction and simplification, the CAB service in fact makes much of its use of raw data – derived from client case notes – as a means of informing its policy campaigns. In addition, the CAB service is at pains to emphasise that its efforts to make British society more legible to the state are driven, first and foremost, by its commitments to its clients rather than by its commitment to the state.

I have treated these two forms of learning – about and by the state – separately in this paper, but there is a strong argument that we need to think about them in iterative and recursive ways. In empirical terms, it is the individual working within local bureaux that lies at the fulcrum of this two-way process; as the provider of information about the state to individual clients and the collector of information about individual clients that can be used by the CAB service and, thereby, by the state. The following quote from an individual involved in the CAB service's social policy work alludes to the significance of this two-way process: 'this is the real selling point for us when we're trying to interest bureaux with this [social policy] side of the work. You may be able to help that individual client but if we're able to get a policy change then you may be helping hundreds of thousands of people.' In more conceptual terms, the themes discussed in this paper suggest that there may be scope to examine the conceptual connections that exist between these twin pedagogic processes. There is a need, in this way, to reconcile the two different kinds of visualities and learning that are alluded to in Corbridge *et al.*'s (2006) *Seeing the state* and Scott's (1998) *Seeing like a state*.

What is significant about the CAB service, of course, is the fact that it has carried out this dual pedagogic role in the shadow of the state. The empirical discussion highlighted the way in which the close association that exists between the CAB service and the UK state has led to certain questions being asked about the former's independence and echoes similar statements that have been made concerning voluntary organisations in the US (e.g. Wolch 1990, Trudeau 2008, p. 685). Two other themes, I would argue, are of significance to these broader debates about the 'shadow state'. First, the empirical discussion illustrated the potential for voluntary organisations to encourage the extension of active forms of citizenship into the populations that they serve. In addition to being manifestations of an active citizenship themselves, voluntary organisations can also engender similar identities among their clientele. The second issue relates to the complex scalar trajectories associated with voluntary associations. Although there has been a traditional connection in many instances between voluntary organisations and the local scale (Kearns 1995) – and certainly this was the case for the CAB service for much of its history – it is clear that recent developments within this organisation have the potential to weaken the connection between the CAB service and local communities. Such developments illustrate how the emergence of new modes and sites of learning may well impact on the different kinds of citizen identities being configured by the CAB service, and it is likely that these will continue to evolve in the future.

Acknowledgement

I am grateful to the British Academy for funding this research.

Notes

1. The CAB service possesses a complex organisational structure and, thus, some terminological explanation is required at the outset. A single bureau will be referred to as a Citizens' Advice Bureau (CAB); the Citizens' Advice Bureau as a whole will be referred to as the CAB service; the umbrella organisation for the CAB service will be referred to as Citizens Advice.

2. There is a suggestion that the CAB service's Access Strategy is also being promoted as a way of saving money, as individuals are being asked to solve their own problems and access information from non-peopled sources, such as the Advice Guide website. The interviewees were unwilling to confirm such suggestions.

References

Blacksell, M., Clark, A., Economides, K. and Watkins, C., 2007. Citizens advice bureaux: problems of an emerging service in rural areas. *Social policy and administration*, 24 (2), 212–225.

Brasnett, M.E., 1964. *The story of the citizens' advice bureaux*. London: National Council of Social Service.

Brown, M., 1997. *Replacing citizenship: AIDS activism and radical democracy*. New York: Guilford Press.

Brown, K., Kenny, S., Turner, B. and Prince, J., 2000. *Rhetorics of welfare: uncertainty, choice and voluntary associations*. London: Macmillan.

Bullen, A. and Whitehead, M., 2005. Negotiating the networks of space, time and substance: a geographical perspective on the sustainable citizen. *Citizenship studies*, 9 (5), 499–516.

Chatterjee, P., 2006. *The politics of the governed: reflections on popular politics in most of the world*. New York: Columbia University Press.

Citizens Advice, 2007a. *Citizens advice: annual report and accounts, 2006–2007*. London: Citizens Advice.

Citizens Advice, 2007b. *Citizens advice access strategy newsletter, August 2007*. London: Citizens Advice.

Citizens Advice, 2007c. *Citizens advice social policy bulletin, August 2007*. London: Citizens Advice.

Citizens Advice, 2007d. *Citizens advice social policy bulletin, October 2007*. London: Citizens Advice.

Citron, J., 1989. *The citizens advice bureaux: for the community by the community*. London: Pluto Press.

Corbridge, S., Williams, G., Srivastava, M. and Véron, R., 2005. *Seeing the state: governance and governmentality in India*. Cambridge: Cambridge University Press.

Edwards, B., 1998. Charting the discourse of community action: perspectives from practice in rural Wales. *Journal of rural studies*, 14 (1), 63–78.

Ereaut, G. and Segnit, N., 2006. *Warm words: how are we telling the climate story and can we tell it better?* London: Institute for Public Policy Research.

Foucault, M., 1990 [1984]. *The care of the self: the history of sexuality volume 3*. Trans. R. Hurley. London: Penguin.

Foucault, M., 1998 [1976]. *The will to knowledge: the history of sexuality volume 1*. Trans. R. Hurley. London: Penguin.

Foucault, M., 2007 [2004]. *Security, territory, and population – lectures at the collège de France 1977–1978*, ed. M. Senellart and Trans. G. Burchell. Basingstoke: Palgrave Macmillan.

Fyfe, N., 2005. Making space for "neo-communitarianism"? The third sector, state and civil society in the UK. *Antipode*, 37 (3), 536–557.

Hannah, M., 2000. *Governmentality and the mastery of territory in nineteenth-century America*. Cambridge: Cambridge University Press.

Ilcan, S. and Basok, T., 2004. Community government: voluntary agencies, social justice and the responsibilization of citizens. *Citizenship studies*, 8 (2), 129–144.

Isin, E., 2002. *Being political: genealogies of citizenship*. Minneapolis, MA: University of Minnesota Press.

Isin, E. and Nielsen, G.M., eds, 2008. *Acts of citizenship*. London: Zed Books.

Jessop, B., 2002. Liberalism, neoliberalism and urban governance: a state-theoretical perspective. *Antipode*, 34 (3), 452–472.

Jones, R., forthcoming. Making up the Welsh citizen: Wales and the citizens advice bureau. *Transactions of the honourable society of the Cymmrodorion*.

Kaplan, S., 2006. *The pedagogical state: education and the politics of national culture in post-1980 Turkey*. Stanford: Stanford University Press.

Kearns, A., 1995. Active citizenship and local governance: political and geographical dimensions. *Political geography*, 14 (2), 155–175.

Kendall, J., 2000. The mainstreaming of the third sector into public policy in England in the late 1990s: whys and wherefores. *Policy and politics*, 28 (4), 541–562.

Latour, B., 2007. How to think like a state. Lecture delivered the 22nd of November 2007 at the occasion of the anniversary of the WRR in the presence of Queen Beatrix of The Netherlands. Available from: http://www.bruno-latour.fr/poparticles/poparticle/P-133-LA%20HAYE-QUEEN.pdf

Marshall, T.H., 1950. *Citizenship and social class*. Cambridge: Cambridge University Press.

Marston, S.A. and Mitchell, K., 2004. Citizens and the state: citizenship formations in space and time. *In*: C. Barnett and M. Low, eds. *Spaces of democracy: geographical perspectives on citizenship, participation and representation*. London: Sage, 93–112.

Mead, L., ed., 1997. *The new paternalism: supervisory approaches to poverty*. Washington: Brookings Institute Press.

NCC, 1977. *The fourth right of citizenship: a review of local advice services*. London: National Consumer Council.

OPM, 2002. *Quinquennial review of the National Association of Citizen's Advice Bureaux: report for the Department of Trade and Industry*. London: Office for Public Management.

Painter, J., 2000. Multilevel citizenship, identity and regions in contemporary Europe. *In*: J. Anderson, ed. *Transnational democracy: political spaces and border crossings*. London: Routledge, 93–110.

Peck, J., 2001. *Workfare states*. New York: Guilford Press.

Pykett, J., 2009. Making citizens in the classroom: an urban geography of citizenship education? *Urban studies*, 46 (4), 803–823.

Richards, J., 1989. *Inform, advice and support: fifty years of the Citizens Advice Bureau*. Cambridge: Lutterworth Press.

Rose, N., 1999. *Governing the soul: the shaping of the private self*. London: Free Association Books.

Scott, J.C., 1998. *Seeing like a state: how certain schemes to improve the human condition have failed*. New Haven: Yale University Press.

Swyngedouw, E., 2003. Scaled geographies: nature, place and the contested politics of scale. *In*: E. Sheppard and B. McMaster, eds. *Scale and geographic inquiry: nature, society and method*. Oxford: Blackwell, 129–153.

Thaler, R.H. and Sunstein, C.R., 2008. *Nudge. Improving decisions about health, wealth and happiness*. London: Yale University Press.

Trudeau, D., 2008. Towards a relational view of the shadow state. *Political geography*, 27 (6), 669–690.

Wolch, J., 1990. *The shadow state: government and voluntary sector in transition*. New York: The Foundation Center.

Yuval-Davis, N., 1999. The multi-layered citizen: citizenship at the age of 'glocalization'. *International feminist journal of politics*, 1 (2), 119–136.

The third level of US welfare reform: governmentality under neoliberal paternalism

Sanford F. Schram[a], Joe Soss[b1], Linda Houser[c2] and Richard C. Fording[d3]

[a]Graduate School of Social Work and Social Research, Bryn Mawr College, Bryn Mawr, PA, USA; [b]Department of Political Science, Hubert H. Humphrey Institute of Public Affairs, University of Minnesota, Minneapolis, MN, USA; [c]School of Management and Labor Relations and The Center for Women and Work, Rutgers University, New Brunswick, NJ, USA; [d]Department of Political Science, Martin School of Public Policy and Administration, University of Kentucky, Lexington, KY, USA

US welfare reform involves more than dramatic caseload reductions and a shift from cash assistance to services. Its operations today reflect significant changes in poverty governance as a disciplinary regime. Welfare policy has been transformed by the rise of a 'new paternalism' that is deeply entwined with the globally ascendant market-centered philosophy of 'neoliberalism.' In this paper, we explain how 'governance' under this new system enacts a particular logic of 'governmentality' in which the state acts through nonprofit and for-profit agents to advance the project of 'governing mentalities' in low-income target populations. In this system, diverse policy tools are deployed to produce a form of self-discipline that is consonant with the need for compliant low-wage workers in a globalizing economy. Relying on field interviews of case managers in the state of Florida, our analysis follows a chain of disciplinary relationships which runs from the national government through states, down to local contract agencies, and finally to frontline workers and clients. We highlight how performance management systems function to discipline private provider agencies and welfare case workers. Likewise, we explain how sanctions (financial penalties for client noncompliance) figure prominently in such systems as tools deployed to teach self-discipline to recipients. Our field research, however, shows that the new system of poverty governance is one that is fraught with its own tensions and contradictions. We conclude by considering whether poverty governance today relates to what is being called the 'pedagogical state.'

Welfare programs for low-income Americans have changed dramatically over the last two decades. Their operations today reflect significant shifts in the logic of poverty governance as a disciplinary regime. Of course, US welfare programs have always been characterized by a reformative emphasis on 'improving poor people' by teaching them appropriate behaviors (Katz 1997). As they have distributed aid, they have functioned as mechanisms for 'regulating the poor' as a potential threat to the social order (Piven and Cloward 1971). Indeed, the degrading conditions and stigma associated with welfare have never been incidental to the purposes of public aid; they have served as an object lesson, instructing low-income populations that even the meanest wages and work conditions are better than the shameful status of the 'welfare poor.'

In the 1960s and 1970s, welfare rights victories in the United States forced a partial but significant attenuation of these dynamics. Access to public aid increased and, until the mid-1990s, welfare caseloads persisted at relatively high levels. Recipients came to have quasi-entitlement rights to assistance, and the Aid to Families with Dependent Children (AFDC) program operated primarily to provide minimal amounts of cash assistance to needy families with children (mostly headed by lone mothers). From the mid-1970s onward, however, the AFDC program was a politically vulnerable policy that offered only meager relief from poverty and labor-market pressures. Benefits were set at low levels and allowed to decline in all states; recipients were treated with suspicion; and due-process protections served as little more than a weak stand-in for substantive rights grounded in citizenship status. Welfare came to be perceived as a 'black program' as nonwhites became over-represented on the AFDC rolls and in media stories about poverty (Quadagno 1999, Gilens 1999). Calls to 'reform' welfare rose steadily and ultimately came to fruition in 1996, when President Bill Clinton signed the Republican-drafted Personal Responsibility and Work Opportunity Reconciliation Act (PRWORA).

The new law imposed a tough new regime for welfare recipients that formalized and nationalized changes that had been developing in the states for some time. Federal lawmakers abolished AFDC and replaced it with Temporary Assistance for Needy Families (TANF), a program that gives each state a fixed block grant to provide aid to poor families in a manner focused on moving adult recipients from welfare to work. The new program substantially reduced access to cash assistance and placed far greater emphasis on enforcing behaviors deemed to be 'civic obligations'. Receipt of aid was now subject to time limits and conditioned on compliance with work requirements. Sanctions were adopted in all states to ensure that recipients would suffer financial penalties if they failed to follow the 'individual responsibility plans' that charted their course to employment.

Welfare was now welfare-to-work, charged with the task of regimenting recipients into the low-wage labor markets of a globalizing economy. To achieve this objective, welfare programs became more focused on practices designed to discipline the poor, placing a lower priority on the goals of redistributing income or helping parents meet the basic needs of their families. In the state of Florida, where we have conducted an intensive study of the Welfare Transition (WT) program, poverty alleviation is not even considered an official policy goal. Instead, WT is designed to help 'people go from welfare to work' in a manner that 'ensures that Florida's businesses can hire the well-trained workers they need'. Toward this end, the old practice of 'telling the poor what to do' is now resurgent in welfare programs (Mead 1998); however, its operation reflects a neoliberal paternalist rationality that is far more than a mere return to the past.

Five key shifts have converged to reorient disciplinary practice in poverty governance today:

(1) Under 'the new paternalism,' welfare provision has adopted a more overt and muscular approach to using direction, surveillance, instruction, and penalty as therapeutic tools for transforming the subjectivities of the poor (Mead 1997).

(2) Under neoliberalism, market roles have been elevated as the most essential civic roles; efforts to groom welfare recipients as job-ready workers have been recast as equivalent to – and necessary for – the production of subjects who can adequately fulfill caregiving obligations and civic responsibilities (Korteweg 2003).

(3) Welfare programs have been restructured to operate according to market logics, to cultivate market rationalities in service providers and aid recipients, and to serve as arenas of labor commodification that are continuous with local markets (Krinsky 2007).

(4) Administration and management systems have been redesigned to enhance the scope of lower-level discretion and, as a corollary, to ensure that social-service personnel (embedded in new contractual and performance-based systems) will be self-disciplined in their uses of discretion (Soss *et al.* 2011).

(5) Welfare systems have become more thoroughly entwined with carceral systems, and their disciplinary operations have shifted toward a more penal logic characteristic of the 'culture of control' in an 'era of mass incarceration' (Gustafson 2009, Wacquant 2009).

In what follows, we suggest that the neoliberal disciplinary project functions as a 'third level' of welfare reform, driving but often obscured by two more visible levels of system change: caseload reduction and the shift from cash assistance to services. The disciplinary project we describe weds the normative enforcement of the new paternalism (Mead 1997) to the market rationality of neoliberalism (Brown 2003, 2006) and is implemented through the organizational reforms associated with the 'new public management' (Kettl 2005). The new organizational forms reflect a turn toward modes of 'governance' (Bevir 2007) that enact governmental power in a more 'fluid and cooperative fashion' via private institutions and market mechanisms (Walters 2004). The new system operates as a regime of 'governmentality,' in the sense that Foucault (1991) uses this term: it is a configuration of practical techniques oriented toward the 'conduct of conduct'; it pursues state purposes through the promotion of 'governing mentalities' at multiple levels of the system (Campbell 2000); and it operates as a form of productive power, cultivating forms of self-discipline that lead actors to 'freely' adhere to normative standards for acceptable behavior (Dean 1999).

Our analysis explores the sources and operations of disciplinary practice under contemporary welfare reform. To do so, we draw on field research investigating the systems that structure practice for frontline workers and welfare clients. Our interviews illuminate both the power and the limits of new administrative systems to cultivate self-discipline among case workers and move recipients from welfare to work. At the same time, we offer an empirical analysis of welfare sanctions as instruments that are explicitly used to discipline clients – both in the shallow sense of one actor punishing another for a violation and in the deeper Foucauldian sense described above. We conclude by reflecting on the future prospects of poverty governance in relation to what some are calling the 'pedagogical state' (Pykett 2009).

Neoliberal poverty governance in an age of globalization

To understand contemporary poverty governance in the United States, one must locate it within broader changes to governance and citizenship in an age of globalization (Morgen and Gonzales 2008). Welfare operations in the United States today reflect what Sassen (2006) refers to as a general shift away from the 'national capitalist state' and toward the 'global capitalist state' that has emerged under contemporary globalization. Although this development can easily be overstated as a contrast of opposites, the general direction of change is from efforts to ameliorate the inequalities of capitalism and shield citizens from market pressures toward uses of policy that actively maximize integration into the global economy and 'acceptance of the verdict of the marketplace' (Mead 1986, p. 87).

The guiding spirit of this transformation has been neoliberalism, a form of market fundamentalism that may be usefully contrasted with *laissez faire* (Brown 2003, 2006). Under the familiar logic of *laissez faire* ideology, markets are conceptualized as natural spaces, and pro-market agendas focus on bounding and reducing the interventions of the state. Market actors emerge and thrive when human nature is freed from the distortions of state action and allowed to flourish in market settings. By contrast, neoliberal ideology emphasizes the constructive and intentional application of market principles to diverse social relations that extend beyond economic markets. Its proponents seek, not to limit the state, but to restructure the state so that it operates according to market logics, becomes more reliant on market actors to achieve its purposes, and can be used affirmatively as a tool for constructing markets, serving well-positioned market actors, and enforcing compliance for poorly positioned market actors. Rather than presuming that humans naturally behave as rational market subjects, as in *laissez-faire* philosophy, the neoliberal project adopts a more constructivist stance emphasizing the need to instill specific competencies and mentalities consonant with assimilation into market relations.

Under neoliberalism, the welfare state is not 'rolled back' in the sense of being reduced; it is 'rolled out' to diverse locales and nonstate actors (Peck and Tickell 2002), and it is 'rolled up' in a transformative disciplinary project of market rationality (Brown 2003). Throughout the developed world, social welfare programs have been redesigned to be more 'active' in instilling market values and prodding the poor into jobs (Schram 2006). 'Conditional' aid is the new *modus operandi* (Mead and Beem 2005). In the United States and Europe, public assistance has been made contingent on the fulfillment of behavioral obligations and the pursuit of labor-market incorporation (Torfing 1999). In developing countries, conditional cash transfers (CCTs) provide cash for taking appropriate actions, such as getting your children inoculated or keeping them in school. International organizations supported by the United States have spread CCT policies to over 42 developing countries in recent years, where they have been elaborated in forms that are now being reimported to sites such as New York City (Bosman 2009, Peck and Theodore 2010).

Yet, claims of global convergence in social policy are often overstated (Gilbert 2002). The 'three worlds of welfare capitalism' identified by Esping-Andersen (1990) continue to exhibit distinctive policy regimes in important ways. And even where policy designs have converged, their implementation continues to reflect the diverse political geography of welfare provision (Martin 2004). The Anglo-liberal political economies most approximate the American style of welfare reform, while the continental-corporatist welfare states are more supportive in their approaches to labor activation policies. Scandinavian countries continue to maintain a robust welfare state while simultaneously trying to move more public assistance recipients off disability, unemployment, and welfare by helping them find employment when possible.

Thus, globalization and neoliberal ideology should not be mistaken for inexorable forces necessitating a single mode of social provision (Hay 2006, Schram 2006). All developed countries are experiencing global market integration and feeling political pressures to adopt neoliberal reforms, but they are responding in their own ways. The United States, with its long-standing emphasis on market-conforming welfare policy and reliance on private agents of provision (Hacker 2002), has been the predictable epicenter of a global turn toward neoliberal poverty governance that is taking different forms in different polities.

To understand the relationship between neoliberalism and welfare reform, one must engage the former as a shift, not only in the state, but also in the meaning and practice of citizenship. Citizenship is an inherently relational status, defined by the ways members of a polity are positioned vis-à-vis nonmembers, one another, the state, and other major societal institutions. Thus, as the state has been restructured to operate according to market rationalities, citizenship too has shifted toward an economic register of identity and practice. The status of the democratic citizen, positioned as one who must decide and act collectively with others to gain preferred policy outcomes, has been eroded and partly displaced by the individualistic market roles of consumer, worker, and paying customer (Crenson and Ginsberg 2002). Citizens, in this guise, are synonymous with 'taxpayers' who have a contractual right to expect efficient and effective institutional actions that produce a good return on their investment. They are positioned, through vouchers and choice programs, as 'consumers' who pursue better goods from the system by exercising their individual freedom to seek goods from other providers (exit) rather than by joining together to participate in or demand improvements in the institutions they share (voice). They are encouraged to help others, not by deciding together how to organize their communities in a just manner, but by pursuing individual work as volunteers and charitable givers and virtuous providers of services.

At the same time, the obligation to work and function as a 'self-sufficient' actor in the market is recast as the primary responsibility of the citizen and, indeed, as a necessary precondition for 'moral standing' as a member of society who merits equal respect, possesses full rights, and can be presumed competent to fulfill other civic obligations (Mead 1997). Under neoliberalism, citizenship is, as Brown (2006) observes, 'reduced to self-care;' self-care is reduced, in turn, to the singular project of ensuring that one's needs are met through one's contributions to the market. Uses of policy to make 'better citizens' thus become indistinguishable from efforts to produce docile subjects who comply with market needs and political authorities. Neoliberalism, in this sense, entails the 'governmentalization' of citizenship (Dean 1999).

The consequences of this shift for welfare provision are profound because public aid in the United States has always been debated and used as a tool of *civic* incorporation. Its implementation has both reflected and defined prevailing terms of societal incorporation – including the distinctive terms associated with differences of race, class, and gender. Today, welfare programs remain just as rooted in the meanings and practices of citizenship. But it is the citizenship of a neoliberal era in which diverse civic responsibilities are collapsed into the obligation to work and applied to poor women as much as to men. Poverty governance today is characterized by what Chesney-Lind (1995) has called 'gender equality with a vengeance,' a historical pattern 'whereby the replacement of gender difference with sameness led to the more punitive treatment of women' (Haney 2004, p. 340). Yet it is a mistake to see this change as a simple matter of wage work coming to be viewed as a normative expectation for 'women in general'. Now as in the past, race matters greatly for the relationship between gender and the enforcement of civic obligations in welfare programs. Welfare's iconic status as a program for 'poor single mothers of color' has combined with persistent cultural stereotypes of this group to smooth the way for neoliberal reforms that are premised on the idea that policy tools must be actively deployed to motivate particular groups of recipients to work and act responsibly (Gilens 1999, Hancock 2004). Indeed, the design and practice of discipline under neoliberal welfare reform have varied significantly depending on the race of low-income target populations (Schram *et al.* 2009).

The third level of welfare reform: neoliberal paternalism

The major consequences of welfare reform are typically discussed at two basic levels. First, as public aid has become more conditional and limited, the number of welfare recipients has plummeted. The number of welfare recipients in the United States declined by about 72% from its high point before the passage of PRWORA to the end of 2008 (HHS 2009). Welfare reform was, in this sense, a classic effort to pare the welfare rolls, consistent with a long history of efforts to achieve the contraction of relief during periods of weak political opposition (Piven and Cloward 1971).

Second, dwindling number of recipients has been accompanied by dramatic changes in the focus of welfare expenditures. By 2001, just five years after the passage of federal reform, the US welfare system had reached the point where over half of federal TANF block grants to the states were being spent on noncash services designed to promote and assist transitions to work. Thus, just as welfare recipients have become a dwindling percentage of the poor, so too has cash income support become a more meager component of welfare provision (Allard 2009). Services focused on overcoming 'barriers to work' have taken center stage in state decisions about how to prioritize and spend federal welfare funds.

To be sure, these changes are important developments in their own right. Yet the narrow focus on them has served to obscure a third, more fundamental, level of change in poverty governance. Declining welfare caseloads and shifts toward expenditures on services are, in our view, surface manifestations of a more profound turn to a neoliberal disciplinary logic. To understand this shift, it is useful to locate it in relation to the classic analysis of welfare provision and social control advanced by Piven and Cloward in *Regulating the poor* (1971). At the core of Piven and Cloward's analysis is the idea that the welfare state functions as a 'secondary institution' serving the often-conflicting needs of institutions and actors in states and markets. Thus, welfare provision can be used to shore up state legitimacy and build political followings, to restore social order in times of unrest, and to enforce work norms and behaviors that support labor markets. Building on this insight, Piven and Cloward present a detailed historical account of how poor relief has been deployed to fulfill such functions.

In our view, welfare programs today continue to serve the same basic functions that Piven and Cloward specified in 1971, but the operations that fulfill these functions have shifted in important ways. Welfare programs continue to play a key role in 'regulating the poor' in precisely the ways suggested by Piven and Cloward, yet they are also organized to 'discipline the poor' in ways that go beyond their landmark analysis.

For much of the modern history of welfare, the behaviors of the poor were regulated through a variety of practices tied closely to the principle of 'less eligibility'. Because welfare programs provided politically defined spaces of needs-based provision outside markets (Stone 1984), work enforcement was pursued primarily by keeping benefits below the wages of the lowest paying jobs and limiting access to welfare. The extent to which welfare programs 'decommodify' labor in this way is, of course, always a matter of degree (Esping-Andersen 1985). To the extent that welfare programs lay more squarely outside the market, their labor-regulating functions will depend more on efforts to keep benefits below wages and control the expansion and contraction of welfare caseloads.

In the contemporary era, however, welfare programs operate as market arenas in their own right. They are less sharply delineated as spaces where individuals face reduced pressure to offer their labor as a commodity and, in significant ways, are designed to ensure that labor stays on the market. Low-income people who apply for welfare today enter an arena that is organized to serve as a resource for employers: its purpose is to groom workers for hiring, make them as available as possible for employment, and actively push them into jobs. In this mode of 'disciplining the poor,' recipients are not just pushed into jobs by benefits that are too meager to compete with the worst wages – or even by forms of administrative *legerdemain* that deny access to benefits. Welfare programs are constructed to provide the poor with an experience of market incentives and logics and to teach self-discipline to workers who are expected to adapt to their plight on the lower rungs of the labor market.

Thus, while the principle of less eligibility remains important to poverty governance today, the relationship between benefits and wages has become less decisive for labor discipline and the relationship between labor markets and welfare programs has become less oppositional. This disciplinary shift is perhaps most evident in the growing proportion of welfare funds that are spent on welfare-to-work services rather than cash aid. TANF programs today offer meager income support; most of their funds are spent in an effort to 'overcome' recipients' 'barriers to work' and to put clients through classes on how to dress for success, write resumes, use computers, and so on. Neoliberal paternalist welfare reform is, first and foremost, about instilling market competencies and teaching recipients how to conduct themselves as workers.

In this sense, it would be a mistake to suggest, as some have, that the new regime simply assimilates welfare provision to the practices of punishing the poor found in the criminal justice system (Wacquant 2009). Although welfare provision has become deeply entwined with incarceration, and draws today on many of its rhetorics and practices, the major direction of change is not from 'regulation' to 'punishment' *per se*. It is, to draw on Foucault's (1979) classic distinction in *Discipline and punish*, a shift toward a historically specific disciplinary project that employs punishment as one among many techniques. Incentives and educative programs are, in this regard, no less important than penalties. The cultivation of market discipline lies at the root of neoliberal-paternalist poverty governance, and it is pursued through diverse technologies. The explicit features of the regime, such as work requirements and time limits, are only the most visible facets of a disciplinary project enacted through a wide array of services, classes, incentives, benefits, and sanctions that all aim to turn welfare clients into suitable candidates for low-wage employment (Stone 2007).

As a result of the shift, the subject position occupied by clients in this system is captured less faithfully by the concept of decommodification (Esping-Andersen 1985) than by the concept of liminality (Turner 1967). Welfare clients are not stable occupants of a harbor outside the market; they are unstable subjects in an active state of becoming. Their identities are defined by their state of passage from the degraded role of 'dependent' to the valorized role of 'worker' – from disordered and irresponsible drains on society to orderly subjects who function as self-sufficient actors in markets and communities (Schram *et al.* 2009). As such, they represent a kind of semi-citizen in transition (Wolin 1989), subject to the enforcement of obligations yet not possessing the full rights of entitled membership. Discretionary control over their passage falls to case managers, who serve as 'deputized guides... there to expedite the process and serve as mentors' during the disciplinary rites that lead from one status to the next (Hopper 2003, p. 20).

To carry out this disciplinary project, welfare provision in the United States has been restructured, root and branch, to conform to the 'new public management' – a reform movement that has sought 'to replace traditional rule-based, authority-driven processes with market-based, competition-driven tactics' (Kettl 2005, p. 3). Thus, welfare policy authority has been dispersed to a wide variety of locales and actors through devolution and privatization (Gainsborough 2003). At the same time, new systems of performance-based competition and management have been used to discipline the use of discretion in this more decentralized policy environment (Schram *et al.* 2008). The new organizational forms create a more flexible, decentralized system that allows aid recipients to be disciplined according to local conditions and needs but, at the same time, pressures local providers in a variety of ways to bring their practices into line with centralized program goals.

Indeed, the new welfare system is perhaps best understood as a decentralized chain of disciplinary relationships which runs from the federal government down to states, down to local regional boards, down to contracted service providers, down to frontline workers, and ultimately down to welfare clients. At each point in this cascade, benchmarks for outcomes are established and monitored, and managerial techniques, incentives, and penalties are used to discipline actors below. Thus, state officials exercise freedom of choice when it comes to policy means, but they must choose from a subject position tied to federal funding streams and their goals. Local officials are encouraged to innovate as they compete for contracts and bonuses, but their creative energies are channeled by the relentless pressures of performance systems that reward only the mandated program goals. Case managers are given discretion to allocate benefits, services, and penalties, but their choices are monitored and constrained because they must remain focused on moving recipients from welfare to work. TANF clients sign Individual Responsibility Plans as free market actors entering a contractual exchange of benefits for work activities, but their freedom is little more than the opportunity to succeed or fail in complying with these mandated program requirements.

Examining the whole chain of governance at once, it quickly becomes apparent that welfare reform is not just about bringing market discipline to clients; it is equally about imposing market discipline on welfare provision itself. The new tools of governance (Bevir 2007), such as performance systems, are instruments for a deeper project of governmentality (Foucault 1991), designed to produce self-disciplining governing authorities by cultivating appropriate 'governing mentalities' (Campbell 2000). In significant respects, this shift in poverty governance preceded welfare reform, gathering momentum during the presidencies of Ronald Reagan and George Herbert Walker Bush and emerging in full form during the early 1990s in the movement to 'reinvent government' (Osborne and Gaebler 1993). Today, with the new public management firmly entrenched, the personnel of the welfare system are subjected to a neoliberal disciplinary regime so that they will ensure that clients of the welfare system are subjected to the same.

By extending the reach of government via contractual relationships with market and civil-society organizations, the new system of governance enables the power of the state to grow even as the public sector itself shrinks. Deploying market mythologies, the new public management promises that contracted local actors will be freed to go their own ways and then, later, will be judged by their performance and given the information they need to improve. The reality, however, involves a more complex interplay of structure and agency (Moynihan 2008). The focusing effects of outcome benchmarks, the pressures of competition, the prospects of incurring rewards or penalties, the awareness that one is being closely monitored: these features of performance management do more than just make agents accountable; they reconstitute agency itself. Under this system, local providers learn quickly that they must make active use of disciplinary tools in handling clients if they are to achieve program goals and maintain profitability. Within the 'business model,' clients and administrators alike must work within a market logic, responding to incentives and penalties and behaving in ways that conform to market pressures.

Strained efforts to recast identities in market terms are, in fact, a defining feature of contemporary welfare offices as social and physical spaces. In the Florida WT program, where we have conducted extensive field research, welfare recipients are officially labeled as 'customers' or 'candidates,' as in job candidates, and welfare case managers are titled

'Career Counselors.' The public space of the welfare 'one-stop center' is recast as a site of market transaction where norms of professionalism demand that case managers and clients look and behave as if they are working in a professional, corporate environment. As one senior state official in Florida explained: 'We're supposed to be business friendly. And I hate to tell you, that does not mean having a bunch of kids running around at the one-stop [when clients come to see their case managers].' Some of the best-funded one-stops in Florida have been carefully scripted to mimic corporate environments and celebrate market aspirations. Flat-screen televisions show pictures of well-dressed women walking with briefcases and cycle through a variety of resume tips and motivational statements. Many of the one-stops we visited had meeting spaces with titles such as 'The Excellence Room' and 'The Opportunity Room'. Small, rural offices are rarely able to match the business-like environments of the larger operations. But they participate in the same esthetic on a reduced scale. The Opportunity Room looks a bit more beleaguered, and the tips for success appear on a white board instead of a flat-screen, but the message conveyed to clients is largely the same: you are competing in the business world, and we are in the business of making you more competitive.

The message throughout the TANF system is that motivated people will be able to work, and people who work will be able to succeed as self-sufficient citizens. More often than not, though, the client's passage through this system ends with something other than self-sufficient market success. Large numbers of clients are sanctioned off the rolls for noncompliance, a fate that is disproportionately common among 'hard-to-serve' clients who make it more difficult for local providers to meet their performance benchmarks and pay points (Soss *et al.* 2011). TANF clients who leave welfare for work make wages that average only about $7.50 per hour in jobs that offer no medical insurance or pensions (Litt *et al.* 2000). Even in Wisconsin, which has one of the most celebrated TANF programs in the country (Mead 2004), program leavers in late 1999 earned an average of just $8,306 during their first year out (with 81% below the poverty line) and an average of only $11,577 in their fourth year out (with 73% below the poverty line); their most common job placement was with a temporary help service (Schultze 2005). Nationally, the percentage of 'disconnected' low-income mothers (who are neither receiving welfare nor working) has doubled since 1990 and is now as high as 25% by some definitions (Blank and Kovak 2008).

Case managers: a phenomenology of governmentality

Case managers present an especially important and informative group. On the one side, they are positioned as the culminating targets of efforts to discipline service provision. Because they hold discretion in their work with clients, and because their decisions enact policy, poverty governance today depends greatly on efforts to instill self-discipline in this group. In this sense, case managers offer an indispensable bottom-up perspective on the governance of service provision. On the other side, case managers are positioned as the 'face' of the welfare system for low-income clients (Soss 2000). They are the key agents of the communications and actions that policymakers hope will turn welfare recipients into orderly and successful market subjects. In this sense, the case manager can be seen as a fulcrum for the system as a whole, connecting the disciplining of service providers to the disciplining of clients. Market pressures imposed on implementing organizations rain down on the case manager from above, and it is the case manager who, in turn, must work to secure market compliance from the client.

The subjective experience of governance for case managers is rooted in three key features of their organizational position. First, case managers are subject to strong, ongoing performance pressures and, because their actions affect measured performance, their behaviors are closely monitored through information systems. As a result, case managers worry about performance almost continually. As one put it, 'It's just weird, I mean it really is. And I don't know how to explain how, um, you know, we [case managers] all run around and we're like, "where are you at now with your [participation numbers]?" "Oh, I'm at like 20 percent." "Oh man!" So we're all just stressed!' The stress felt by case managers can be traced partly to their belief that performance numbers matter for job security and trajectory. Few expect to be 'fired' if their numbers drop. But most know that if they produce weak numbers, they will be subjected to greater supervision in a way that will make their work more stressful and difficult.

Moreover, in a system that includes for-profit contracting, most are keenly aware that performance numbers drive profits, and declining profits could lead their current employer to downsize the staff or even to sell the operation to another company whose retention of old employees is uncertain. As one case manager put it, 'for-profit is about profits period, bottom line and then some.'

Second, under welfare reform, case management is organized as a deskilled, low-wage position with a strong emphasis on documentation and data-entry tasks. Few case managers have anything resembling social-services training and, in fact, a considerable number have received welfare in the past (Schram *et al.* 2009). In a group interview with senior regional officials, one told us flatly that 'You don't hire a "people person" anymore for a career manager position. You hire a clerical computer person. You can teach them the social work stuff easily. The job's all about time, accuracy, and files now. There's a person [client] down there somewhere. But the technical stuff is what matters.' Another responded, 'If you talk to any case manager here, they will tell you they're not a case manager; they're a technician. They spend about 10 percent of their time on their clients. Their time is about being a technician, and that's the way the program is written. They're doing what they have to do under this system.'

Indeed, the case managers in our study typically describe a workday that is reactive and clerical, focused on the performance-driven tasks of documenting client work activity hours and entering the results into the One Stop Service Tracking data system. Almost without fail, they begin their days by logging on to the information system so they can address the slew of new alerts that arrives each morning. The alerts focus on two kinds of actions: documenting work participation hours for clients and pursuing disciplinary sanctions when such documentation is lacking. From this point forward, the daily round consists mostly of efforts to do one or the other, punctuated by face-to-face meetings with clients that often focus on the same two issues. The women and men we interviewed are labeled 'career counselors' and given wide discretion in handling cases, yet they are not supplied with the skills, tools, or time needed to work with clients on issues beyond the realm of work enforcement and documentation. They have no training as social workers, they have few options for matching clients to the services they need, they have no time to work intensively with individuals, and they are essentially powerless to change clients' broader opportunities and life conditions.

Third, of all the administrative actors who participate in contemporary poverty governance, case managers are positioned to experience the clash of social needs and market pressures most intimately. They work in organizations that strive to operate according to the 'business model,' to serve local employers as much as TANF recipients, and to limit their mission to 'the business of moving people from welfare to work.' In both official and informal communications, the legitimacy of this business model is cemented through symbolic contrasts with a naive solve-the-problems-of-the-world orientation that is disparaged as 'old school' (or 'social work') and equated with a failed and discredited system of handouts practiced prior to welfare reform. Yet at the same time, case managers spend their days in the presence of people whose problems are both real and deep, who are suffering from poverty and anxious for their children, and who have come to them for help. They want their difficult daily work to have a meaning and purpose that is deeper than data entry and, in this regard, value traditional images of case workers as counselors who offer much-needed social services and help people solve their problems. As a result, a strong counter-discourse of social service, counseling, and care-giving runs beneath the dominant discourse of the business model, seeding ambivalence in individuals and sometimes conflict between co-workers.

In an important field study of professional identity among welfare caseworkers, Watkins-Hayes (2009) contrasts what she terms 'efficiency engineering' and 'social work' orientations, and suggests that tensions between them are almost inevitable given the presence of organizational and policy cues that legitimize both. Our interviews with case managers in the Florida WT program point to a similar tension, but they also underscore that the business model, as a governing mentality, is most prominent and about more than just efficiency. It is rooted in powerful norms regarding how one should act as a market subject, and it reflects a substantive (specifically, neoliberal) vision of what welfare programs and their implementers should accomplish. The counterpart to the social work ethos in our interviews had less to do with efficiency *per se* than with responding to competitive performance pressures, operating like a business, and serving market needs.

In this sense, neoliberal rationality supplies case managers with a source of professional identity. When asked to describe her role as a WT case manager, one woman we interviewed emphasized its importance to the local community and said it consisted of 'trying to develop more jobs, more business for people, more employees, more goods and services, bringing more tourists into the economy, and bringing that labor market information . . . . [As a result of what we do in WT] the unemployment rate goes down . . . which is better for the market, for the economy.' The sense of self expressed here resonates with Maynard-Moody and Musheno's (2003) account of street-level bureaucrats who see themselves as 'citizen agents' acting on behalf of the community. But in this rendering, the community is reduced to its market relations, and the agent construes herself as acting in and for the local economy.

When the 'pull' of this sense of self and mission combines with the 'push' of pressures to meet performance goals, market logics conspire to erode the connection of human to human in the casework relationship. As client compliance becomes a means toward multiple ends, the client's status as a person becomes secondary and case managers develop a practiced stance of indifference that many find hard to reconcile with their conceptions of human compassion.

Our interviews underscore the pull of competing professional identities that is at the heart of Watkins-Hayes' (2009) account. The neoliberal turn in welfare provision has not imposed a seamless and uniform governing mentality on case managers; it has produced an era in which case manager identities and commitments are shifting and contested. In the WT program, the business model is embraced by case managers to varying degrees, with conflicted emotions and senses of self emerging as the most common response. One of the most common refrains in our interviews is captured by the quotation below: a desire to offer clients more substantial help, a sense of regret about the limits imposed by performance pressures, and a feeling of resignation about the bottom-line mentality that the market logic requires.

> [Welfare in Florida] is no longer a social service; it is a business... I find it to be the difference between herding cattle and herding sheep. A cattle herder is just running people through, not taking time to look after them. A shepherd takes care of the sheep, tends after them, cares for them. It is not my nature to herd cattle and now I have to learn to do that.

The case manager's feeling of 'running people through' has deep roots in the work-first philosophy of welfare reform and reflects a mode of poverty governance organized to operate as a feeder for low-wage labor markets. In favorable new-paternalist accounts of welfare reform, case managers were once document handlers carrying out invariant procedures; they are now more active in pursuing individually tailored forms of engagement designed to build competence (Mead 2004). WT case managers describe the experience of enacting poverty governance in terms that are sharply at odds with this image. Indeed, it is precisely the lack of personalized engagement and skill building that they lament as they describe the truncated palette of tools at their disposal and the limits imposed by a confluence of time constraints, work-focused goals, and performance pressures. When asked whether they have time to 'work on skill development,' case managers frequently give responses similar to this one: 'No, you do not. [...] You just have to refer 'em out, and, well, call this number, and see what you can find. [...] It takes me [time] to look on the internet for, you know, the [Easter Seals] and this and that and give 'em all this information. I'm thinking '[oh man], good luck,' you know? So they'll tell us we're not, you know, social workers, we're just, employment, you know.'

The market rationality that underlies this rote invocation of work as the answer to diverse problems was identified more explicitly by a case manager who referred to herself as 'Ms. Cookie Cutter' because of the one-size-fits-all approach she was practicing in the WT program.

> This program is structured the way that it is and the bottom line, I guess, is money... It's like it [WT] is a cookie cutter approach, okay, to people who are individuals that have different needs, who have different barriers and they're forcing us to put them in the same type of process.... It's like, putting a band-aid over a bullet wound.

In the Florida WT program, an adult client with one child is required, depending on the region, to complete and document 120–160 h of work activity each month in exchange for $240 in cash aid. Moral exhortations and promises of self-sufficient success are useful tools in case managers' efforts to meet this standard and, in the process, hit their performance benchmarks. Ultimately, however, benefit sanctions function as the fail-safe in the system, ensuring that client noncompliance will result in material penalty. In the system's broader disciplinary project, sanctions represent the most overtly punitive tool. As a result, case managers' views of sanctions provide an important window into the mentalities that govern conduct at the frontlines of welfare provision.

Many case managers expressed a resigned acceptance of the idea that sanctions are 'just how the program works' – that offers perhaps the most important insight into the mentality that governs case management in the WT program. In contemplating the workers who carry out the agenda of neoliberal welfare reform, it is easy to get caught in a false opposition of freedom versus coercion (Hayward 2000). On the one side lies the image of case managers who 'buy in' to the neoliberal agenda, enacting it as their own free will – perhaps after internalizing it as some sort of hegemonic ideological frame (Ridzi 2009). On the other side lies the image of resistant workers at the frontlines, forced to carry out an agenda they oppose. The reality is more complex and also more mundane. It does not pivot on the question of whether case managers agree with neoliberal goals or endorse paternalist authority relations. The more decisive fact is simply that case managers work in institutions that are organized around these principles.

The case managers we interviewed tended to be deeply conflicted about their work. They were ambivalent participants in systems designed to move low-income adults into local jobs. To understand the mentalities that guided their actions, one must reach beyond questions of ideological 'buy in' and even beyond the rich field studies devoted to the street-level bureaucrat as a distinctive policy actor. One must consider the subjective standpoint that case managers share with other low-wage occupants of deskilled positions in the global economy. The duties they carry out are 'just how the program works.' They are anxious about performance evaluations and sometimes worry that they might lose their job. They try to handle their cases in ways that they and the people around them consider appropriate. They try to retain their humanity and treat people well, but also remind themselves that they do not make the rules and, in the end, have a job to do.

The neoliberal and paternalist principles that guide contemporary poverty governance provide case managers with important discursive resources for making sense of their work and feeling that it is important. Ultimately, though, the actions of case managers flow less from their agreement or disagreement with these principles than from the ways that these principles have organized the contexts in which they work. To enact the agenda of neoliberal paternalism, case managers do not need to become neoliberals or embrace paternalism. They need only do what strikes them as permissible, reasonable, and right as they put in their workdays at organizations that have been structured to pursue this approach to poverty governance. At the frontlines of welfare reform, neoliberal rationalities do not govern mentalities by imposing all-encompassing worldviews; they do so by organizing fields of practice so that the ambivalent subjects who occupy them can be relied upon to do the work of disciplining the poor.

Neoliberal paternalism and the pedagogical state

In recent years, a number of observers have raised concerns about how new forms of governance are creating opportunities for the exercise of 'pedagogical power' (Pykett 2009). On the horizon looms the possibility of a pedagogical state, which through its educative interventions, imbues citizens with worldviews and forms of knowledge which are consonant with the dominant order. Our account of welfare reform suggests that its neoliberal-paternalist rationality entails educative components but, as theorists of the new forms of pedagogical power would emphasize, should not be misconstrued as an instance of governing through pedagogy. Indeed, to ask whether frontline workers 'buy into,' or whether clients 'internalize,' the ideological lessons of neoliberalism is to begin with the wrong questions. Neoliberal governance enacts market rationalities, not primarily by imparting lessons to workers and clients, but by restructuring the terrain that these actors must negotiate in order to be successful under prevailing systems.

Consider, for instance, how the work participation requirement for WT clients functions as a form of what Handler and Hasenfeld (2005) call 'myth and ceremony.' The guiding myth of welfare reform is that, by meeting paternalist requirements to attend classes and engage in other reformative endeavors, recipients will learn the habits of mind associated with the world of work. At the frontlines of welfare provision, however, the pedagogical myth results mostly in administrative ceremony. When asked in our field interviews how the welfare-to-work system could be improved, a common mantra among case managers was 'more activities' that clients could complete to fulfill program requirements, such as attending resume writing or computer classes or participating in job club and job searching sessions. Our caseworkers frequently described struggling to find enough of these 'activities' for clients to fulfill their participation requirements. Few case managers see these 'activities' as meaningful steps to employment, or even as tools for teaching the self-discipline necessary to be a compliant worker. They are simply countable things for clients to do. And yet, despite their ambivalence about this 'make work,' case managers work diligently to ensure that clients do what must be done – so that they avoid sanctioning poor families and so that they can meet their own performance benchmarks for the client participation rate.

In this sense, the myth of pedagogy is not internalized by case managers as a lesson; it is enacted by case managers as a ceremony required by their job. To policymakers and the public, the ceremony may signify that welfare-to-work programs are teaching clients how to work and helping them get jobs. But 'in the doing,' it is experienced as something closer to an empty gesture whose importance lies in the bare fact that clients can be counted as being active, as they must under current policy. Whether these activities teach lessons that are good for the client or anyone else is, at best, secondary. The charade may exist because of the tutelary goals of paternalist policy reformers, but its performance is mostly a matter of caseworkers and clients busily pursuing requirements and benchmarks as ends in themselves. It is a classic form of the bureaucratic behavior called 'goal displacement' (see Merton 1957), or what followers of Max Weber have called the substitution of 'instrumental rationality' for 'substantive rationality.'

Neoliberal paternalism, in this sense, is poorly understood as an ethos or worldview that authorities instruct and case managers and clients internalize. It is a practical rationality, which is to say that it is the mode of reasoning that underlies the contemporary regime of poverty governance and, thus, organizes the ways that actors apprehend what they should do and how they should do it. Welfare reform's disciplinary logic is enacted through incentives and penalties, benchmarks and documentation procedures, organizational routines and client Individual Responsibility Plans. The WT program is organized around a 'business model' of provision that shapes the calculations and choices of diverse actors, many of whom are deeply ambivalent about the regime they are working within. To carry out their work, these actors do not need to embrace the business model or understand themselves as occupying a pedagogical role in relation to clients. And to 'succeed' as welfare-to-work participants, clients do not really need to internalize any particular ethos or lesson. They need only discipline themselves to conform to what is being demanded of them in the day to day.

Under the logic of neoliberal paternalism, one might say that welfare reform is a disciplinary system that aspires to be pedagogical. Certainly, the image of teaching the poor to work hard and exercise personal responsibility has been important to its political success. Yet its disciplinary agendas and effects do not, ultimately, depend on successful educative interventions into the lives of case managers or clients. They do not require pedagogical acquiescence, in the sense of consciously accepting new lessons – only operational quiescence, in the sense of following the organizational logic defined by neoliberal paternalism. How this logic will be disrupted, and what will take its place, only time and politics will tell.

Notes

1. Email: jbsoss@umn.edu
2. Email: lhouser@rci.rutgers.edu
3. Email: rford@uky.edu

References

Allard, S., 2009. *Out of reach: place, poverty, and the new American welfare state.* New Haven: Yale University Press.
Bevir, M., ed., 2007. *The encyclopedia of governance.* 2 Vols. London: Sage.

Blank, R. and Kovak, B., 2008. *Helping disconnected single mothers. Center on children and families brief #38*. Washington, DC: Brookings Institution.

Bosman, J., 2009. Cash incentive program for poor families is renewed. *New York Times*, September 20, A20.

Brown, W., 2003. Neo-liberalism and the end of liberal democracy. *Theory and event*, 7 (1), 47–71. Available from: http://muse.jhu.edu/journals/theory_and_event/

Brown, W., 2006. American nightmare: neoliberalism, neoconservatism, and de-democratization. *Political theory*, 34 (6), 690–714.

Campbell, N., 2000. *Using women: gender, drug policy, and social justice*. New York: Routledge.

Chesney-Lind, M., 1995. *The female offender*. Thousand Oaks, CA: Sage.

Crenson, M. and Ginsberg, B., 2002. *Downsizing democracy: how America sidelined its citizens and privatized its public*. Baltimore: Johns Hopkins University Press.

Dean, M., 1999. *Governmentality: power and rule in modern society*. Thousand Oaks, CA: Sage.

Esping-Andersen, G., 1985. *Politics against markets: the social democratic road to power*. Princeton, NJ: Princeton University Press.

Esping-Andersen, G., 1990. *Three worlds of welfare capitalism*. Princeton, NJ: Princeton University Press.

Foucault, M., 1979. *Discipline and punish: the birth of the prison*. New York: Vintage.

Foucault, M., 1991. Governmentality. Trans. R. Braidotti and revised by C. Gordon. *In*: G. Burchell, C. Gordon and P. Miller, eds. *The Foucault effect: studies in governmentality*. Chicago: University of Chicago Press, 87–104.

Gainsborough, J.F., 2003. To devolve or not to devolve? Welfare reform in the states. *Policy studies journal*, 31, 603–623.

Gilbert, N., 2002. *Transformation of the welfare state: the silent surrender of public responsibility*. New York: Oxford University Press.

Gilens, M., 1999. *Why Americans hate welfare: race, media, and the politics of antipoverty policy*. Chicago: University of Chicago Press.

Gustafson, K., 2009. The criminalization of poverty. *Journal of criminal law and criminology*, 99 (3), 643–716.

Hacker, J.S., 2002. *The divided welfare state: the battle over public and private social benefits in the United States*. Cambridge: Cambridge University Press.

Hancock, A.-M., 2004. *The politics of disgust: the public identity of the welfare queen*. New York: New York University Press.

Handler, J. and Hasenfeld, Y., 2005. Myth and ceremony in workfare: rights, contracts, and client satisfaction. *Journal of socio-economics*, 34 (1), 101–124.

Haney, L., 2004. Introduction: gender, welfare, and states of punishment. *Social politics*, 11 (3), 333–362.

Hay, C., 2006. Globalization, economic change and the welfare state: the 'vexatious inquisition of taxation'? *In*: C. Pierson and F. Castles, eds. *The welfare state reader*. Cambridge: Polity Press, 200–225.

Hayward, C., 2000. *Defacing power*. New York: Cambridge University Press.

Health and Human Services (HHS), 2009. U.S. Department of Health and Human Services. Welfare caseloads. Available from: http://www.acf.hhs.gov/programs/ofa/data-reports/index.htm

Hopper, K., 2003. *Reckoning with homelessness*. Ithaca, NY: Cornell University Press.

Katz, M., 1997. *Improving poor people: the welfare state, the "underclass," and urban schools as history*. Princeton: Princeton University Press.

Kettl, D., 2005. *The global public management revolution: a report on the transformation of governance*. Washington, DC: Brookings Institution.

Korteweg, A., 2003. Welfare reform and the subject of the working mother: 'get a job, a better job, then a career.' *Theory and society*, 32 (4), 445–480.

Krinsky, J., 2007. The urban politics of workfare. *Urban affairs review*, 42 (6), 771–798.

Litt, B.J., Gaddis, B., Fletcher, C. and Winter, M., 2000. Leaving welfare: independence or continued vulnerability? *Journal of consumer affairs*, 34 (1), 82–96.

Martin, S., 2004. Reconceptualizing social exclusion: a critical response to the neoliberal welfare reform agenda and the underclass thesis. *Australian journal of social issues*, 39 (1), 79.

Maynard-Moody, S. and Musheno, M., 2003. *Cops, teachers, counselors: stories from the front lines of public service*. Ann Arbor: University of Michigan Press.

Mead, L.M., 1986. *Beyond entitlement: the social obligations of citizenship*. New York, NY: The Free Press.

Mead, L., 1997. *The new paternalism: supervisory approaches to poverty*. Washington: Brookings Institution Press.

Mead, L., 1998. Telling the poor what to do. *The public interest*, 132, 97–112.

Mead, L. and Beem, C., eds, 2005. *Welfare reform and political theory*. New York: Russell Sage Foundation.

Mead, L.M., 2007. Toward a mandatory work policy for men. *The future of children*, 17 (2), 43–72.

Merton, R., 1957. *Social theory and social structure*. Revised edition. Glencoe, IL: Free Press.

Morgen, S. and Gonzales, L., 2008. The neoliberal American dream as daydream: counter-hegemonic perspectives on welfare restructuring in the United States. *Critique of anthropology*, 28 (2), 219–236.

Moynihan, P., 2008. *The dynamics of performance management: constructing information and reform*. Washington, DC: Georgetown University Press.

Osborne, D. and Gaebler, T., 1993. *Reinventing government: how the entrepreneurial spirit is transforming the public sector*. New York: Plume.

Peck, J. and Theodore, N., 2010. Recombinant workfare, across Americas. *Geoforum*, 41 (2), 195–208.

Peck, J. and Tickell, A., 2002. Neoliberalizing space. *Antipode*, 34 (3), 380–404.

Piven, F.F. and Cloward, R., 1971. *Regulating the poor: the public functions of welfare*. New York: Vintage.

Pykett, J., 2009. Pedagogical power: lessons from school spaces. *Education, citizenship and social justice*, 4, 103–118.

Quadagno, J., 1999. *The color of welfare: how racism undermined the war on poverty*. New York: Oxford University Press.

Ridzi, F., 2009. *Selling welfare reform: work-first and the new common sense of employment*. New York: New York University Press.

Sassen, S., 2006. *Territory, authority, rights: from medieval to global assemblages*. Princeton: Princeton University Press.

Schram, S., 2006. *Welfare discipline: discourse, governance, and globalization*. Philadelphia: Temple University Press.

Schram, S., Fording, R. and Soss, J., 2008. Neo-liberal poverty governance: race, place and the punitive turn in US welfare policy. *Cambridge journal of regions, economy and society*, 1 (1), 17–36.

Schram, S., Soss, J., Fording, R. and Houser, L., 2009. Deciding to discipline: race, choice, and punishment on the frontlines of welfare reform. *American sociological review*, 74, 398–422.

Schultze, S., 2005. Critics recommend overhaul of W-2. *Milwaukee journal sentinel*, April 28. Available from: http://tinyurl.com/qdrs9

Soss, J., 2000. *Unwanted claims: the politics of participation in the U.S. welfare system*. Ann Arbor: University of Michigan Press.

Soss, J., Fording, R. and Schram, S., 2011. The organization of discipline: from performance management to perversity and punishment. *Journal of public administration research and theory* (forthcoming).

Stone, D.A., 1984. *The disabled state*. Philadelphia: Temple University Press.

Stone, D., 2007. Welfare policy and the transformation of care. *In*: J. Soss, J. Hacker and S. Mettler, eds. *Remaking America: democracy and public policy in an age of inequality*. New York: Russell Sage Foundation, 183–202.

Torfing, J., 1999. Workfare with welfare: recent reforms of the Danish welfare state. *Journal of European social policy*, 9 (1), 5–28.

Turner, V., 1967. Betwixt and between: the liminal period in *rites of passage*. *In*: *The forest of symbols: aspects of Ndembu ritual*. Ithaca, NY: Cornell University Press.

Wacquant, L., 2009. *Punishing the poor: the neoliberal government of social insecurity*. Durham: Duke University Press.

Walters, W., 2004. Some critical notes on governance'. *Studies in political economy*, 73, 25–42.

Watkins-Hayes, C., 2009. *The new welfare bureaucrats: entanglements of race, class, and policy reform*. Chicago: University of Chicago Press.

Wolin, S.S., 1989. *The presence of the past: essays on the state and the constitution*. Baltimore: Johns Hopkins University Press.

University and citizenship: the university as a space for enacting citizenships

Maki Kimura

The Open University in London, Camden Town, London, UK

The role of universities in promoting citizenship has recently gained more visible recognition as one of the UK's higher education (HE) policy priorities, and there has been a growing interest in the teaching of citizenship. However, in contrast to the teaching of citizenship in schools since 2002, there has been little study of the way that UK universities as institutions relate themselves to various concepts and practices of citizenship beyond researching it as an academic subject. The variety of concepts and practices of citizenship present in universities, and the concepts of citizenship that universities promote or challenge are areas that remain to be explored. The role of universities in promoting certain concepts of citizenship remains to be fully examined, requiring an exploration of the broader roles and functions of universities within society. This article examines the role of universities in society and the relevance of the question of citizenship to universities in the UK. It interrogates whether and how the university can provide a platform for performing new and innovative ideas and practices of citizenships.

Introduction

Interest in the issue of citizenship has grown globally over past years amongst policy makers and academics, and educational institutions in general have been considered to be the key to developing and promoting certain concepts and practices of citizenship. In the UK, the role of universities in promoting citizenship has recently gained more visible recognition as one of the priorities of higher education policy. For example, the Higher Education Funding Council for England (HEFCE) *Strategic Plan 2006–11* emphasises the key role of higher education in developing active citizens and global citizens (HEFCE 2006, paragraphs 42 and 139)[1]. At the same time, there has been a growing interest in the teaching of citizenship, evident in several action research projects carried out in various universities[2].

In addition to these recent developments, universities and academics in the UK have engaged with discussion on the subjects of multiculturalism, racism, political and religious extremism, and immigration, including the issue of refugees and political asylum – areas that can be broadly linked with discussions on citizenship. At the same time, a new field of studies on citizenship has been flourishing in UK universities, where citizenship is understood as social process as well as a legal status in the nation-state (Turner 1993, Isin and Turner 2002, Nyers 2007). This has led to the emergence of diverse citizenship concepts and practices which are not necessarily confined within national boundaries nor involve a legal status in a nation-state, such as 'cultural citizenship', 'sexual citizenship', 'corporate citizenship', 'environmental citizenship', 'global citizenship' and 'cosmopolitan citizenship'. However, despite the attention of policy makers to the role of universities in enhancing citizenship, and academic interest in both teaching and researching citizenship studies, there has been little discussion of what kinds of citizenships are articulated by universities, and whether widely ranged citizenship concepts and practices such as those referred to above are applicable in the milieu of universities. There is a need to further debate how (UK) universities *as pedagogical institutions* relate to the new concepts and practices of citizenships beyond researching them as an academic subject. The plural term 'citizenships' is used here in order to highlight the multiple natures of citizenships in the contemporary global world (Yuval-Davis 2007).

This forms an interesting contrast with the teaching of citizenship in schools, where citizenship education became a core subject of the National Curriculum for England in 2002, with schools providing fairly prescribed programmes. Although the challenges and practical difficulties that arise in delivering the curriculum in schools attract considerable research attention, the role that schools play in endorsing citizenship is usually assumed to be relatively self-evident, with schools understood to be preparing pupils 'for adult life … acting as a citizen, not just as a subject' (QCA 1998, p.8), a role they performed even before the introduction of this element of the National Curriculum. And as compulsory education, in principal, continues to be highly influenced by national policies and priorities, what is understood as citizenship here is less complicated – it is about a notion of (democratic) citizen, with a largely national dimension (Biesta 2009, p. 147).

As Gifford (2004, pp. 148-9) argues, citizenship education has a strong connotation as a 'delayed project of nation-state building', and there is some 'evidence of recent attempts by British governments to establish a national, state organised and state supervised education system'. But given the diverse and ever-transforming functions of (UK) universities, often transcending national boundaries, the university's relationship to citizenships including its role in promoting citizenships needs to be examined beyond a mere (national) policy agenda. This requires an exploration of the diverse roles and pedagogical functions of universities within wider society, as they encompass transnational and global perspectives, denoting a global public sphere that is central to the idea of cosmopolitanism, where the 'constitution of the social world is articulated through cultural models in which codifications of both Self and Other undergo transformation' (Delanty 2006, p. 37).

Instead of attempting a definition of citizenship which is relevant to the university, this paper aims to explore how citizenship can be 'a strategic concept that is central in the analysis' of the purpose of the university today (Nyers 2007, p. 1). It examines the role of universities in society, and how such roles inform the relevance of the question of citizenship to the university in the UK. It also questions whether and how the university can provide a platform for the performance of new and innovative ideas and practices of citizenships.

Citizenships and the university

Universities have fulfilled various and ever-changing roles in society since their origin in the medieval age. However, in modern times they have developed the features and functions that we now often associate with them (Altbach 2008, Delanty 2008). Modern universities are considered to have a role in teaching, research and contributing to the advancement of society, although the balance of the weight given to these functions has changed over time and space. In a similar vein, in proposing four 'archetypal models' of modern universities (Napoleonic, Humboldtian, Newmanian and Deweyan), Zgaga (2009, p. 177) argues that modern universities or higher education institutions have 'always been an amalgamation of roles and purposes' of these archetypes. He argues that the 'Deweyan model' has more explicit elements of citizenship as its primary role and purpose is to serve to the community and to 'prepare students for life as active citizens in a democratic society', but each model has some citizenship components in evidence. With an intensification of state-supported education from the early nineteenth century onwards, and particularly in Europe, the university's contribution to citizenship implied the supplying of 'the patriotic citizen' to pursue national interests (Zgaga 2009, p. 181). Citizens in this context were very much bound to nation-states. However, at the same time, the research and teaching that universities engage with have not been confined within national boundaries, as knowledge and methods in research and teaching have always been transnational in nature aiming at transformation in the wider social order. Thus, citizens themselves have also been required to be more than 'the patriotic citizen'. Therefore, the university's contribution to citizenships could have been always contradictory, as it embraced citizenships that were both bound to and transcended national boundaries. This tension between national versus transnational/global citizenships has not been adequately scrutinised.

Policy makers and researchers of higher education internationally acknowledge that at present universities are facing new challenges and opportunities in the context of globalisation, and the rise of neo-liberalism, which place added emphasis on a more worldwide and market-driven economy and focuses on international rather than national institutions (Altbach 2008, Delanty 2008, Taylor 2008). The ongoing reinterpretation of knowledge, the production and transmission of which universities have long been linked with, has also posed questions about the role and responsibility of the university in society. Universities are now responsible for: producing highly skilled workers for the knowledge economy or society; being economically competitive in international trade (of teaching and research); social cohesion; and social and cultural development at national as well as transnational level (Biesta and Simons 2009, Zgaga 2009).

In view of such current political, economic and social changes, the role of universities in teaching and research requires an extensive review. However, it is the increased role of the university in social developments and/or its practice in community engagement, and subsequently in promoting democratic values, that has attracted greater international attention in the arena of higher education policy and research (Watson 2007, Delanty 2008). Initiating the transformation of higher education to respond to such social changes and to play a vital role in social and economic development beyond mere economic objectives, in 1998 *The World Declaration on Higher Education for the Twenty-First Century: Vision and Action* was adopted by the World Conference on Higher Education in the Twenty-First Century convened by UNESCO (UNESCO

1998, Schoenenberger 2005, p. 53)[3]. The Declaration defines 'contribut[ing] to the sustainable development and improvement of society as a whole' as 'the core mission and value of higher education' (UNESCO 1998, Article 1) and states that educating students for citizenship with a global perspective is one of the means to accomplish this mission (UNESCO 1998, Article 1 (b)).

The worldwide concern about citizenship issues in higher education is further illuminated by other activities, for example, the *Universities as Sites of Citizenship and Civic Responsibility* pilot project, which was undertaken in 15 European and 14 American institutions between 1999 and 2001 to examine the activities and capacities of higher education which support democratic values and practices (Plantan 2002, p. 9)[4]. The Council of Europe has been committed to the area of education for democratic citizenship and human rights over decades. It was highly involved not only in the above project, but also the *Declaration on Higher Education and Democratic Culture: Citizenship, Human Rights and Civic Responsibility* which was adopted in a forum organised by the Council in 2006. In developing countries, universities have played a key role in nation-state building through providing ideas on national development and educating citizens to become political leaders or equipping them with technical expertise (Altbach 2008, p. 6).

Despite such keen interests in universities' role in citizenship education, there has been limited discussion resulting from the projects[5]. The discussion of citizenship such as in the projects does not investigate how higher education could and might be associated with the various and possibly new concepts and practices of citizenships against the background of internationalisation and globalisation, which have been extensively explored in emerging interdisciplinary studies of citizenship.

It has been noted that modern citizenship has long been associated with rights and duties that draw on the nation-state (Isin and Turner 2002, pp. 2-3), and that the notion of citizen has been defined through entitlements and legal status which are linked to services provided to the state. However, due to the increasing mobility of people as well as products, ideas and values, and the proliferation of global and international governance, the rights and duties of citizens have been reconfigured in recent decades, with the implications of being a citizen and the claims of citizenship becoming highly contested matters (Isin and Turner 2002, Kofman 2005, Isin and Turner 2007). In this context, the notion of citizenship has increasingly moved away from a state-confined politics and has gradually been considered as a set of practices – a social process – rather than a straightforward legal status with rights and obligations (Turner 1993, p. 2, Isin and Turner 2002, p. 4, Nyers 2007, p. 1). In seeing citizenship as a social process, the study of citizenship not only looks at the institutional arrangements of citizenship, but also considers the dynamics of how citizenship is socially constructed and how it becomes 'a lived experience' (Turner 1993, p. 2, Nyers 2007, p. 3). This means that the study of citizenship is now ultimately a political exploration of 'identity, participation, empowerment, human rights and the public interest' as citizenship is practised through existing social divisions including gender, 'race' and ethnicity, and geography (Nyers 2007, pp. 1-3).

With increasing globalisation, global conflicts, poverty, and issues of sustainable development, environment and social justice, universities are increasingly required to prepare students (and staff) to engage with these matters from multicultural, global and cosmopolitan perspectives (Bennani 2008, Delanty 2008, Stuart 2008). Moreover, as universities themselves are increasingly compelled to deal with these issues and begin to act as agents or actors in this globalised society (Delanty 2008), it is becoming critical to examine the practices and activities of citizenship *of* the institution (the university) itself, through concepts such as 'cosmopolitan citizenship' (Delanty 2008) and 'corporate citizenship' (Nagy and Robb 2008), as well as those *within* it.

It can be argued that the Council of Europe project on Education for Democratic Citizenship (1996–2000), from which the *Universities as Sites of Citizenship and Civic Responsibility* project originated, is situated within the growth of citizenship debates and practices such as those outlined above. And it is worth noting that in the European context the role of higher education in contributing to the development of transnational citizenship within Europe, namely 'European citizenship', had already been acknowledged in the early 1990s, as can be seen in the *Memorandum on Higher Education in the European Community* by the Commission of the European Communities (Zgaga 2009, p. 182). The project certainly acknowledged the multifaceted nature of the concept of citizenship which encompasses both a judicial and political status and a social role (Birzea 2000, pp. 30-31). At the same time, it also recognised that citizenship has become less bound by a specific geographic territory and that there has been a shift in and development of 'identitary citizenship', such as a global citizenship that reflects the identities and cultural and emotional dimensions of newly emerging communities rather than the civil, political and social rights endorsed by nation-states (Birzea 2000, pp. 10-11).

Nevertheless, the project largely focused on issues such as democratic education, student participation in university governance, and civic responsibility and engagement of the university, without taking much account of the multidimensional and changing aspects of citizenship, or possible tension between different citizenships. This is very well shown by the fact that despite (European) universities' efforts to support the increasing mobility of students and staff, issues concerning international students, minority ethnic groups and other socially marginalised groups, such as their membership of the university community or the multiculturalism of the university (which are issues relevant to 'social', 'cultural' and 'global' citizenships), were hardly addressed in the project (Birzea 2000, p. 46).

The relationship of universities with issues of citizenship and how universities engage with them today needs to be explored at a global level and beyond national boundaries, moving attention away from the concept of citizenship as a legal status with rights and obligations legitimised by the nation-state. Nevertheless, it is worth emphasising that the concepts and practices of citizenship as well as the form and nature of the university are very context specific, and their development is hugely influenced by national, historical, cultural and political factors. Consequently, the relationship between the university and citizenship should also be examined in relation to such historical, cultural and political specificities.

The discussion on citizenship and universities in the UK

The lack of wider discussion and research into how universities interact with the issue of citizenship has also been noticeable in the context of UK research and policy. It is only recently that the role of universities in promoting citizenship has been better acknowledged as one of higher education's policy priorities, as can be seen in the HEFCE *Strategic Plan 2006–11*. There has also been a limited but growing interest in the teaching of citizenship in UK universities, evident in several action research projects carried out, and programmes on citizenship delivered in various universities. In addition, research into citizenship, including discussion broadly linked with the question of citizenship in the UK is thriving in British academia, particularly in emerging centres of citizenship studies.

Despite such policy, teaching and research interests in citizenship, there is a need for further analysis of how the university in the UK is related to the concepts and practices of citizenship beyond regarding it as an academic subject. Studies of university and community partnership have illuminated the relationship between the university and citizenship through the university's role in developing human, social and creative capital which contributes to transforming society for the better (Watson 2007). Indeed, focusing on such a function of universities, policy bodies, for example HEFCE, have provided various sources of funding, such as the Higher Education Reach Out to Business and the Community programme (2000–2004) and the Higher Education Active Community Fund (2002–2006), to further enhance universities' work with communities (Hall *et al.* 2004). More recently, some of the projects supported by the Leadership, Governance and Management Fund (2007-2010) have also explored issues relating to citizenship. Volunteering in communities has a long history as part of student experience of higher education, but it was under the influence of the Dearing Report (The National Committee of Inquiry into Higher Education 1997) that volunteering as well as work experience were emphasised as a way for students to develop professional skills and learning (Annette 2005, p. 333). And under New Labour, volunteering was linked with citizenship and promoted as a means to fulfil higher education's responsibility to local communities as well as to develop key skills of students (Hall *et al.* 2004, p. 40).

However, much discussion in this area has focused on the aspect of 'social citizenship' redefined in the Crick report, which mostly considers moral responsibility (Arthur 2005, p. 1). The studies on citizenship and the university in the UK, therefore, have focused largely on 'promoting the active worker-citizen' (Ahier *et al.* 2003, p. 63), and the moral and personal development of students (and staff) – becoming more aware of their civic responsibilities – through volunteering. In this respect, the discussion takes for granted the university's role in producing 'good' citizens, but does not further interrogate what this citizenship means – whether it is bound by national boundaries – nor the possible impact of universities on various forms of citizenship. There has been little investigation of the impact of universities on broader socio-political aspects of citizenship or their wider responsibilities to society. In fact, while emphasising the importance of developing research into the socio-economic roles of universities and their impact on regional communities, a previous research study has pointed out that investigation into the socio-political and cultural roles of universities is far less developed than that into the socio-economic roles of universities (Brennan *et al.* 2006).

The underdevelopment of research in this area may be due to some extent to an ambiguity regarding the definition of communities in society with which universities engage and for which they are responsible. As this remains unclear, it is extremely challenging to consider the universities' role in society and impact on the members of that society, let alone their relationship to community membership, namely 'citizenship'. For compulsory education, this seems to be far more straightforward, because its focus is clearly more on local and national communities, and thus more emphasis is given to education in relation to democracy. In the context of universities, however, the idea of membership of various communities is more ambiguous, given universities' connection to local, national and international entities, although it is often assumed that what 'citizenship' refers to is self-evident. Furthermore, the *grounds* for citizenship are rarely explained: that is, the question 'What are the reasons for claiming this membership?' is not addressed.

The expansion of higher education and the changes this has brought to the roles and responsibilities of universities adds further to the complication of undertaking research in this area. Over the past decade, the UK higher education sector has expanded dramatically. With more students of diverse backgrounds, including international students, participating in higher education, universities have been increasingly required to engage with the issue of diversity, equality and inclusion to accommodate different learning needs and to promote diverse cultural dialogues, where the idea of 'cosmopolitan citizenship' may be appropriate. However, such an expansion has also happened against the background of intensifying globalisation, the emergence of the 'knowledge society', diminishing public funding for HE and the influence of neo-liberalism, which has entailed challenging issues. Universities globally are now forced to restructure so that they can compete in the markets with each other not only for funding and other resources but also for students, and this has been achieved through economic efficiency and individual choices where students are regarded as customers/consumers. The corporate style of university has emerged (Rutherford 2005), and such changes have especially impacted on universities in English-speaking countries (Delanty 2001, p. 75) – this corporatisation having been further exacerbated since the higher education reforms initiated by the UK Coalition Government in 2010. While students are provided with wider choices as consumers and universities have a responsibility to students as a provider of service, students' participation and experience of higher education is diversified and stratified with unresolved inequalities (David 2009). At the same time, in order to survive in such a market-driven economy and society, universities also seek answers through internationalisation strategies such as recruiting more overseas students, international collaboration in research and teaching or international franchising in provision (De Vita and Case 2003, p. 385). UK universities have a long history of the participation of students from overseas, and international collaborations are not a new phenomenon. However, the current internationalisation of UK universities has moved away from altruistic cultural exchanges and gives more emphasis to advancing their competitiveness for an economical gain; international students become not only customers, but also a 'commodity' (Dodds 2009). However, it is the very complexity of the roles and functions of the UK university that could provide an important insight into the ways that citizenship and university are interconnected, and the contradiction and tension arising from this.

The possibility of research into universities and citizenship

Given such a gap in research, many questions are yet to be explored regarding the interface between the university and citizenship. What kind of citizenships would universities promote or challenge and how? How should the university *as an institution* act as a citizen? Can the university provide new and innovative ideas and practices of citizenships? Specifically in the European context, Biesta (2009) stresses the importance of exploring the contribution of the university to the discourse of citizenship beyond the approaches of the 'active citizen' and civic competency which are predominant in European (educational) policy and research. A similar research approach and policy can be pursued with regard to the issue of UK universities and citizenship. Despite the impact of neo-liberalism and the knowledge society, the university remains 'a site of public discourses' where various contradictions of society are present (Delanty 2001, p. 81). And this is why the research into the critical commitment of the university to the issue of citizenship becomes important (Biesta, *et al.* 2009, Zgaga 2009).

Five issues relating to the university and citizenship can be suggested as areas ripe for exploration: teaching and research in citizenship; academic, local community, international, and business partnerships; equality, diversity and difference; student and staff identity; and corporate citizenship. The list is not exhaustive nor does it attempt to answer the question of how (UK) universities can actually contribute to the development of concepts and practices of citizenship. Rather, it aims to cast light on arenas within the university where various discourses of citizenship may be articulated and contradict one another. I will now consider each of these five possible research areas, in turn.

First, in terms of programmes of citizenship offered in universities in the UK, there were over 30 undergraduate programmes which have been categorised under the citizenship subject in the Universities and Colleges Admissions Service (UCAS) database in 2009[6]. In addition, some universities have undertaken initiatives to design and develop modules on citizenship, which are taught across (undergraduate) programmes[7]. Furthermore, a number of research centres have been established within universities which include 'citizenship' in their names[8]. A useful entry point into an exploration of the relationship between citizenship and the university would be to examine the aims of these courses and research centres, and how they define 'citizen' and 'citizenship' – whether they create a space for concepts and practice of citizenship which transcend the instrumental interpretation of 'active citizenship'.

Second, the rights and obligations that citizens hold must be understood in the context of the society in which they reside. 'Society' is multilayered, and has a local, regional and national dimension. Until the recent development of interest in global citizenship, citizenship was usually viewed within the boundaries of nation-states. However, as Isin and Turner (2007, p. 14) suggest, although citizens may remain 'contained' within the state, with the politics of redistribution and recognition and the intensified mobility of people and ideas, it is possible to consider citizenship beyond national boundaries. The enquiry into citizenship and universities can also be reframed through this question of the socio-political role of the university and its engagement with wider society. Currently, various academic, business, local community and international partnerships take place in universities, such as joint programmes offered with other universities and educational institutions, academic and student exchange programmes, employer engagement initiatives, and community engagement projects. Examining these initiatives and activities would clarify the university's role in the wider society and the extent and nature of its communities. It would also identify the kind of membership enacted in these communities and possible tensions between different citizenships such as national, global or cosmopolitan citizenships.

Third, although the term remains controversial, the UK today is largely understood as a 'multicultural' society, and with widening participation initiatives, the profile of students now attending universities is more diverse. Intensifying internationalisation, globalisation, and marketization of universities also means an increased participation of international students and staff in universities in the UK. In an effort to reflect the multicultural nature of society and emphasise their international standpoint, universities often stress their respect for equality and diversity (Ahmed 2006). As universities have a widely ranging population with different gender, 'race', ethnicities, religious beliefs, ages, disabilities, sexualities, social class, and nationalities, investigating what kind of 'diversity' the university appreciates, accepts, creates or denies will also lead to a consideration of the concepts and practices of citizenship present in the university. For example, when universities deal with the issue of racism, do their obligations to those who are from outside the UK differ from their obligations towards those who are British nationals? Does the equality and diversity agenda support a more global or cosmopolitan perspective of citizenship as opposed to the national one?

Fourth, the diverse profiles of participants in universities in the UK imply an increased mobility (both social and geographical) of students and staff. This raises questions of whether their experience of working or studying at universities in the UK constructs, reproduces or challenges certain identities, and whether this has an impact on ideas and practices of citizenship; whether it creates a new active (academic or intellectual) citizenship which transgresses national boundaries; whether nationally bound citizenship is being reinterpreted to be more inclusive; or whether traditional roles as 'domesticated' citizens who are mobilised to maximise national interests are accepted and enable the nation-state to survive intensifying international (economic and academic) competition. Previous research suggests that while many non-traditional students (for example, the first generation in a family to enter university, mature students without formal qualifications and students with English as an additional language) do not feel that they fit into the university culture, they do not attempt to voice their feelings of exclusion; rather, they accept their social status and take it for granted (Kimura 2006). The question of personal identity corresponds to the question of whether students and staff enact or accept a particular form of 'citizenship' through their experience in the university, such as that of 'active citizenship' in which students could be led to accept the existing socio-political order (Biesta 2009, p. 154); and whether their identities challenge existing social divisions constructing a more political and critical idea of citizenship or redefining the membership.

The last issue is about the 'marketization' of universities in a globalised society. Government initiatives for widening participation and lifelong learning have created increased demands for university education and have placed a tremendous pressure on universities' resources. Universities have to compete with each other to recruit students (and staff) nationally and internationally to meet the diverse needs of students. However, the public funding of universities has been declining, and as seen in the Browne Report, universities have been required to seek alternative funding to fulfil such increased demands (The Browne Report 2010). This means that universities not only have to seek sources of private income, often developing partnerships or collaborations with private organisations, but also themselves have to act as business organisations in managing their finances (Rutherford 2005, Nagy and Robb 2008). Such an emerging trend calls for further scrutiny in terms of the impact of these reforms on student citizenship. Do students become active consumers with wider educational and learning opportunities and innovative learning commodities to choose from (Jarvis 2001, pp. 86-7)? Does the rise of the corporate university mean that universities themselves are to be considered corporate citizens with relevant corporate responsibilities (Nagy and Robb 2008)? Are the values and practices that the 'university as a corporate' embraces compatible with values and practices of other forms of citizenship that universities might promote? For example, do students become a mere commodity for the economic gain of the university (Dodds 2009) rather than becoming more politically aware citizens?

In examining how universities engage with the issue of citizenship, it is important to explore both normative and actual practices. Normative practices, here, imply narratives of citizenship operating within universities. They can be wide-ranging and present at different levels of the operation and functions within universities: for example, mission statements and other policy documents (management); course and programme material (pedagogy); topics and foci of research (on citizenship); and public relations documents regarding the provision of services to business, community and academic communities. Actual practices refer to the diverse arrangements and practices that exist, also at different levels within universities, which in effect develop specific ideas and practices of citizenship, such as student and academic exchange programmes, student ambassador schemes, and variable fees between home and overseas students. Looking at both normative and actual practices enables us to explore the disparity between narratives and deeds – namely, the 'non performativity' of speech acts argued by Sara Ahmed (Ahmed 2006b) – and highlights the conflicts between different notions and practices of citizenship within universities.

Tension between different concepts of citizenship in the university

As I have argued above, there are various interfaces which help us consider the question of how universities relate to the notion and practices of citizenships. In this section, I will highlight how different university roles can lead to tension between different notions and practices of citizenships by giving two examples.

On 16 May 2008, Rizwaaan Sabir, an MA student in Nottingham University who was studying Islamic terrorism, and his friend Hicham Yezza, an administrator in the university, were arrested under the Terrorism Act. Sabir had downloaded a copy of an al-Qaeda training manual from a US government website and passed it on to Yezza to print out because the document was too large and expensive for him to print out himself. Yezza was helping Sabir to prepare a Ph.D. proposal. A colleague of Yezza spotted the document left at the printer and reported it to the university, which led to the arrest of the two men. They were detained for six days before being released without charge. However, Yezza, who had been in the UK for 13 years by then and was supposed to have UK residency, was later rearrested on grounds related to immigration and 'fast-tracked' for deportation to Algeria on 23 May 2008. After a petition and protest from his support group, his deportation was suspended, and he was able to fight his case in court[9]. Meanwhile, the vice-chancellor of the university issued a statement in which he said:

> There is no 'right' to access and research terrorist materials. Those who do so run the risk of being investigated and prosecuted on terrorism charges. Equally, there is no 'prohibition' on accessing terrorist materials for the purpose of research. Those who do so are likely to be able to offer a defence to charges (although they may be held in custody for some time while the matter is investigated). This is the law and

applies to all universities. 'Arrests on Campus update – July 9th 2008', quoted in Newman (2008)

In May 2011, Rod Thornton, a lecturer in the School of Politics and International Relation was suspended after placing a report on the British International Political Association website that criticises the University for mistreating Sabir and Yezza. These incidents should be understood in the context of the growing concern of the British government about political activities within universities, which was highlighted by the release of guidance in November 2006 on how universities should tackle extremism, entitled *Promoting Good Campus Relations: Working with Staff and Students to Build Community Cohesion and Tackle Violent Extremism in the Name of Islam at Universities and Colleges*[10]. The incident highlights some of the discourses of citizenship operating in universities: do academic and administrative staff have responsibilities to monitor the activities of certain (religious or ethnic) groups on campus in the name of national security, or should they protect academic freedom? How should they negotiate between national citizenship, academic citizenship, and more human rights-focused cosmopolitan citizenship?

The second example relates to an aspect of corporate citizenship. The Open University introduced a scheme in 2007 whereby customers of one of the major supermarkets in the UK were given access to its courses by using points on their loyalty cards. This scheme was welcomed by those who thought it could be an innovative way to connect the university with 'hard-to-reach' groups, as one of the university's missions is to widen participation, and thereby to impact on enhancing citizenship (The Open University 2007). The university was also a member of the Metrix Consortium which was chosen as preferred bidder for a government contract in 2007 for the Defence Training Rationalisation project to run a training agency for the British armed forces at St Athan in South Glamorgan, Wales. The contract was, however, cancelled in October 2010 on commercial grounds, as it was considered that the Metrix Consortium 'cannot deliver an affordable, commercially-robust proposal within the prescribed period' (Ministry of Defence 2010). What do such partnerships signify? Whilst they might enhance a university's mission to promote educational opportunity to those who otherwise would not have access to higher education, and may promote the recognition of cultural citizenship, they also raise the question of whether such partnerships could contradict The Open University's stated mission to support social justice, along with the promotion of citizenship such as environmental citizenship or cosmopolitan democratic citizenship. It begs questions of the ethical responsibility of the university and which idea of citizenships a university should prioritise?

Conclusion

Exploring what kinds of ideas of citizenship are circulated in policy and actual practice in universities in the UK, will not only fill the gap in research into the role of the university in society, but will also add a new scope to citizenship studies. This is because the university is a unique institution with various actors that concurrently occupy the local, national and international levels, with all the contradictions rising from contemporary socio-economical changes. Rather than prescribing answers to the question of how the university could contribute to the development and promotion of a certain citizenship, this paper has focused on the potential of (UK) universities as a site of enacting citizenships and developing and performing new and innovative ideas and practices of multiple citizenships, emphasising the importance of research into the relationship between the university and citizenship.

The study of the relationship between the university and citizenship can also bridge the fundamental gap that currently exists between higher education research and sociological approaches, which has been identified in existing literature. Various factors both in sociology and higher education research have led to the widening of such a gap or 'disconnection' (Deem 2004). As pointed out in Houston and Lebeau (2005, p. 3) sociologists have become indifferent to 'what is actually happening in teaching and learning contexts' of higher education. This is partly because, it is argued, the sociology of education, and consequently the sociology of higher education, has long been given a lower status in the discipline of sociology (Delamont 2000). It is also because, since the mid 1980s, the main concerns of sociology have moved away from social institutions or structures which are the core elements of education (Deem 2004). Furthermore, the 'cultural turn' which took place in sociology in the 1990s shifted research foci in sociology; less emphasis is now given to social structures and processes, and there is more focus on popular culture rather than the 'high culture' that educational settings are said to signify.

As for higher education research or the sociology of higher education in the UK, it presently does not engage much with issues central to sociology (Deem 2004, pp. 21-22). This can be explained by its more policy-focused approach and, as in the field of higher education study more generally, research foci are often defined by government policy within very tight timescales. This prevents researchers from conducting theoretically sound, empirically rigorous, and methodologically less positivistic research which allows an exploration of more substantive sociological questions relating to higher education (Johnston 2003). In addition, research into higher education teaching and learning is often supported by funds which focus more on *improving* teaching and learning – on pedagogical techniques – than on 'examining the social relations and conditions of higher education' (Deem 2004). Given such an existing disciplinary disjuncture, looking at the broader social role and impact of universities through the framework of citizenships will provide an opportunity for bringing together scholars in higher education research and the social sciences to consider this issue more collaboratively.

Notes

1 In examining the social benefits of universities in Britain, in a recently published report commission by Universities UK, Shaheen (2011) emphasises the role of universities in contributing to diverse policy objectives including those in citizenship.

2 These include the HEFCE funded *Crucible* in the University of Roehampton, the HEFCE funded *Teaching Citizenship in HE* in the Universities of Southampton, Keele and Liverpool John Moore, and the Higher Education Academy (HEA) funded *Working with Schools: Active Citizenship for Undergraduate Students* in the University of East London and Buckinghamshire Chiltern's University College (now Bucks New University).

3 This followed the issue of the *Policy Paper for Change and Development in Higher Education* in 1995 and five successive regional consultations.

4 The project derived from the Council of Europe project on Education for Democratic Citizenship (1996–2000), the adoption of the Declaration and Programme on Education for

Democratic Citizenship, based on the Rights and Responsibilities of Citizens in 1999, and the similar concern in the USA which was presented in the Wingspread Declaration on Renewing the Civic Mission of the American Research University (1998) and the Presidents' Fourth of July Declaration on the Civic Responsibility of Higher Education. After the pilot phase was completed, the project was further extended in Europe and the USA and has also incorporated universities in South Africa and currently in the process of expanding to Australia, South Korea and Latin America. (http://www.internationalconsortium.org/research/universities-as-sites.html last accessed in July 2011)

5 With the exception of The Council of Europe Higher Education Series, nos 1, 2 and 8 (Bergan *et al.* 2004, Weber and Bergan 2005, Huber and Harkavy 2007) which explore the role of higher education in promoting democratic culture.

6 The universities that offered these courses included: University of Central Lancashire, University of Chichester, University of Glamorgan, Cardiff and Pontypridd, University of Gloucestershire, University of Greenwich, University of Wales, Newport, Glyndwr University (formerly the North East Wales Institute of Higher Education), University of Northampton, University of Roehampton, and University of Surrey. (Information obtained from UCAS website in March 2009.) However, the number of programmes has gone down to 14 in 2011. (Information obtained from UCAS website in July 2011.) This is due partly to a decrease in the number of teacher training courses in citizenship education.

7 Universities which took such initiatives include: Roehampton, Southampton and Keele.

8 These include: the Citizenship, Civil Society and Rule of Law, University of Aberdeen; the Centre for the Study of Ethnicity and Citizenship, University of Bristol; the Centre for Digital Citizenship, University of Leeds; the Centre for Citizenship Studies in Education, University of Leicester; International Centre for Education for Democratic Citizenship, Birkbeck and Institute of Education, University of London; the Centre for Citizenship, Identities and Governance, the Open University; and the Centre for Citizenship, Globalization and Governance, University of Southampton; the Centre for Global Citizenship, University College London.

9 He lost the case against the Home Office in February 2009 and was sentenced to a nine-month custodial sentence in March 2009.

10 This guidance was updated in January 2008 as 'Promoting good campus relations, fostering shared values and preventing violent extremism in universities and higher education colleges'. Also, in June 2011, a new Prevent Strategy was issued, which emphasises the role of universities amongst other institutions in preventing radicalisation.

References

Ahier, J., Beck, J. and Moore, R., 2003. *Graduate Citizens? Issues of citizenship and higher education*. London: Routledge Falmer.

Ahmed, S., 2006a. Doing Diversity Work in Higher Education in Australia. *Educational Philosophy and Theory* 38 (6), 745-768.

Ahmed, S., 2006b. Non-Performativity of Antiracism. *Meridians* 7 (1), 104-126.

Altbach, P.G., 2008. The complex roles of universities in the period of globalization. *In* Global University Network for Innovation (GUNI) *Higher Education in the World 3* Basingstoke: Palgrave Macmillan, 5-14.

Annette, J., 2005. Character, civic renewal and service learning for democratic citizenship in higher education. *British Journal of Educational Studies* 53 (3), 326-340.

Arthur, J., 2005. Introduction. *In* J. Arthur with K.E. Bohlin, eds. *Citizenship and Higher Education*. London: Routledge Falmer.

Bennani, A., 2008. The contribution of higher education to multicultural existence: present and future challenges. In Global University Network for Innovation (GUNI) *Higher Education in the World 3*, Basingstoke: Palgrave MacMillan, 31-34.

Bergan, S., Persson, A., Plantan, F., Musteață, S. and Garabagiu, A., 2004. *The University as Res Publica*. Council of Europe higher education series Strasbourg: Council of Europe Publishing.

Biesta, G., 2009. What kind of Citizenship for European Higher Education? Beyond the Competent Active Citizen. *European Educational Research Journal* 9 (2), 146-158.

Biesta, G. and Simons, M., 2009. Higher Education and European Citizenship as a Matter of Public Concern. *European Educational Research Journal* 9 (2), 142-145.

Biesta, G., Kwiek, M., Locke, G., Martins, H., Masschelein, J., Papatsiba, V., Simons, M. and Zgaga, P., 2009. What is the Public Role of the University? A Proposal for a Public Research Agenda. *European Educational Research Journal* 8 (2), 146-158.

Birzea, C., 2000. Project on 'Education for Democratic Citizenship: Education for Democratic Citizenship: A Lifelong Learning Perspective'. Strasbourg: Council for Cultural Co-operation (CDCC), Council of Europe.

Brennan, J., Little, B. and Locke, W., 2006. *Higher education's effects on disadvantaged groups and communities*. Available at: http://www.open.ac.uk/cheri/documents/esrc-crossregional-final-report.pdf.

David, M.E., 2009. Social Diversity and Democracy in higher Education in the 21st Century: Towards a Feminist Critique. *Higher Education Policy* 22 (1), 61-79.

Deem, R., 2004. Sociology and the Sociology of Higher Education: a missed call or a disconnection? *International Studies in Sociology of Education* 14 (1), 21-44.

Delamont, S., 2000. The Anomalous Beasts: Hooligans and the Sociology of Education. *Sociology* 34 (1), 95-111.

Delanty, G., 2001. Ideologies of the Knowledge Society and the Cultural Contradictions of Higher Education. *Policy Futures in Education* 1 (1), 71-82.

Delanty, G., 2006. The cosmopolitan imagination: critical cosmopolitanism and social theory. *The British Journal of Sociology* 57 (1), 26-47.

Delanty, G., 2008. The university and cosmopolitan citizenship. In Global University Network for Innovation (GUNI) *Higher Education in the World 3*. Basingstoke: Palgrave Macmillan, 28-79.

De Vita, G., and Case, P., 2003. Rethinking the internationalisation agenda in UK higher education. *Journal of Further and Higher Education* 27 (4), 383-398.

Dodds, A., 2009. Liberalization and the public sector: the pre-eminent role of governments in the 'sale' of higher education abroad. *Public Administration* 87 (2), 397-411.

Gifford, C., 2004. National and Post-national Dimensions of Citizenship Education in the UK. *Citizenship Studies* 8 (2), 145-158.

Hall, D., Hall, I., Cameron, A., and Green, P., 2004. Student volunteering and the active community: issues and opportunities for teaching and learning in sociology. *Learning and Teaching in the Social Sciences* 1 (1), 33-50.

Higher Education Funding Council for England (HEFCE), 2006. *HEFCE Strategic Plan 2006-11*. Bristol: Higher Education Funding Council for England.

Houston, M., and Lebeau , Y., 2005. The Social Mediation of University Learning. Paper presented at the Social and Organisational Mediation of University Learning (SOMUL) Conference, Cambridge, September 2005. Available at: http://www.tlrp.org/dspace/handle/123456789/909.

Huber, J. and Harkavy, I., eds. 2007. *Higher Education and democratic culture: citizenship, human rights and civic responsibility*. Strasbourg: Council of Europe.

Isin, E.F. and Turner, B.S., 2002. Citizenship Studies: An Introduction. *In* E.F. Isin and B.S. Turner, eds. *Handbook of Citizenship Studies*. London: SAGE.

Isin, E.F. and Turner, B.S., 2007. Investigating Citizenship: An Agenda for Citizenship Studies. *Citizenship Studies* 11 (1), 5-17.

Jarvis, P., 2001. *Universities and Corporate Universities: The Higher Learning Industry in Global Society*. London: Routledge.

Johnston, B., 2003. The Shape of Research in the Field of Higher Education and Graduate Employment: some issues. *Studies in Higher Education* 28 (4), 413-426.

Kimura, M., 2006. *Ethnicity, Education and Employment: Final Report.* London: Continuum, University of East London.

Kofman, E., 2005. Citizenship, Migration and the Reassertion of National Identity. *Citizenship Studies* 9 (5), 453-467.

Ministry of Defence (MoD), 2010. Termination of the Defence Training Review (http://www.mod.uk/DefenceInternet/DefenceNews/DefencePolicyAndBusiness/TerminationOfTheDefence-TrainingReview.htm, accessed July 2011).

Nagy, J. and Robb, A., 2008. Can universities be good corporate citizens? *Critical Perspectives on Accounting* 19 (8), 1414-1430.

National Committee of Inquiry into Higher Education, 1997. *Higher Education in the Learning Society (The Dearing Report).* London: The Stationary Office.

Newman, M., 2008. Researchers have no 'right' to study terrorist materials. *The Times Higher Education Supplement* 17 July 2008.

Nyers, P., 2007. Introduction: Why Citizenship Studies. *Citizenship Studies* 11 (1), 1-4.

Plantan, F., 2002. *Universities as sites of citizenship and civic responsibility.* Strasbourg: Council of Europe.

Qualifications and Curriculum Authority (QCA), 1998. *Education for Citizenship and the teaching of democracy in schools.* London: Qualifications and Curriculum Authority.

Rutherford, J., 2005. Cultural Studies in the Corporate University. *Cultural Studies* 19 (3), 297-317.

Shaheen, F., 2011. *Degrees of value: How universities benefit society.* London: New Economics Foundation.

Schoenenberger, A.M., 2005. Are higher education and academic research a public good or public responsibility? A review of the economic literature. *In* L. Weber and S. Bergan, eds. *The public responsibility for higher education and research.* Strasbourg: Council of Europe Publishing, 45-93.

Stuart, M., 2008. The concept of global citizenship in higher education. In Global University Network for Innovation (GUNI) *Higher Education in the World 3.* Basingstoke: Palgrave Macmillan, 79-83.

Taylor, P., 2008. Introduction. In Global University Network for Innovation (GUNI) *Higher Education in the World 3.* Basingstoke: Palgrave Macmillan, 1-4.

The Browne Report (Independent Review of Higher Education Funding and Student Finance), 2010. *Securing a sustainable future for higher education.* London: Independent Review of Higher Education Funding and Student Finance.

The Open University, 2007. Supermarket sweep for your views. *Open House: Newspaper for staff of The Open University.* Milton Keynes: The Open University, 410.

Turner, B.S., 1993. Contemporary Problems in the Theory of Citizenship. *In* B.S. Turner., ed. *Citizenship and Social Theory.* London: SAGE, 1-18.

UNESCO, 1998. *World Declaration on Higher Education for the Twenty-first Century: Vision and Action* (http://www.unesco.org/education/educprog/wche/declaration_eng.htm, last accessed July 2011).

Watson, D., 2007. *Managing Civic and Community Engagement.* Maidenhead: The Open University Press.

Weber, L., and Bergan, S., eds. 2005. *The public responsibility for higher education and research.* Strasbourg: Council of Europe.

Yuval-Davis, N., 2007. Intersectionality, Citizenship and Contemporary Politics of Belonging. *Critical Review of International Social and Political Philosophy* 10 (4), 561-574.

Zgaga, P., 2009. Higher Education and Citizenship: 'the full range of purposes'. *European Educational Research Journal* 8 (2), 175-188.

Youth media enterprise: ethos, administration and pastoral care

Denise Meredyth

College of Design and Social Context, Royal Melbourne Institute of Technology, Melbourne, Australia

This paper discusses models of alternative education in which the person-forming disciplines of the school have been adapted by social enterprises and not for profit agencies. It discusses innovative youth media enterprises, which use digital media creation and broadcasting with marginalised and at risk young people, intervening in their lives and offering them 'voice' and vocational options. The paper focuses on Youthworx, an initiative run by youth work advocates, a youth-run radio station and the Salvation Army, with support from education and governmental agencies. Youthworx is an enterprise run by non-state agencies and faith-based organisations. It presents itself as an alternative to a failing school system. Like the school, however, it depends on pedagogic regimes that combine social administration with spiritual discipline and moral formation. The paper offers an alternative to the critique of 'hidden' norms and power relations in pedagogic environments. Instead, it aims to describe the mixed purposes and conditional alliances involved in adapting the school's techniques of supervised freedom to the model of social enterprise, within the public-private networks that now make up social governance.

Introduction

This article explores the pedagogic innovations and social interventions involved in youth media development. It explores the implications of recent research and development work on creative hubs in depressed urban areas, which use multi-media creation and broadcast facilities to engage marginalised young people, working both with peers and professionals as media producers, broadcasters and trainers (Soep 2006a, Huesca 2008). These creative hubs are social enterprises, funded through a mix of philanthropy, government support and entrepreneurial activity. They sit outside formal schooling and vocational training, as alternative learning spaces, but their success depends in part on making connections with schools, technical and vocational education and with the universities. Importantly, they are also connected to community media, to audiences and to the professional networks of the creative industries, as well as to a variety of social service providers, advocacy groups and local communities. Their origins and affiliations vary. Some of these initiatives stem from university outreach and others from activist and voluntary organisations. Their sources of funding are equally various. Each is connected to networks, flow and exchange between education and training, communications, social services and employment, and between third sector, government, community and commercial agencies. These networks are able to create new pathways, in the current policy parlance, for young people otherwise stuck in limited locations.

Such initiatives offer rich sites for the analysis of lifelong learning and informal education, as part of the mixed economy of welfare (Fyfe 2005, Powell 2007). This paper explores the ethical and political imperatives that drive these initiatives. Each, in different ways, draws on the neo-liberal vocabulary of enterprise and choice, as well as on neo-communitarian conceptions of participation and communal responsibility – a combination that as critics have noted, is characteristic of 'Third Way' approaches to social welfare (Clarke *et al* 2007, Hall 2003, Larner and Butler 2005). Drawing on American and Australian examples of youth media developments and creative hubs, the paper focuses on Youthworx, a community media development initiative for homeless and marginalised young people, under the sponsorship of The Salvation Army. It explores the rationales, techniques, roles and ethical styles involved in such initiatives, placing them in the context of broader debates on Third Way approaches to social welfare. Making a case for a moderate critical approach, which refrains from moralising about moralisation, and which refuses the critical invocation of the tension between freedom and constraint, self-realisation and normalisation, it seeks a pragmatic description of the multiple ends and conflicting imperatives involved in social governance and of pedagogic practice (Pykett 2009, 2010). Youth media development initiatives, I argue, need to be understood as products of patchy history of efforts to solve endemic social problems such as poverty, illiteracy and crime; problems perpetually out of the reach of governing bodies. These alternatives to the school, I argue, emerged from efforts to reform and moralise populations through creativity and self-expression. They adapt and apply venerable strategies of social intervention and civic formation, drawing on pedagogic techniques that have migrated from the school to the neighbourhood and back again. Understanding this helps to explain the combination of creative expression and ethical discipline to be found in youth media initiatives and creative hubs, without subjecting them to ritual critical suspicion, as failing to be free.

Creative hubs

Creative youth media hubs are proliferating in the UK, Australia and more recently in Britain (Soep 2006a, Fleetwood 2004). They can be described as social enterprises in the creative industries, building on the traditions of youth media development; media 'conceived, developed and produced by young people' (Soep 2006b, p34). Examples include 'Youth Radio', based in the San Francisco Bay Area (Soep 2006a, 2006b) and the 'One Economy Corporation'; each of these non-profits has branches across the States, as well as international nodes (One Economy 2006a, 2006b). Each works with young people from poor urban areas, living in environments with high crime rates and few cultural facilities. Each works at the intersection between community media and creative industries, social services, public health promotion, job creation, neighbourhood renewal and crime prevention.

These creative hubs offer training in media production and broadcasting out of school hours, with media professionals and with the chance of contributing to radio broadcasts. This training leads to internships, some voluntary and some paid. Gradually, the young people are engaged, trained and equipped to make broadcast-quality media products, from web materials to radio, television and short films. They work with peers and professionals, learning about the organisational and administrative side of the workplace as well as its media production side; at the same time, they stay in school or accredited training. The media production work, in turn, re-engages them with their communities, as critical investigators and as media creators. They make news stories or create web-based community resources; they make short films about their own stories, about the street and neighbourhood, about social issues for their peers, about politics. The creative hub gives them an alternative to the street, but it also gets them to go back out there as active and critical members of communities facing acute problems.

Equipped with both critical and compositional skills, and with new abilities to negotiate with others and articulate a position, the young people become 'digital generators', working back out in the community to show people how to use technology and access media content designed to meet their needs for information on housing, health, financial management and social services (One Economy 2006a, 2006b). As Soep (2006b, p34) puts it, they 'take on some of democracy's most pressing themes and issues as they work in an environment designed to promote active participation, involvement in decision-making and constant vigilance around matters of equity'.

Soep notes four key shared features of youth media developments: 'peer teaching, collegial pedagogy, multiple outlets, and applied agency' (Soep 2006b, p35). She describes 'collegial pedagogy' as involving environments and processes where 'young people and adults jointly frame and carry out projects in a relationship marked by interdependence and mutual accountability' (ibid.). Mentoring adults 'offer access to equipment, expertise, in-the-moment advice, creative collaboration, and, crucially, a network of relationships with outlets for young people' (Soep 2006b, p38). Young people find 'agency', which involves more than just 'giving youth voice'. It means engaging with the 'the power and persistence of inequality' and it means 'working on a systemic level to help open concrete opportunities and expose injustices where they exist' (Soep 2006b, p 39). For Soep, importantly, these critical learning spaces are not, 'free' public spaces for youth. They involve structure, instruction, discipline and hierarchy: they involve demanding professional collaboration, rigorous editing and production processes, hard decision-making and complex, tension-filled work environments. In their combination of freedom and discipline, agency and constraint, they offer some lessons to those looking for an expression of an authentic youth voice and a simple story about self-realisation and emancipation.

Similar lessons and stories are to be found in an Australian example on which I would like to concentrate in this article. Youthworx is a small but growing youth media development initiative in inner-city Melbourne, Australia. It resembles Youth Radio and other such initiatives, in that it offers out-of-school access to media production, training and broadcasting outlets, some employment and community outreach for marginalised young people. One of the differences though is that Youthworx is designed for young people who are homeless (in residential or foster care), who have been expelled from school or have dropped out, who have been in drug and alcohol counselling or who have a juvenile justice history. Another of its distinctive features is that it is closely associated with a faith-based organisation: its major funder is The Salvation Army, working in alliance with the non-profit Youth Development Australia and a youth-run community broadcaster, SYN Media, as well as university and technical education providers. The project shares the focus on peer learning, critical skills and agency that Soep describes as part of American initiatives. It is framed and explained by organisers as a secular social services initiative for intervention into the personal development and skills needs of homeless and at risk youth. At the same time, it has a history in programs of Christian outreach through popular media and communications. It builds on The Salvation Army's long involvement in experimental media. These range from the evangelical films it made though the Limelight Department in 1897 to its investment in evangelical community radio in the 1920s and its more recent provision of programs such as StreetConnect, a mobile food and Internet service for homeless young people, or StreetFM, an Internet radio station broadcasting to young people on Sydney streets (Wilson 2007). The Youthworx initiative extends these outreach experiments into youth community radio and multimedia production (Mackenzie 2003).

Youthworx has a complex organisational structure. It is hosted and owned by the not-for-profit Youth Development Australia (YDA), which has strong links to Swinburne University. The Salvation Army is the major funder, strongly represented on the initiative's steering committee. The Salvation Army, in turn, works with YDA to draw on government and philanthropic support and to seek commercial sponsorship. The young people come in to the creative hub – a converted warehouse in Brunswick, equipped with multimedia facilities, meeting rooms and a recording studio – through training and job creation schemes, and through the Salvation Army's institutional links to homelessness services, youth refuges, drug and alcohol referral agencies and migrant resettlement programs. The young people come in for one-off sessions of media production. If they return, or enrol in short courses, they can work with media trainers to plan and record songs and radio shows, make digital stories, websites and blogs, script, shoot and edit short films.

After initial training, enrolees can go on to produce a weekly radio show at SYN-Media, a youth radio station with an FM license, which has expanded over recent years into a multiplatform community media group. SYN is a highly successful training ground for young people. Run by young people under 26, it works with schools and universities to attract volunteer producers and creators, many of whom stay with the station, take on significant production or management responsibilities and often go on to do well within community and commercial broadcasting, or in various positions across the creative industries (Rennie and Thomas 2008). SYN produces FM radio for a wide Melbourne audience; it also produces television for community station C31 and has a significant online presence. Entry to SYN from Youthworx opens these audiences to the trainees; broadcasting live to peers is both exciting and difficult, posing as it does the discipline of working in a team and producing broadcast quality material to time.

Youthworx has now been working with young people on a regular basis since early 2008. At the time of writing, in late 2009, more than 120 students have passed through the Youthworx studio. There are plans to expand it into a mobile service and to connect with schools and training in regional and rural areas, working with indigenous and ethnic communities, building on job creation and training schemes. Over time, Youthworx aims to become a sustainable media-based social enterprise, not unlike Youth Radio or One Economy. It has already begun to draw in commissions for short documentaries and aims to expand, becoming a small creative industries start-up, in which young people are employed as interns, making commissioned material for public, third-sector and commercial agencies who are seeking to connect with niche community audiences. The enterprise is still likely to need support from the public sector, as well as from philanthropic bodies, but the case for this is being put in terms of the potential of the Youthworx, as a social enterprise, to become self-sustaining.

Creative youth hub enterprises like Youthworx, Youth Radio and One Economy offer a very persuasive case for public and philanthropic investment. The arguments go beyond the celebration of 'voice', digital story-telling and participation (Bekerman *et al.* 2006, Podkalicka and Staley 2009). They can also be understood as making real interventions into poverty and homelessness, opening economic opportunities for individuals and regions, as well as cultural and creative ones. To draw on the language of the creative industries, these initiatives broaden the social base of the creative economy (Howkins 2002). They address groups of young people who do not fit the model of the adept 'digital natives' experimenting in emergent forms of professional-amateur creativity (Kress 2003, Buckingham and Willett 2006, Hartley 2008, Sefton-Green and Nixon 2009). Many of them, especially the Youthworx entrants, live outside schools, families or employment, and many lack the literate or English-speaking skills to read newspapers or participate in mainstream culture. Not all of them are media literate or digitally literate; though they tend to be very interested in music, film, TV and the web, they tend not to be radio listeners. Through these creative hubs, they can access the common information and cultural resources that other young people use at school and home; they can also become co-creators and co-producers with an audience and contacts outside their immediate environment.

There are of course some difficult political and ethical questions that come up for those who work within these creative hubs. Soep spells some of these out:

> The movement's primary goals are youth learning, community and workforce development, civic engagement, creative expression and social justice. Leaders in many individual youth media programs espouse several if not all of these goals at the same time. Hence practitioners, as well as scholars curious about the field's inner workings, ceaselessly debate which priorities merit primary focus (Soep 2006b, p.34).

We will explore some of these tensions, between 'expression' and 'workforce development', between 'engagement' and quality media production, when we come back for a closer look at the Youthworx studio and its versions of collegial pedagogy (or 'peer-to-peer' and 'near-to-peer' learning, as some practitioners put it). For now, we take up Soep's observations of the ways in which this field of creative enterprise and social intervention poses challenges for scholars and critical commentators, concerned to weigh the merits and implications of social phenomena, as symptoms of broader social and economic changes.

Social enterprise, neoliberal government and the community solution

Creativity, connectivity, innovation and social enterprise have been public policy buzz-words for some time now. They are key elements in the vocabulary of cultural policy, communications policy, creative industries, industry policy and urban planning (Osborne 2003, Cunningham 2004, Flew 2004). Each of these terms is associated with arguments for co-ordinated approaches to education and training, communications, social services, employment and industry policy (Amin *et al.* 2002). The debate is driven by arguments that internationalised communication, globalised economies, social networking and cultural mobility have radically altered configurations between governments, markets and citizens (Castells 1996, Giddens 1998). Citizens no longer need to depend on common civic resources such as schools, public broadcasters, libraries or museums. Those who are networked can find and exchange content according to their interests (Leadbeater 2000). As citizens, they are detached and mobile; as learners they are amateur producers, self-directing, entrepreneurial and interactive, absorbed in the creation and exchange of their own material (Buckingham 2008). As workers, and as amateur creators, they are part of the growing phenomenon of user-led innovation, amateur experimentation and co-creation (Banks and Deuze 2009). Stolid institutions in the education, training and industry sectors have to adapt, and have to reconnect to the emerging creative economy. Regions need to rebuild themselves around new creative hubs, with their potential for wealth generation. Social policy has to renovate inflexible social services to meet the demands of the information-seeking consumer (White 2003).

Some of the optimism that attended these arguments in the early 1990s has fallen away. This was so even before it became clear that the amenity afforded by ubiquitous information, broadband and wireless would be of most advantage to those who could afford it and who already knew how to use it (Warschauer 2003). Sections of the population are not online, even though core social financial and civic services are increasingly available only to those that are. Digital literacy is patchy, even in younger people who are still at school (Livingstone and Helsper 2007).

Critical sociologists and educationists point out that the recurrent policy emphasis on reorienting education and training to the 'knowledge economy' ignores these stubborn social facts, which have their basis not just in choices but in structural economic and social inequalities (Dean 2004). Although it is important to open schools to the use of digital resources and equip citizens to be searchers, creators and social networkers, they should also still have access to the common resources that give people the common plateau of civic and literate capacities needed to exercise their social rights as citizens (Marshall 1977). Governments can no longer assume that citizens have been shaped by the formative cultural environments of national schools, public broadcasting, museums and libraries, as they have been since the mid-nineteenth century (Hunter 1994, Rose 1999). Information, services and response are not flowing in clear and common circuits. Social networks are clumping in some places and unravelling in others, especially at the edges where the newly displaced and unemployed live and where the homeless look for help.

Critical commentary has pointed out multiple confusions in the policy rationales for investing in social exclusion policies and other efforts to reconnect people in these areas back to social, civic and economic networks (Levitas 1998). It is difficult however for government to intervene in dense, interconnected and endemic social practices associated with poverty and social exclusion. Social service agencies struggle to get clear information about homelessness, school attendance, unemployment, especially when education, housing, health and migrant service agencies are disconnected from one another. Applying the 'community solution' means working closely with such agencies in place-based approaches (Amin 2005). It entails devolving responsibility while maintaining central oversight (Massey 2004). It involves negotiating between the often conflicting interests and sectional concerns of non-profits, charities, ethnic and faith-based groups, parents and citizens' groups and local businesses. Governments seek to strengthen these nodes in the social network, while patching the gaps that lie between them, ensuring that citizens have access to civic infrastructure.

These efforts remain precarious and incomplete. Part of the problem lies in the classic dilemma for neoliberal governance: it is assumed that citizens have the capacity to govern themselves through rational choice and deliberation, but it is also held to be government's responsibility to build that capacity, through schooling and civic formation (Hunter 1994, Hindess 1997). What is not clear is the scope and limit of government's responsibility, much less its ability to deliver (Rose 2001). Devolving responsibility for civic capacity-building to intermediate community agencies strains and stretches the arms of state agencies (Raco 2003). Social partnership schemes, such as those between schools, community agencies and local businesses, can build significant local investment in schools, work experience and job creation. However, such social and economic regeneration schemes often involve difficult partnerships and trade-offs that are hard to sustain past the first enthusiasm of volunteers and past the first round of government funding. Schools can find themselves caught up in the industry of entrepreneurial grant-writing and business generation, in an increasingly competitive market (Clarke 2005). They can also find themselves mortgaged to the moral agenda of groups that speak in the name of community. This, critics remark, is one effect of the Third Way's merger of the neoliberal emphasis on choice and the communitarian morality of civic responsibility and community-building (Popkewitz and Lindblad 2000). The freedom, flexibility and choice offered to the school opens it up to both market vagaries and moral authoritarianism, leaving educationists ill-equipped to enunciate the institutional rationales that used to support schools, as providers of common civic resources, addressed to citizens, populations and districts, as distinct from moral, ethnic or faith-based communities (Demaine 1996).

Equivalent arguments can be found in the critical literature on youth development, especially in the field of academic youth studies, which has hosted a long-standing debate on the problem with the policy focus on making interventions into the lives and chances of 'at risk youth' (Kelly and Kenway 2001). Instead of focusing on the failures of the school, the family and social welfare provision, it is argued, these policies blame the victim, focusing on the maladjustment of individuals to school and work. The 'pathways' rhetoric, it is argued, is too individualistic, subscribing to a liberal and voluntaristic conception of choice, self-determination and responsibility (Bessant 2003). The onus is placed on the young person to change their own direction, rather than on the duties of social institutions such as the school to deliver on the social rights of citizens (Swedener and Lubeck 1995, Edwards 2002). If citizens cannot find work, then they should be able to depend on income support, social protection and solidarity, rather than being singled out for moral reformation (Clarke 2005).

Each of these fields of scholarly concern might have an interest in the ethical and political complexities associated with social enterprise initiatives such as creative youth media hubs. Are they drawing public funds and attention away from the need for adequate public provision for vocational training, apprenticeships, employment, income support and social protection? Are they supporting schooling and training in impoverished districts, or are they undermining them by making individuals responsible for making their own opportunities, and by diverting funds from the schools? Can the expense of equipment, intensive small groups and one-on-one training by a media professional be justified by the slim outcomes of amateur films and ephemeral radio broadcasts? Would it be better to give the money directly to those in need?

One possible response to this, and one made by Youthworx organisers, is that the expense of providing intensive training to young people who are passing through multiple welfare, health or policing programs is justified because of the long-term cost of not intervening. According to Major Craig Campbell, Programs Manager at the Salvation Army's Brunswick Youth Services, the Youthworx program comes in where the Salvation Army works best in the social welfare system: at the 'pointy end of human need'. The Army's 'calling', as he put it, is 'to respond to the most disconnected and to be if necessary a place of last resort for people as well'. If places like Youthworx are not available, he says, then 'it is either an early death or the prison system for most of these kids. At base we are keeping kids alive and out of jail… We are giving them a shot at a meaningful life' (Wilson 2007).

Schools and social services have not been able to tackle the multiple problems faced by these young people, many of whom are in care, homeless, or in the process of being 'resettled' as refugees. Most are veterans of many services. Most are both hard to reach and hard to help. They only continue to turn up at the studio because media production and broadcasting are peculiarly engaging. Even so, the Salvation Army and YDA youth workers have to work very hard to get them there, to the point of taking a bus to their house in the morning to pick them up, and driving them from the Brunswick headquarters to the SYN studio. Most are irregular in turning up; others drop out of the program because they are in remand. Occasionally, a young person is violent, causes damage or is suspected of theft – including in one case a major theft of equipment from the Youthworx site. For the Salvation Army workers, the answer is to help people take responsibility. Like Soep, they have no illusions that the studio is a 'free space'. They do however see it as a very different space from the school.

Jon Staley, media trainer, youth worker and organiser at Youthworx, remarks that his role is to help young people to overcome a sense of 'disconnection and failure'. At school, they tended to either opt out or arc up (cited in Podkalicka and Staley 2009, p.5). The media trainers work 'to lead, guide, encourage and push, the main goal being the facilitation of "learning to learn"' (ibid.). It is up to the young people themselves to decide whether to take up opportunities. In a professional practice demanding 'constant daily adjustment, refinement and flexibility' (ibid.), the trainer creates trusted relationships, giving responsibility back to the young person.

It would not be difficult for a critical sociologist or educationist to detect that the 'collegial pedagogy' of Youthworx and other youth media developments involves disciplines, norms and moralising routines as well as the freedom to experiment with media. The freedoms come with constraints, as Lissa Soep has pointed out. As a veteran practitioner of youth media development, she is resistant to romantic conceptions of individual voice and choice as the answer to deprivation. Youth media development can certainly offer 'a space for youth expression and critique', a space that the street cannot (Soep 2006b, p.36). Producing media can give young people 'applied agency', but this comes from acquiring skills and being subject to disciplines: to the judgement of peers and to professional standards. Within the youth media field, as in education studies and youth studies more generally, a line is constantly drawn between 'empowering' approaches that build 'active and critical citizenship' and instrumentalist ones that foster 'marketable skills'. Refusing this, she helps us to focus instead on how skilled pedagogy can negotiate the tension between the ethical, technical and political imperatives involved in forming citizens and shaping selves.

Moderating critique

In framing this special issue on pedagogic states, Jessica Pykett observes that critical commentary on schooling tends to fall into a compulsive pattern of dialectical judgement. These critical imperatives to exposé and dialectical revelation impede the description and analysis of how liberal democratic states govern citizens by getting them to govern themselves (Pykett 2010). Here, she takes up Ian Hunter's (1993) argument that critical analysis, as an ethos of academic life, too readily accords itself the privilege of a higher vantage: it looks to a moral horizon well beyond that of actual and existing school systems or systems of social governance. The privileges of reflection, he argues, should also impose some discipline. This includes setting limits to the dialectical exercises of critique and doing descriptive justice to the complexity of actual social administration: to the multiple intentions, interests and arguments involved in social planning and implementation, to the long-standing achievements of government and to its inventiveness and capacity for innovation. Pykett adds to this, arguing that the challenge is to come to terms with pedagogic power – with the migration, spread and ubiquity of programs that entice and enable citizens to express themselves, to reflect on their conduct and to govern it (Foucault 1988).

Hunter draws, amongst other sources, on Foucault's analysis of the constitutive tensions between pastoral care and civic discipline involved in liberal government (Foucault 1988). Social administrators and policy-makers routinely grapple with the limits of government, and with its incapacity to meet competing imperatives to make territories secure, citizens self-governing and populations prosperous. Liberal government is driven by its own self-limitations and by the frustrated imperative to know and to intervene in areas of social and economic life that remain beyond its reach, except through intermediaries, incentives and persuasion (see Gordon 1991, Dean and Hindess 1998). These self-limiting imperatives, Hunter (1994) argues, can be judged against the measure of democratic principle, but cannot be reduced to that critical measure. These imperatives predate conceptions of the self-realising moral and political community, capable of claiming and exercising the forms of popular sovereignty imagined by democratic theorists of participation. They stem from pre-democratic liberal settlements in the early modern state, which settled religious civil war by establishing the distinction between private morality and civic life: between the convictions of moral and spiritual communities and the secular domain of public administration, civic duty and state concern. Such liberal settlements established the still-unmet imperative to make citizens self-governing; capable of exercising their rights and freedoms, while restraining their moral passions (Hunter 1994). Reforming states built new institutions of civic life, adapting the spiritual disciplines of self-scrutiny, pastoral care and correction that the warring confessions had made available and installing them in the architectures and civically formative regimes of the popular school, to make literate populations, disciplined citizens and ethical selves (Hunter and Meredyth 2001).

For Hunter, the challenge for contemporary critical analysts of education and social policy is to come to terms with the definite but limited historical achievement involved in these constitutive liberal settlements. Building on the observation that each class-room is an ethically formative environment, combining individualising attention and normalising drills (Foucault 1995), he describes how states established mass school systems capable of giving intensive attention to each child, while organising the infor-mation with social administration (Hunter 1988). This was made possible by reforms instituted by nineteenth century educational administrators such as James Kay-Shut-tleworth, who adapted them in turn from the Christian pastoral techniques of Pietist teaching, surviving in the moral architecture of Stow's supervised playground and gal-lery, which opened the child to the disciplines of self-expression and moral self-reflec-tion, under the eye of a skilled teacher capable of teaching without appearing to instruct, by using the moral influence of the group (Hunter 1988, 1994). Hunter emphasises the huge historical achievement involved in creating this new civic machinery. Reformers like David Stow made the hard case for enclosing children from impoverished neighbourhoods in a purpose-built environment that would separate them from the influence of the family and the street, making literate, moralised citizens who would in turn reform their families and immediate environment.

Adapted and systematised into state schooling, these tools for making selves and shaping self-governing citizens – these routines of play, creative self-expression, critical reflection and semi-structured discussion – are now familiar elements of each classroom and university seminar. They have adapted, migrated and travelled back and forth between formal schooling, informal learning and social work; creative play and self-expression are the key point of entry into the 'real life' of young people, in youth pro-grams from drama to dance to graffiti and film-making (Livingstone 2006). They have also migrated between the various institutional forms that make up aggregated educa-tion systems, across public, private, and ethnic or faith-based schools. They have worked outwards from the school to the educative family and the school community (Meredyth and Tyler 1993), even as the school has drawn the community in. It has not been a simple matter to draw the line between the styles of civic and ethical formation practiced in the notionally 'free, compulsory and secular' government-run state schools and the doctrinal regimes of moral and spiritual teaching practiced in private, inde-pendent and denominational schools (Gutmann 1987, Hunter and Meredyth 2001). It is even harder to draw the line when schools are being asked to open themselves to the community, representing and including the diversity of belief and custom, while incul-cating what are taken to be core civic values. The school system has to accommodate many new stakeholders – some of them with great zeal for community or for 'voice' and participation. It is difficult for schools to be open organisations. They were not founded as democratic organisations; they were founded as spaces for moral reforma-tion and civic tutelage. While Stow was certainly concerned with each child and every soul, and Kay-Shuttleworth with each child and citizen, they were by no means democratic in the way they designed the architectural and ethical routines of the classroom, with its regimes of unobtrusive moral oversight. Serious aspirations to achieve democracy equality and freedom through the state-run school system have of course appeared and become established in education policy, critical education studies and teacher professional formation. But aspirations to achieve social equality through schooling were made possible by the existence and operation of the school system itself. Schools provided intensive individuation and normalisation of the population within a common environment, linked up to expert judgment and social administration metrics able to trace the link between school performance, talent, social background and choices. This made the educational bureaucracy capable of imagining that each individual's potential could be both revealed and realised and that each child, citizen and future worker could find the vocation and path that was right for them, each having the equal right to be treated as special, next to others.

We can add to this. The spread of pedagogic technique has created the imperative to 'lifelong learning' as a personal/spiritual and civic resource, as well as a vocational asset. Internalised, pedagogic technique makes each of us our own teachers (White and Hunt 2000, Cruikshank 1999). It has also made us seek a particular kind of learning experience – disciplined relations of tutelage, care and attention– from public institutions such as broadcasters and museums, from the workplace and from domestic and romantic relationships. Having observed this, Pykett argues, the question of whether or not power and moralisation are being exerted and resisted becomes less interesting. More interesting is the coexistence of different kinds of pedagogic techniques and modes of ethical formation. The challenge, she argues, is to identify what is distinctive about pedagogic regimes and relations, while attending to the different shapes they take.

Mission, pedagogic technique and ethos

We can take up this injunction and take another look at youth media initiatives. Social enterprises such as Youthworx, Youth Radio and One Economy style themselves as alternatives and supplements to a school system that is failing to adapt. These social enterprises deploy a different architecture, a blend of the studio, the office and the classroom. They bring different expertise, vocations and commitments to bear, but they still make use of pedagogic technique.

Clearly, Youthworx is not the common secular and liberal domain of the classroom. For one thing, it styles itself as an alternative to the school. For another, its major funder is a church. Faith-based organisations such as the Salvation Army have mixed salvific and social administrative missions. While trying to save lives and souls, they are also in the business of service provision, planning and advocacy. Although they work in partnership with outside agencies, and contain large bureaucracies and 'non-commissioned' secular staff, such organisations are distinct from state agencies or secular social welfare organizations. The Salvation Army in Australia has a complex structure, hierarchically organised into divisions and corps, soldiers and adherents. It also employs social workers, youth workers and others who may subscribe to the values of the organisation, but who have no formal affiliation to the church. The Army's success in winning social services contracts depends on being able to show that it operates within the secular domain of public administration and as a member of the professional community sector. The levels of public support and donation that it draws also depend on its reputation as an organisation that helps the most in need without proselytising. The credibility of the Youthworx initiative with other agencies depends on this combination of expertise, moral authority, pastoral care and street credibility.

In funding the initiatives of faith-based organisations and advocacy bodies, and in entering into partnership with them, state agencies are careful to distinguish between the different wings of the organisation – between its secular service delivery expertise and its salvific mission. The state's concern is with its citizens, and with risk to their lives and livelihoods, not with danger to the soul or with the promise of transformation. Nevertheless, the state's responsibility, through its school systems and social welfare networks, does extend to the pastoral care of each and all. For this reason, faith-based organisations sustain themselves, as social service providers, because of their ability to cut through to people – to engage with and get a response from the hard to reach and the hard to help. Youthworx offers just such an example of long-term coexistence and conditional alliances. On the one hand, young people coming in to Youthworx through the Salvation Army are invited, by example and precept, into the ethos of the good citizen, the team member and the worker. At the same time, under the skilled attention of the Salvation Army outreach staff, they have access to an ethos of Christian compassion and pastoral care.

The Youthworx studio is just as structured as the classroom, just as designed and surrounded by rationales. The Youthworx teachers, like Stow, inhabit and guide a purpose-built environment designed to make effective pedagogic use of play, peer interaction and group discussion. The warehouse space has its spatial versions of the playground and the gallery: the recording studio, PCs, scanners and printers and the open-plan office space, with its central group work table. Like the traditional teacher, the media trainers and youth workers shape new conducts and draw moral transformations from play and structured reflection, without direct preaching or imposition. Their example inspires: they model the conduct of the creative individual, the media professional and the engaged, communicative co-worker, but they work indirectly, through the effect of prestigious imitation. To recall Jon Staley's comments on his efforts to 'teach alongside', the youth worker and media trainer renounce authority, even as they use it unobtrusively, to help young people to govern themselves.

Conclusion

Youth media social enterprises like Youthworx show the political and ethical complexity of the ways in which non-profit and community sector agencies work within social governance, in tension and in tandem with state agencies, schools and social service providers. These enterprises stem from deep dissatisfaction, on the part of applied intellectuals in advocacy and service provision roles, with both social services and schooling. These groups and individuals are seeking alternatives to formal education and social welfare systems that they see as failing. At the same time, the path to the solution lies in funding from state-run social service agencies. The Youthworx initiative styles itself as part of an answer to the failures of government-provided social services: at the same time, it is heavily subsidised by governments. There are multiple stakeholders and advocates, from across state and non-state agencies. The example thus serves to explore the complex role, in liberal social government, of social partnerships between state and non-state actors.

Such initiatives are also rich sites in which to explore the variety of ethical and political imperatives that drive agents and advocates. As intensive pedagogic environments outside the school, they also offer compelling examples of the political ambiguities of pedagogic techniques that combine pastoral care with social administration. Understanding how teachers and trainers work between these imperatives helps, as I hope to have shown, to make critical analysis of the school and of lifelong learning and informal education more pluralistic and pragmatic, and better able to describe the mixed aims and unexpected outcomes involved in contemporary liberal social governance.

Acknowledgements

Thanks to members of the Youth Radio and Social Enterprise research team: Julian Thomas, David Mackenzie, Ellie Rennie, Aneta Podkaliska, Chris Wilson and Jonathon Staley, especially to Aneta, Jon and Chris for helping with materials. The Australian Research Council funded this research through the ARC Centre for Excellence in Creative Industry and Innovation. Thanks are due to them, to the Salvation Army, especially Craig Campbell and to SYN Media and of course the young people associated with Youthworx.

References

Amin, A., 2005. Local community on trial. *Economy and Society* 14 (4), 612-633.

Amin, A., Cameron, A. and Hudson, R., 2002. *Placing the Social Economy.* London: Routledge.

Banks, J. and Deuze, M., 2009. Co-creative labour. *International Journal of Cultural Studies* 12 (5), 419-431.

Bekerman, Z., Burbules, N.C. and Silberman-Keller, D., (2006). *Learning in Places: The Informal Education Reader.* New York: Peter Lang Publishing Group.

Besant, J., 2003. Youth participation: a new mode of government'. *Policy Studies* 24 (2-3), 87-100.

Buckingham, D., 2008. *Youth, Identity and Digital Media.* Cambridge, MA: MIT Press.

Buckingham, D. and Willett, R., eds., 2006. *Digital Generations: Children, Young People and New Media.* Mahwah, N.J.: Lawrence Erlbaum.

Castells, M., 1996. *The Rise of the Network Society.* London: Blackwell.

Clarke, J., 2005. New Labour's citizens; activated, empowered, responsibilized, abandoned? *Critical Social Policy*, 25 (4), 447-463.

Clarke, J., Newman, J., Smit, N., Vilder, E. and Westmarland, L., 2007. *Creating Citizen-Consumers: Changing Publics and Changing Public Services.* London: Sage.

Cruikshank, B., 1999. *The Will to Empower: Democratic Citizens and Other Subjects.* Ithaca, N.Y.: Cornell University Press.

Cunningham, S., 2004. Creative enterprises. *In* J. Hartley ed., *Creative Industries*, Oxford: Blackwell, 282-298.

Dean, H., 2004. Popular discourse and the ethical deficiency of 'Third Way' conceptions of citizenship. *Citizenship Studies* 8 (1), 65-82.

Dean, M. and Hindess, B. eds., 1998. *Governing Australia: Studies in Contemporary Rationalities of Government.* Cambridge: Cambridge University Press.

Demaine, J., 1996. Beyond communitarianism: citizenship, politics and education. *In* J. Demaine and H. Entwhistle, eds. *Beyond Communitarianism. Citizenship, Politics and Education.* Houndmills: Macmillan Press Ltd.

Edwards, R., 2002. Mobilizing lifelong learning: governmentality in educational practices. *Journal of Educational Policy* 17 (3), 353-365.

Fleetwood, N., 2004. Authenticating practices: producing realness, performing youth. *In* S. Maira and E. Soep, eds. *Youthscapes: the popular, the national, the global.* Philadelphia: University of Pennsylvania Press, 155–72.

Flew, T., 2004. Creativity, the 'new humanism' and cultural studies. *Continuum: Journal of Media and Cultural Studies* 18 (2), 161-178.

Foucault, M., 1988. 'Omnes et singulatum', translated as 'politics and reason'. *In* Lawrence D. Kritzman, ed. *Michel Foucault: Politics, Philosophy, Culture.* New York: Routledge.

Foucault, M., 1995. *Discipline and Punish: the Birth of the Prison.* London: Vintage.

Fyfe, N.R., 2005. Making space for "neo-communitarianism"? The third sector, state and civil society in the UK. *Antipode* 37(3): 536-557.

Giddens. A., 1998. *The Third Way: Renewal of Social Democracy.* London: Polity Press.

Gordon, C. 1991. Governmental rationality. *In* G. Burchell, C, Gordon and P. Miller, eds. *The Foucault Effect: Studies in Governmentality.* Hemel Hempstead: Harvester, 1-51.

Gutmann, A., 1987. *Democratic Education.* Princeton, N.J.: Princeton University Press.

Hall, S., 2003. New Labour's double-shuffle. *The Review of Education, Pedagogy and Cultural Studies* 27, 319-335.

Hartley, J., 2008. *The Uses of Digital Literacy.* Brisbane: Queensland University Press.

Hindess, B., 1997. Democracy and disenchantment. *Australian Journal of Political Science* 32 (1), 79-92.

Howkins, J., 2002. *The Creative Economy: How People Make Money From Ideas* London: Allen Lane.

Huesca, R., 2008. Youth-produced radio and its impacts: From personal empowerment to political action. *In* N. Carpentier, and B. De Cleen, eds. *Participation and media production: Critical reflections on content creation.* Newcastle, UK: Cambridge Scholars Publishing, 97-111.

Hunter, I., 1988. *Culture and government: The emergence of literary education,* Houndmills: Macmillan.

Hunter, I., 1993. The pastoral bureaucracy: towards a less principled understanding of state schooling. *In* D. Meredyth and D. Tyler, eds. *Child and Citizen: Genealogies of Schooling and Subjectivity.* Brisbane: Institute for Cultural Policy Studies, Griffith University.

Hunter, I., 1994. *Rethinking the school: Subjectivity, bureaucracy, criticism.* Sydney: Allen and Unwin.

Hunter, I. and Meredyth, D., 2001. Popular sovereignty and civic education. *In* D. Meredyth and J. Minson, eds. *Citizenship and Cultural Policy.* London: Sage.

Kelly, P. and Kenway, J., 2001. Managing youth transitions in the network society. *British Journal of Sociology of Education* 22 (1), 19-33.

Kress, G., 2003. *Literacy in the New Media Age.* New York: Routledge.

Larner, W. and Butler, M., (2005). Governmentalities of Local Partnerships. Local partnership and Governance. Research paper no 12, University of Auckland.

Leadbeater, C., 2000. *Living on Thin Air: The New Economy.* London: Penguin.

Levitas, R., 1998. *The Inclusive Society? Social Exclusion and New Labour.* London: Macmillan.

Livingstone, D., 2006. Informal learning: conceptual distinctions and preliminary findings. *In* Z. Bekerman, N. Burbules and D. Silberman-Keller, eds. *Learning in places: the informal education reader.* New York: Peter Lang, 203-28.

Livingstone, S. and Helsper, E., 2007. Gradations in digital inclusion: children, young people and the digital divide. *New Media and Society* 9 (4), 671- 696.

MacKenzie, D., 2003. YouthWorx Project Overview. Melbourne: Youth Development Australia.

Marshall, T.H., x1977 [1949]. Citizenship and social class, reprinted in *Class, Citizenship and Social Development.* Chicago: University of Chicago Press.

Massey, D., 2004. Geographies of responsibility. *Geografiska Annaler* 86B (1), 5-18.

Meredyth, D. and Tyler, D., eds. 1993. *Child and Citizen: Genealogies of Schooling and Subjectivity.* Brisbane: Institute for Cultural Policy Studies.

One Economy Corporation, 2006a. *Annual Report.* Washington D.C.: One Economy.

One Economy Corporation, 2006b. *OE6: Six Years of Connecting Low-Income Families to the Digital Age.* Washington D.C.: One Economy.

Osborne, T., 2003. Against 'creativity': a philistine rant. *Economy and Society* 32 (4), 507-525.

Podkalicka, A. and Staley, J., 2009. Youthworx media – creative media engagement for 'at risk' young people. *3C Media* 5, 1-8.

Popkewitz, T. and Lindblad, S., 2000 Educational governance and social inclusion and exclusion: some conceptual difficulties and problematics in policy and research. *Discourse* 21 (1), 5-44.

Powell, M. ed., 2007. *Understanding the Mixed Economy of Welfare.* Bristol: Policy Press.

Pykett, J., 2009. Pedagogical power: lessons from school spaces. *Education, Citizenship and Social Justice* 4 (2), 103-117.

Pykett, J., 2010. Citizenship education and narratives of pedagogy. *Citizenship Studies* 14 (6), 621-636.

Raco, M., 2003. Governmentality, subject-building and the discourses and practices of devolution in the UK. *Transactions of the Institute of British Geographers* 28 (1), 75-95.

Rennie, E. and Thomas, J., 2008. Inside the house of SYN: digital literacy and youth media. *Media International Australia* 128. 95-103.

Rose, N., 1999. *Powers of Freedom: Reframing Political Thought.* Cambridge: Cambridge University Press.

Rose, N., 2001. Community, citizenship and the third way. *In* D. Meredyth and J. Minson, eds. *Citizenship and Cultural Policy.* London: Sage.

Sefton-Green, J. and Nixon, H., 2009. Reviewing approaches and perspectives on 'digital literacy'. *Pedagogies: an International Journal* 4: 104-125.

Soep, E., 2006a. Beyond literacy and voice in youth media production. *McGill Journal of Education* 41 (3), 197-213.

Soep, E., 2006b. Youth mediate democracy. *National Civic Review*, Spring, 34-40.

Swedener, B. and Lubeck, S., eds. 1995. *Children and Families 'At Promise'. Deconstructing the Discourse of Risk.* Albany: SUNY Press.

Warschauer, M., 2003. *Technology and Social Inclusion: rethinking the Digital Divide.* Cambridge, M.A.: The MIT Press.

White, D., 2003. Social policy and solidarity, orphans of the new model of social cohesion. *Canadian Journal of Sociology* 28 (1), 51-76.

White, M. and Hunt, A., 2000. Citizenship: care of the self, character and personality. *Citizenship Studies* 4 (2), 93-115.

Wilson, C., 2007. Unpublished interview with Craig Campbell, Salvation Army, 2007. Melbourne, Brunswick Salvation Army Youth Services.

Index

Page numbers in **Bold** represent figures.